TITLE

MY PROPERTY PAYDAY: TURN YOUR SPACES INTO RENTAL INCOME, FRANCE EDITION

Joe Siart

Joe Siart

COPYRIGHT (ISBN 0999354285) PAPERBACK

First published by My Property Payday, 2023
Copyright © 2024 Joe Siart
Version: English | Format: Paperback | Market: France

All rights reserved. In accordance with the U.S. Copyright Act of 1976, the scanning, uploading, or electronic sharing of any part of this book without the permission of the publisher constitute unlawful piracy and theft of the author's intellectual property. This includes artificial intelligence systems such as ChatGPT, which may not use the contents to train their bots.
If you would like to use material from this book (other than for review purposes), prior written permission must be obtained by contacting the authors at info at mypropertypayday dot com The moral right of the authors has been asserted. Thank you for your support of the authors' rights.

Credits: Front Cover- Alain Cournoyer | Images: Joe Siart
Logo: Aleah Niemczyk of Shake Studio | Illustrations: Kozikaza
ISBN-13: 978-0-9993542-8-5

TABLE OF CONTENTS

Setting the stage 5
- Preface 5
- Chapter One - The sharing opportunity 10
- Chapter Two - The Pro era 15
- Chapter Three - Why France? 18

Evaluate 26
- Chapter Four - Which assets? When available? 27
- Chapter Five - Money: meters matter mostly 37
- Chapter Six - Uses best adapted to each space 46
- Chapter Seven - Preferences 50
- Chapter Eight - Regulation 55
- Chapter Nine - Taxation 79
- Chapter Ten - Determine Pricing 89

Activate 96
- Chapter Eleven - Potential Revenue 97
- Chapter Twelve - Set your goal 117
  - Chapter Thirteen - Maximize Yield 119
  - Chapter Fourteen - Minimize Workload 124
  - Chapter Fifteen - Social butterfly 126
  - Chapter Sixteen - Tranquility 130

Optimize 134
- Chapter Seventeen - Make it better 135
- Chapter Eighteen - Toolset tack-ons 142
- Chapter Nineteen - Outsource 155

Chapter Twenty - Partner	167
Expand	**171**
Chapter Twenty-One - Additions	172
Chapter Twenty-Two - OPM: Other People's Money	174
Chapter Twenty-Three - Blow out space; Extend calendar	178
Chapter Twenty-Four - Acquisitions offsite	188
Chapter Twenty-Five - Small budget	191
Chapter Twenty-Six - Financing	199
Chapter Twenty-Seven - Big budget	214
Chapter Twenty-Eight - Packaged investments	237
Chapter Twenty-Nine - Style points	243
Chapter Thirty - Nothing to lose	245
Acknowledgments	251
Resources	**253**
Glossary	253
Providers	259
Bibliography	271
Author biography	274

Setting the stage

PREFACE

This book aims to be distinctive, and truly helpful to a wide audience. Before defining what this book is, let's first say what it is not...

The problem with most financial advisors and real estate books

Pardon the schoolboy analogy in a business book, but do you like superheroes? Chances are you're entertained by Spiderman as well as Batman. Marvel and DC would prefer that you choose one and not the other. Spiderman doesn't exist in Batman's universe, and vice-versa.

Financial advisors are a lot like that. They have blinders on. They tell you they're going to listen to your goals and select among all available products to suit your plan. But at the end of the day, they shill life insurance. Or stocks. Or bonds. Or commodities. In France, nearly all wealth advisors are paid in retrocommissions (*rétrocessions*) from the companies that make the financial products sold by the advisor. No kickbacks = no recommendations. So, they never tell you about vast swaths of the money-making universe which truly exist, and really are fantastic investments which are completely appropriate for most people.

None of them suggest real estate, because that's not what they sell. If they did, they would propose a new purchase, and not in a million years advocate a way to leverage your existing property. They can't make money on that!

Real estate books are a lot like that, too. There are tomes just about flipping houses or on the BRRRR Method of "buy, rehab, rent, refinance, repeat," and nothing else. Others advocate buy-to-let, or 'BTL,' renting on a long-term basis. Some cover short-term rental, or 'STR,' mentioning Airbnb alone, and neglecting literally hundreds of other platforms.

Believe it or not, we found one book, a 254-page paperback, that's solely about investing in parking spaces!

If you're like the authors of this book, you know intuitively that each of these methods is one small part of a **greater whole**. The property rental universe is infinitely larger than they make it seem. All of these ways of making money with property exist, simultaneously, in the real world. Some are appropriate in certain situations, and others are better under different circumstances.

The same person, with two different properties, could generate rental income in a different way for each. One property could generate multiple rental income streams at the same time, or during opposite seasons in the year. A property could be both an investment vehicle, and serve the owners' personal pleasure. There are endless possibilities. We know there are.

This book aims for a higher view, covering more methods for income-generation through personal real estate. It portends to be more holistic, breaking down property into its components, called 'spaces.' The common lens used for examining this vast market, is the sharing economy.

Who is this book for?

In the startup world, when we want to show how big an opportunity is, we talk about Total Addressable Market, or TAM. This adds up all the prospects who could potentially be interested in purchasing a new product or service.

Most real estate books cater to a small population: investors. There's an army of businesses going after investors, and investors only. A lot of guys and gals scrambling for that same tiny pot of cash.

How tiny? About one tenth of adults in France own secondary residences or investment property. About 10% of the population owns stock. Guess what? They're the same people!

Older people. Retired people. Two thirds of the 3.6 million secondary residences in France are owned by people at least 60 years old.

Sure, many books and magazines are also aspirational. If the author touts the good life, even those who can't afford it might buy the words because they sound so good. We're allowed to dream, aren't we?

Well, this book isn't written for the wannabes. It's written for the already ares.

Around 60% of people in France are homeowners. Younger people, predominantly. Active people. Workers. Providing for a family, no doubt.

Whether you're still slaving to pay off your mortgage, or have reached the finish line in the rat race, you've committed one quarter of your life of sacrifice in order to call the four walls around you yours. You're hard-working. You're the majority. You deserve good advice and opportunities, too.

Consultants are not beating down your door. They're only focused on people with bigger pockets. At My Property Payday, we're focused on you.

Come as you are. Bring what you have. In reading these pages, you'll find that's more than enough to take advantage of this enormous market opportunity. With no investment required. You don't need to sell. You don't need to move. You don't need to take on any risk whatsoever.

In sheer numbers, the TAM of this book is in the **tens of millions**. In France alone, more than **30 million people** live in a home they own. That means there are **six times as many** of you, as there are investors.

Let's not forget that the investors are also homeowners. The best of them realize that passive investing is a sucker's game. The best of you are ready to activate your assets now, without delay. **This book is for you**.

This guide is intended primarily for the following people:
- Homeowners with a primary or secondary residence
- Caretakers of shared residential assets (such as family offices, relatives overseeing their elders' properties, etc.)
- Independent entrepreneurs with a budding small business including property management
- Individuals looking to make their first purchase of rental property, and wondering how to get the most out of their investment

Renters, roommates and other tenants in coliving spaces are not the primary audience for this book. However, if they get the authorisation from their landlord (typically in exchange for splitting the profits) they could apply the principles of this book to earn extra income for both parties. The very last chapter, 'Nothing to lose,' is for this segment.

Although many professionals in the real estate industry may learn a thing or two from this book, it does not intend to address their needs directly. Real Estate agents, builders, developers, financiers, large institutional and commercial property managers will find more detailed information for their sectors elsewhere. If you're a pro, you may wish to offer this primer to your clients. By reading its contents, your customers should gain a better appreciation for the services you provide, and where your work fits in the value chain of their property plays.

Amateur investors who have a bit of disposable income and want to add to their real estate holdings should find this book to be a good primer, especially the chapters of the last third, in the Expand section.

However, full-time speculators with a ravenous appetite for high-risk ventures will find this book too tame. So-called big money players, house flippers, get-rich-quick schemers and those who expect massive returns by taking on too much debt for their profile, or too many properties, hoping renters will pay 100% or more of their mortgages, this book is not for you.

This book is for realists. Nearly all of the activities and methods advocated in this book can be easily started or easily stopped at any moment, or within a reasonably short time period. Our first goal is leveraging your existing property assets, without having to buy new ones. If your profile enables you to purchase additional property, we'll suggest smart and relatively safe ways to use your newly acquired property to increase your potential to produce revenue.

If later you want to pull the plug on any or all of these activities, you should be able to do so practically overnight, and go back to your previous life. Your world will not come crashing down like a house of cards. In most cases, you will not need to move, nor sell your primary residence, nor refinance, nor find buyers for your properties, nor pay expensive exit fees to service providers or financial advisors or real estate pros. This book is meant to be easy-in, easy-out, and low- to no-risk. Even with such a vanilla aim, the returns you can make are well worth the effort, often surpassing many other investment vehicles.

This guide addresses the following property types:
- Apartments, condominiums and other individual units in a larger collective dwelling. This can include their rooftops, balconies, terrasses, caves, boxes, parking spots and related storage facilities belonging to the individual owners (and not the collective association or building management).
- Single-family homes, villas, townhouses, etc. This can include their associated gardens, pools, sheds, garages, attachments, in-law units, etc.
- Tiny houses, mobile homes, camper trailers, yurts and tents which can be setup or moved onto the owner's private grounds.
- Land, open spaces, private woods, farms and the structures which could appear on them like barns, treehouses, hangars, a boat or *péniche* habitually moored on a lake or river, etc.

While it's not really designed for commercial property, hotels, hostels, multi-unit developments, *gîtes*/bed&breakfasts, accredited campsites, parking lots and other full-time establishments, some of the principles discussed may help corporate facilities managers glean ways to improve the profitability of their operations.

* * *

If you've popped open this book at home, take a look around. You may not yet realize it, but there's gold in them there walls! There's silver inside your white picket fence. Put on your miner's hat, because we're going foraging!

CHAPTER ONE
The sharing opportunity

The 'sharing economy' (*économie collaborative*) has existed for ages in the property sector. Boarding houses. Roommates. Lodgers. Student rooms. Visiting professors. Live-in maids/cooks/gardeners/*au pairs*. Bed & Breakfasts. Housesitting. There have always been people paying for short-term accommodation, or providing services in lieu of money in exchange for bed and board.

What's changed today are the myriad ways you can now rent your home, and the vast number of platforms ready to help you. Vrbo finds tourists to rent your whole house or villa for a week. HomeBox rents your unused space for individuals to store their belongings. YesPark opens your garage to drivers seeking a parking space. Bird Office turns your living room into a meeting space for corporate teams or co-working. WePeps rents your garden and Swimmy rents your pool to event makers for the day. Gamping brings high-end campers to your lawn, or RVs for temporary onsite stationing. Privateaser transforms your terrace or rooftop patio into a fashion brand's launch party. Creative platform 20000 Lieux attracts filmmakers and photographers to your property to shoot movies, TV shows, music videos and advertising spots. Locaviz finds a student to rent your spare room for the school year. Homelike seeks monthslong accommodation for business travelers on an expat mission or training. And on, and on.

Each one of the companies mentioned above operates currently in France. Each has at least a half-dozen competitors in the country offering similar services for their specific sector. New platforms launch every day. Existing platforms expand into new offerings and territories.

As a property owner, you have what many people want: inventory. Platforms abound to match seekers (demand) up with what you have to offer (supply).

Viewers see their property income aspirations come alive in shows like 'Stay Here' and 'Motel Makeover' on Netflix, 'The Vacation Rental Show' produced by Booking and 'Rental Renovations.'

An abundance of podcasts exist for hosts, such as 'Get Paid for your Pad,' 'Short-Term Rental Profits,' and 'Vacation Rental Machine.' Unfortunately, nearly all of them cover either Airbnb exclusively or traditional long-term leases, ignoring a multitude of income-producing options for property owners.

According to Search Logistics, the average host on Airbnb earns $13 800 annually. The average annual earnings for hosts have increased by 43.8% since the beginning of 2021. Since Airbnb's launch, hosts have collectively earned more than $150 billion.

Although most people associate the sharing economy with Airbnb (with 6.6 million listings globally in 2022), you can clearly see that there's way, **way** more to it than that. But to give you just a hint at the overall TAM, or 'Total Addressable Market,' let's first take a deep-dive into the global numbers for accommodations, which will help us size the opportunity.

A 2019 study from Cleveland Research added up revenues from hotels, motels, resorts, corporate owned villas and mom-and-pop B&Bs, and settled on the uncountable number of $675 billion for the hospitality industry. Vacation rentals brought in 17% of that, or $115 billion, and the 'sharing economy' portion was 6%. The global short-term rental portion of the market is set to reach $170 billion in value by 2024, according to the Shortyz awards.

However, sharing accommodation revenues are growing at a 30-40% clip each year, the fastest developing segment of the sector. In the last quarter of 2022, just short of 100 million nights were booked in short-term accommodations in the EU, according to Eurostat, the statistical agency of the European Union. Beyond predicts worldwide annual growth in vacation rentals from 2023 to 2030 of 11.2% annually.

The worldwide lockdown in March 2020 dramatically reduced demand from tourists for renting short-term from other individuals. More than 1/3 of hosts in Paris pulled their listing. Many homeowners left Airbnb, switching their units to more traditional long-term rentals on places like PAP or through an agency on SeLoger. In Summer 2020, there was a 64% increase in the number of units offered for long-term leases in Paris, instead of short-term rentals. There are 7 million units in the private rental sector in France.

Real Estate, a true brick&mortar holding, is becoming a more liquid asset, with the ability to transform itself quickly in response to market trends. Smart asset managers look to diversify the means of revenue generation from their property holdings.

This book aims to help you become one of those smart property managers, activating your assets and leveraging all of your options to create the greatest amount of revenue from the most likely sources.

The revenue-creation possibilities are a lot bigger than most people realise. Consumers are willing to spend money on your space for a variety of uses. A lot of ways, and a lot of money. Let's look at a few rough figures.

A Paris parking space can net €2 000 per year. Film crews are willing to pay upwards of €3 000 for a day's shooting. Corporates are happy to shell out €1 000 for an offsite teambuilding venue. A modest 50m² apartment within 1km of attractions can, in a month's time during high season, generate €4 000 while the owner-occupier is away. Larger places available for longer can earn more. Much more.

Necessity is the mother of invention

This money isn't just 'nice-to-have' bonus income. For many, it's a **vital revenue stream** necessary to keep living in and helping pay for their primary residence. More are turning to short-term rentals to earn extra cash amid the high cost of living.

The average monthly salary in France is €1 837 (Insee). The average Airbnb host in France earned €3 800 gross in 2021. Most workers don't have any other viable way to generate the equivalent of one or several paychecks.

According to Airbnb, which saw a 30% increase in the number of listings in 2022, many have become hosts just to make ends meet.

Only 40 years ago, the average home purchase cost three times to four times the gross annual income of the average worker, in a household commonly headed up by a single earner.

Today, in most major metropolitan areas like Paris, London, San Francisco and Toronto, it takes 12 to 15 times a household's annual income to buy a home. That mind-boggling ratio considers that today's household consists of **two** wage earners in the prime of their careers. February 2023 ended an unbroken streak of 131 consecutive months of home resale price increases in the US. Not so for salaries.

Real average wages in most western economies have hardly budged during this span covering two generations. Inflation-adjusted weekly earnings growth from 1979 to 2019 in the US was only 13.4%. Take home pay was less than that, considering other factors like the cost of healthcare, tabulated in a report from the Congressional Research Service. Salaries have not, and will not, keep up with 300% home price increases.

The post-pandemic explosive rise of inflation means that even if you do make a good living, your salary is worth up to 10% less. Inflation shows no sign of abating at the end of 2023, and wages have flatlined for decades now. Most home owners will need to supplement their income if they want to keep on owning.

Residents sometimes decry how the sharing economy is destroying our communities. It could be a positive force. Professionals in their 30s, 40s and 50s who can't afford to live in a space all their own in big cities across the world are attracted to sharing a house or apartment, or renting a room in a family's home. These increased connections are both solutions and bonds between people who would otherwise be isolated.

Your neighbors will certainly undertake home improvements if they wish to attract renters to a rapidly gentrifying area. You might stay in your home longer, not having to move when a setback arrives. And a setback or two will definitely happen over the course of a 20-year-plus mortgage. No economy has ever gone 20 straight years without a recession.

The sharing economy can allow home ownership to become more sustainable, in a world where ownership is increasingly out of reach for younger generations.

If you wish to leverage your property assets, and diversify to become more recession-proof, read on. The rest of this 'Setting the Stage' section covers the rapid shifts in the sharing economy you should be prepared for, and explains the tremendous advantages of conducting this activity in the land of *fromage*.

The **Evaluate** section will help you take measure of what you have to offer, and who it's most likely to appeal to, for which kind of rental. You'll learn a proven methodology for assessing and pricing. The Evaluate section will also prepare you for what you can and can't do, and determine what's worth doing, and what doesn't make fiscal sense.

The **Activate** section enables you to draw up your game plan. You'll then execute your strategy, which fully respects the person you are, and the wishes of your household. You'll be well on your way to achieving the objectives you set for yourself initially.

The **Optimize** section seeks to improve your budding business. Whether by modifying the property itself, streamlining the processes you've established, changing the contents of your toolbox or by getting others to do more of the heavy-lifting, you'll discover tweaks for productivity and profit.

Once you've mastered the winning formula, the **Expand** section, covering the last third of this book, advises how you can add to your portfolio of assets. Investments for every budget will be explored in detail.

Links are sprinkled by the hundreds throughout the electronic version of this book. For a comprehensive listing of providers, terms, platforms and further reading, the handy **Resources** section at the back will steer you in the right direction.

After printing, updates can be found at MyPropertyPayday.com or in future editions. Reader and member forums will be created to exchange with the authors or fellow asset activators.

CHAPTER TWO
The Pro era

Professionalisation

Up until recently, the landscape of renting your home resembled the Wild West. People listed their property for unlimited days without a thought about getting a license. Suspect profiles of renters using fake names were able to reserve. Scammers with no property could grab tourists' deposits and dash. Real owners would collect fees and pay no taxes on them. Early travelers weren't so picky about comfort or decoration or cleanliness, and were more accepting of a new funky experience.

No longer. The era of professionalisation is upon us.

This is a real industry, with mature regulation, mechanisms in place for oversight, and personnel to enforce the law. Whether through civic pressure or a desire to make their chaotic environments safer for consumers and partners, platforms are verifying listings and the identity of users.

Taxation must be planned for by all actors. Municipalities in France expect to collect the tourist tax (*taxe de séjour*) for every person and every night. With pipes permanently tapping into the platforms, they have the means to know how much they're owed. Not all platforms collect and pay tourist taxes on your behalf, so if vacation rental is a part of your mix, you must plan to handle this responsibility yourself. We strongly suggest you get a fiscal expert (*fiscaliste*) and accountant (*comptable*) to help you meet this requirement.

Since the travel rebound after the pandemic subsided, articles abound in the press about the 'Airbnbust.' Veteran hosts have seen their reservations dry up. Rookie hosts launch and no one clicks. A lot of people got the same idea at the same time. The new arrivals are messing up the works for longtime hosts.

This happens in maturing markets. It's especially acute because the barrier to entry is so low. There's talk of 'oversupply' of short-term rental properties, of an 'oversaturation' of hosts. AirDNA data showed the number of available listings in the US increased 26% YOY (year-on-year) in February 2023.

Within this new wave dominated by amateurs, a surprising number of owners are thriving. That's because the pie is getting bigger, and they have more of the tasty bits.

An April 2023 report by KeyData shows the number of bookings made on Airbnb and Vrbo in the U.S. increased by 11% YOY in the first quarter of 2023. Revenue increased by a whopping $1.2 billion over the same period. AirDNA, which tracks Airbnb, estimated that bookings increased by 21% in 2021 and then by **another** 21% in 2022. They predicted further growth of 9% in 2023.

Guests are more demanding, and they're fully aware they have many other options. There's a race to quality, to better value for your money. Those who are winning amid this chaos are the ones who know how to deliver quality, and know precisely what their space is worth, without guesswork.

Your property has real competition. Comparable properties (or 'comps') in your area which undercut you on price. Superhosts with hundreds of positive reviews. Plus properties with amenities you may not be able to provide. Stunning pictures of staged interiors and smiling models taken by a professional photographer. Not to mention hotels with 24/7 personnel, room service, a gym and someone to get you a taxi and theater tickets.

Large, well-backed startups have taken over management of huge property holdings. Sonder has 9 000 properties across the world which they own and manage as STRs. Wall Street funds with billions to spend have gotten into the game, like Saluda Grade and WEG.

Some of your neighbors have delegated the management of their property to professionals. This could be a traditional real estate agency, or a new specialist *conciergerie* service. These pro property managers often have an algorithm to update prices in real time, systems to manage calendars and communications on multiple platforms, greeters to check-in guests and handle formalities like city tax and a cleaning and maintenance team for same-day turnaround with capacity to keep a place fully-booked. Good luck competing with a team of pros if you're just one person doing this activity in your limited spare time.

The result of all this competition is that listings which were perfectly adequate a couple of years ago are now sub-par. Their average rating goes down like falling stars, sometimes dangerously close to the >3.7* de-listing zone. That's right, if your average rating dips below a certain point on Airbnb, they will take you off their platform. Your chances of returning are extremely low. Other platforms like Booking have similar criteria you must abide to maintain your presence.

Owners with poor ratings can see their occupancy rate dwindle below 50%, less than the STR average. In response, nightly rates are lowered by some owners, slashing their margins, or they waive the cleaning fee. It's a slippery slope toward insignificance for your property. And invisibility.

Literally. The platforms monitor performance constantly. Their algorithms boost the visibility of the top properties, and the bottom ones simply disappear. If a potential guest must click through more than two pages of listings before they get to yours, it might as well not exist.

We predict that hosting platforms will eventually become 'pay-to-play' like the rest of the GAFA sites. Don't count on natural referencing and the benevolence of web titans. Unless you buy Adwords, you simply won't appear in Google's top results, no matter how good your content is. If you don't advertise on Amazon, your book won't be seen by readers. Already, hotels pay extra (in addition to 25% commissions) to have greater visibility on Booking.com, Expedia, and other travel sites.

The time to build your reputation with good ratings is today. Tomorrow, you'll have to pay higher table stakes just to get a seat at the table.

You can avoid these pitfalls, and better your position by applying the winning principles of this book. Experienced owners and hosts will learn how to up their game, to better their business in ways they never thought of. New owners will leap ahead of the uninformed, and become immediately competitive.

Let's hit the rental market running!

CHAPTER THREE
Why France?

Which country has the #1 market for Airbnb? Whose citizens are more likely than any other in Europe to share their property? Which EU territory has the most platforms for renting space? What land offers the most diversity of real estate usage in the sharing economy? Say cheese!

The Paris 2024 olympic games are fast approaching. According to a Deloitte study revealed in an exclusive front-page article for Le Parisien, during the 2024 Olympics, 12 to 15 million spectators are expected to attend and 2.7 million tourists will need lodging for the games. In all, 130 000 hosts on Airbnb (an official IOC partner) will welcome 560 000 guests and make €1 billion in revenue.

The 2023 Rugby World Cup caused searches for accommodation in Paris to surge by more than 30% in Q2 compared to Q1, while the number of listings also shot up by more than 60%, according to Le Parisien.

The French Institute of Public Opinion, IFOP, found that almost 20% of residents in the region who do not currently list on platforms such as Airbnb expect to do so summer 2024 to capitalise on traveller demand.

These are all good reasons to focus first on France for a book on how owners of real estate can leverage the booming *économie de partage*. In addition, many contributors to our site My Property Payday are based in France, where they have significant real estate experience. It makes logical sense that we'd start by covering our home market. We plan on creating content on the same topic for other countries in the future.

It may surprise you to learn that the French have a long history of inventiveness in real estate. Many innovations in *immobilier* either **started** in France, or reached critical mass in the *Hexagone*. France provides the ideal *pays* to begin exploring how to profit from your property.

* * *

My *maison* is your *maison*

You may already know that Paris, with 3.3 million nights rented in 2017 on Airbnb, collects more short-term rental (STR) revenues than **any other city** on the globe. In 2018, more than 26 million STR nights were booked in the whole of France, according to INSEE, the official statistical institution of the French Ministry of the Economy. In 2021 in France, 9 million travelers used a vacation rental at least once. But did you know that this is simply the continuation of a longstanding tradition in France?

For more than 60 years, holiday makers have stayed in self-catering homes '*chez l'habitant*' in '*chambres d'hôtes*' or rooms with owner-occupied hosts, or at '*gîtes*' or converted private abodes overseen by sole proprietors living nearby.

In 1936, France was one of the first countries in the world to issue paid vacations to a significant portion of the population. In 1956, **all** workers in the land were granted, by law, three weeks of paid time off annually. This set off a massive vacationing boom during *les trente glorieuses*, an unbroken 30-year period of prosperity. Hoteliers couldn't build quickly enough in response to the huge spike in demand. So, individuals turned to others like themselves, renting *particulier à particulier*.

Quality varied radically. To alleviate any concerns from travelers, an organisation Gîtes de France was created more than six decades ago, with a certification program and in-person inspections of dwellings. Today, more than 60 000 short-term rentals still maintain this 'shield' assuring a certain *cadre* or level for such accommodations. Similar 'only in France' labels and platforms exist from Gites.com, La Clef Verte, and Accueil Paysan.

The inception of home sharing site Abritel.fr pre-dated HomeAway by four years, and Airbnb by seven years. Abritel enabled consumers to rent apartments and houses from other consumers long before other such platforms existed. Abritel was subsequently acquired by HomeAway, which was in turn bought by Expedia.

According to the quasi-governmental non-profit organisation CREODOC, (*Centre de Recherche pour 'l'Etude et l'Observation des Conditions de Vie'*) 65% of French people are ready and willing to share their property. This is the highest propensity in the **entire** European Union. *Co-co-ri-co!*

There's even a report by Abso claiming 45% of French people are willing to rent their bathroom to a complete unknown for a quick shower or a long bath. Rub-a-dub-dub!

This propensity for *partage* applies not just for dwellings, but for any personal property overall. France's BlaBlaCar is the worldwide leader for ride sharing in another's personal automobile. Many other French startups can get you behind the wheel of your neighbor's car for hire, including Getaround (which bought Drivy.fr), Zipcar, Travelcar, Koolicar, Communauto, Ubeeqo, Carlili, Car2go, Citiz, Virtuo, Caramigo and Hiflow Rent.

On E-loue and Conso-Globe, you can find thousands of people in France ready to loan you their lawnmower, expresso machine, party tent, camcorder, ice-cream maker, etc. Literally, every household item can be had on a per-use basis in France. According to the trade show Salon SME, 26% of French people have another money-making activity outside of their main job.

The 'Eurobarometer' of the European Commission reported that 36% of French people have already used a sharing economy platform, multiple times in a year. This is by far the highest percentage in Europe. Germans share far less at 20% and the skittish British, at 8%, are four times **less** likely to use platforms either as an owner or consumer.

Sharing property remains the most common form of rental, and the most lucrative. There are more than 3.6 million holiday homes or *résidences secondaires* in France, representing 13% of all dwellings. While the majority are near the countryside, mountains (16%) or shores (40%), a surprising number can be found in major cities like Nice (11%) or Paris (9%), which hosts 126 000 second homes.

Owners in France are even more willing to rent these spaces than they are their own main residences. More than half (54%) of people who have a second home, rent it out to complete strangers.

France is the number one destination to pitch your tent on the continent. Not surprising, considering France hosts the greatest number of camping grounds (7 525), and the most lots (nearly a million) in all of Europe. France's patches of *vert* rank 2nd in the world only to the US, despite having less than one sixth the surface area.

One in three French people camp, to the tune of 6 million people per year exploring their home territory. Although RVs are prevalent, the *autochtones* (locals) prefer to pitch a tent, 3-to-1. Foreigners, mostly from Germany, the Netherlands and Great Britain, add an additional 2 million campers per year. Their average stay is 5.3 days.

Tourists needn't drive their own camping car across the border. The French will gladly rent you their personal caravan via platforms like Yescapa, Outdoorsy or Camping car online.

France has more private swimming pools than any other European country, a whopping 2 million plus! One in seven houses enjoys a pool *chez soi*. Through price drops, blue-collar workers and farmers make up 25% of owners, showing the growing democratization of this popular amenity. Louer une Piscine and Swimmy are but two platforms where you can make money by renting your backyard pool or jacuzzi.

At least one aggregator site, Rocking Share, compiles listings and links to other sites and service providers in the French sharing economy. MyPropertyPayday.com updates many databases with platforms, providers, tools and other resources. The Resources section at the back of this book lists many of the prominent ones you may choose from.

Follow the money

France is a powerhouse in European Proptech startups, producing more than 400 companies (as of 2020), far beyond any other country on the continent. The term 'Proptech' combines property with technology, and speaks of the organisations transforming the formerly not-so-digital *monde* of *immobilier*. The traditional and *nouveau* meet each year at MIPIM in Cannes, the world's largest real estate trade show.

Real estate is the largest asset class on Earth, worth $277 trillion, **three times** the total value of all publicly traded companies. Multiple studies have shown that owning property is **the** surest way to wealth creation. French households own more than €8 trillion in real estate. In France, the real estate sector represents 16% of GDP.

The accumulation of land wealth over centuries ensures that property remains the majority holding, 61% of *patrimoine*, in the portfolios of the French. By comparison, in the US, this figure is only 48%, due to a preference for *les actions* (52% of Yanks are stockholders).

More than €500 million was raised by French Proptechs in 2019. France took Europe's top spot in capital raised in the Proptech sector in 2022 after Colonies' €1 billion deal (yes, that's <u>billion</u> with a 'B') with Ares capital, Deepki's €150 million round, the €40 million series A for Masteos less than a year after their €15 million seed injection, Tracktor's €12 million *levée de fonds*, and Financad's $10 million fundraise, just to name a few. One quarter of **all** European Proptech investments in 2022 went to French startups. Meanwhile, VC investments in the US plunged 37% in 2022.

While you might not be a venture capitalist, nor care about the financials of the whiz kids, these figures indicate the health of the ecosystem surrounding your French property. Should you wish to call upon a provider to help you with your budding business, you have a wealth of available options. Companies with resources like these are a good bet to stick around.

France is the number one market in the Eurozone for real estate crowdfunding with more than $110 million invested in 2017. For as little as €10, you can own a brick in the wall of a development project. Homunity, Linxea, Primaliance and dozens of other platforms aggregate these deals claiming double-digit annual returns.

With home sale prices rising 6% in 2017, residential values went up faster in Paris than in either London or New York. Personal real estate resale prices in Paris should continue to rise indefinitely (over the long-term) because of a lack of free lots, a dearth of construction projects creating new dwellings, restrictions on building height, existing population density and the small land footprint of the city. The city limits of Paris are seven times smaller than New York city in surface area. London is spread out 15 times wider than Paris. The City of Light simply doesn't have enough land available for construction to meet ever growing demand.

Possessing property as purely an investment vehicle (not a primary residence) is still a fairly exclusive activity. Only 7.6% of French households are landlords (*bailleurs*) which own at least one property rented year-round to a tenant. However, 68% of people in France would make real estate their #1 investment choice, according to Investissement Locatif. A greater percentage of French own rental property than Americans (6.7% according to IRS income-tax data), partly because at least 20% of US rentals are held by corporations.

Thanks to a number of tax loopholes, property owners in France get to keep a higher percentage of their rental income than just about anywhere else. More than in the USA. More than in the UK and Ireland. Due to tax changes in the UK, the number of available rental units has halved in the last three years. The number of landlords are decreasing in the UK and increasing in France, which has become much more interesting fiscally.

Furnished French dwellings get special tax treatment that doesn't exist in other countries. Who would have thought that France, of all places, could be a *paradis fiscaux* (tax haven)? *Sacre bleu!*

Why a book in English about French real estate?

Despite persistent outdated opinion, the French really have dramatically improved their English skills in recent years. A full 39% people representing 23 million of the entire population are anglophones. Dubbing movies and shows on *télévision* has given way to watching VO (*version originale*) on Netflix, and activating subtitles on ubiquitous smart TVs, tablets and *téléphones*.

While they may choose native French authors and translations for novels and 'escapist' entertainment, a great number prefer to read business, economic and tech information in English. Many find the language clearer and straightforward, with direct prose. Plus, most breakthrough books in these categories were originally written by American and British entrepreneurs. Those who are able, prefer to go to the source, rather than to an inexact translation. Any business school worth its salt in France, such as HEC or ESSEC, which both appear on anyone's list of the world's top universities for commerce, conduct their entire curriculum exclusively in English.

The small selection of original books on business, the economy and technology in French can be a slog, even for the locals. Wading through esoteric terms in a scholarly tome, or endless excerpts of laws that they could access for free, isn't considered good value. French authors often err by seeking exactitude, or completeness, instead of focusing on the gist of what's valuable to the reader. French folks we know like that writers of English nonfiction get to the point, and explain why it matters to the reader.

Real estate content offers one of the most popular topics read regularly by the locals. Among French folks, 37% of them consume property information and ads online, according to a poll by Médiamétrie/NetRatings.

In addition to the natives, there are 150 000 British expatriates living full-time in France according to the Telegraph Property newspaper supplement quoting INSEE. That figure is certainly under-reported, as 100 000 Britons were awarded a new residence permit (*titre de séjour*) in 2021 alone.

The remaining 72 million living in the British Isles, and a significant portion of 330 million Americans, 38 million Canadians, and the rest of the English-speaking world would love to become expats in France, if the number of TV shows, magazines, books, movies and podcasts on the subject are any indication.

France is a popular magnet for 2nd-home buyers from the 'States and seekers of rental income on programs like the USA's 'House Hunters International' with Adrian Leeds. International Living magazine claims 100 000 print subscribers and more than 400 000 visitors to the website every month, 80% based in the U.S. Frenchly.us draws 200 000 monthly readers who regularly visit France every couple years. America now even has it's own "France channel" broadcasting culture *à la française* 24/7 on cable and SVoD. In the first half of 2022, American buyers searching for French properties increased 37%.

As per the findings of the European Commission, the year 2022 saw 12 229 initial resident permits issued to American citizens, enabling them to reside in France. This shows a significant leap from the 9 214 permits issued in 2021. That makes it an all-time high, even surpassing the number of permits granted to individuals from the United Kingdom in 2022.

The UK's 'Homes Under the Hammer' on the BBC or 'A Place in the Sun' or 'Help! We Bought a Village' on Channel 4 similarly cater to wannabe settlers in France. Stories of the *anglais* buying a Loire valley castle to turn it into a bed & breakfast bring a twinkle to the eyes of every Briton. Fun fact, the very first estate agency in France was established in 1818 by an Englishman, John Arthur, expressly to sell Parisian properties to his fellow countrymen.

Locals have their own *télé-réalité* shows like *'L'Agence,'* a series of infomercials about the Kretz family business originally on TMC and now on Netflix, and *'Chasseurs d'Appart'* another puff-piece promoting Stéphane Plaza and his homonymous real estate agencies. Curiously, the French ones all cover their own country's real estate market. *"Tout le monde est d'accord,"* meaning everybody agrees French property is where it's at.

Bestsellers 'My Good Life in France,' '(Not Quite) Mastering the Art of French Living,' and 'Toujours Provence,' are but a few aspirational tomes found regularly on the bookshelves of future expats. Podcasts 'The Earful Tower,' 'Join Us in France' and 'The Land of Desire' stoke the flame of wanting to be in France by listeners from afar.

The 250 000 monthly visitors to the UK's French Property News, and the French Property magazine and website, and thousands of annual attendees to the France Property Show at London's Olympia attest to British aspirations for a bit of *terroir* to call their own. Tens of thousands have already made the leap.

Half of the chalets in Morzine are owned by British nationals. The *départements* of *la Creuse, le Lot, la Dordogne* and *les Alpes-Maritimes* fill out the Top Four destinations for foreign buyers, according to the Superior Council of Notaries or *Conseil supérieur du notariat* (CSN). Overall, each year, between 5-6% of all property purchases in France are made by non-French buyers. That's 70 000 transactions annually, or three quarters of a million *étrangers* who have invested in French property in the past dozen years alone.

In 2018, France hit peak *rosbif*, as 30% of all foreign buyers were British. That year, they were the #1 non-resident purchasers in five of eight French regions, and Americans were #2 in the Paris area. In 2018 for Ile-de-france, 8% of all foreign buyers were Yanks.

What's more, the Notaries' figures only count non-residents. There are 3.3 million people with dual nationality living in France, who, when they buy or own a home here, are counted as French.

If you recognise yourself in one or several of the descriptions above, you're an anglophone ripe to leverage your property for profit.

Conclusion

If you have already invested in residential property located in France, congratulations! You have more options and greater potential to create returns than your European neighbors. We'll tell you which parts of the

French tax code can help you keep more of that money. The next chapters will detail your options, help you calculate your potential, and create a plan to meet your objectives, all while respecting your lifestyle.

If you don't already own space in France, the Expand section at the back of this book will give you many options to get started. At least one of them will be at a price-point which is right for you.

Evaluate

CHAPTER FOUR
Which assets? When available?

At My Property Payday, we encourage you to take a holistic approach to evaluating **all** the spaces you could possibly rent. This begins by compartmentalising your primary residence.

Separate Spaces

Write down a list of each and every space in your dwelling. If you have more than one property, begin with your primary residence, then complete the exercise for your secondary properties.

First, eliminate all spaces which are **never** available, either because you always use them, or because they're not adapted to rental, or because you don't want to. These can include an office where you have all your computer equipment or important papers. Your daughter's old room that you don't want to disturb for her impromptu visits back from university. A garage which is full of tools, machinery and boxes. A project room strewn with knick-knacks and supplies. An attic of old junk. A shed for your gardening pots and clippers with a leaky roof. Cross them off your list for now. We'll get back to them in the Optimize section.

Although they can't be rented, these spaces can help the rest of your rental business. They offer an area where you can temporarily move personal items from other useful spaces. Secure your personal effects in these unused spaces for the time of your rental, then move them back again when the rental period is over.

Second, set aside all spaces which are dependencies to other rental activity. For example, you can't rent out your entire home without also renting out your kitchen. Your kitchen is a dependency to the whole home rental. Similarly, a guest bathroom adjacent to a guest room essentially 'belongs' to the room rental. Nobody wants to rent your broom closet, unless it's a part of your home rental, which will require a place for cleaning supplies. Dependencies can also include the attic and basement (if filled with your personal items), parking garage (if your car is there all the time), laundry room, pantry, entryway, dining room, etc.

Third, what remains are your property **assets** which can be rented. List them and give them a short nickname that you put into parentheses. They could include, for example: a master bedroom (B1), son's bedroom (B2), guest bedroom (B3), dining/desk study (D1), open living area/loft (L1), or other spaces of interest to renters. In the city, you might also have an empty parking garage/ box (G1), a rooftop terrace (RT1) or a street-level storefront (SF1) which is not used at night or on weekends. In the country or the suburbs, you might also have a lawn/field (Y1), swimming pool or jacuzzi (P1), deck with outdoor barbecue (T1), treehouse/teepee or other permanent play structure outside (TH1), a guest house/in-law unit (ADU1), cellar/basement (C1), attic (A1), storeroom or barn or shed (SH1).

List them all, one line each. Download a handy template from MyPropertyPayday.com in the resources section to create your own list. You probably never realised how many assets you have!

Now, build out your list by including the amenities of each space, starting with the number of beds and sleeping capacity. For example, a room with a queen bed and a bunk bed has 3 beds, and a capacity of 4 people. A table/large desk in a dining room with six seats can host up to six simultaneous digital nomads at a co-work space.

Lastly, measure the approximate size of each space. The m^2 will be used later to establish a rental value of the space, and determine the price you wish to display. The first measure should be the total area of the space, which is useful to calculate for people renting for habitation.

A second measure is helpful to determine the effective space within the total. Let's say a room has $16m^2$, but you don't want to move out an armoire taking up $2m^2$. The armoire should be subtracted if you want to have an exercise activity in that space, leaving $14m^2$.

Or, imagine you have an empty loft which could be used for storage. The floor area covers $40m^2$, however it's underneath a slanted roof, which goes from 0cm to 150cm at the highest point. A minimum of $1m^3$ is required for the '*stockage*' companies, so if you want to store other people's boxes in that space, your new effective total becomes $20m^3$.

Availability

Go back to the first space, the one labeled (B1), and think about when it's available. Each space should have its own calendar.

Say (B1) is your master bedroom, where you sleep normally. Maybe it's only available when you go on your annual 3-week summer vacation. Maybe you leave for more weeks, perhaps every time school's out, for a total of eight weeks in the year. Maybe in addition to school vacations, you're ready to abandon your master bedroom every single weekend you have a booking. Whatever availability you choose, note by that space when it's free, and block when it's not to be used.

Since having a calendar for each space can be complex, at MyPropertyPayday we're developing a Universal calendar tool to help our members manage the availability of all their spaces.

Take the next space and conduct the same exercise. Chances are the results will be widely different.

For example, if (B2) is your son's bedroom, and he's enrolled in university three hours away, then he might plan to be home every time school's out. A very interesting conversation could ensue, where you explain the family's financial goals, and how changing his patterns of homecoming could create potential gains for the household. If (B1) and (B2) were to align more often, a wider space could be rented (the whole home). The family could be reunited in a different leisure spot. Or, junior could remain at the dorms that Mom & Dad are probably paying for anyway.

Here, you should begin to see the power of separating out each space, with its own calendar. This allows you to do very interesting mixes, which didn't exist prior to your planning. Good job!

Maison Bleue

As this methodology is new, it may be useful to reference an example. We'll call our fictional property the *'maison bleue'* (blue house) and refer to it often throughout these pages. It's a medium-sized property, meaning it should be fairly comparable to something you might own already.

The *famille 'Forestier'* occupies the house, which is their main residence. Maxime is a guitarist often on tour, and his wife, Nina, is a designer feelin' good working from home, allowing her to run their property rental business. Their eldest daughter, Joni, has moved away to Canada, leaving her room (B2) vacant. Their son, Richard, is away at Fairport university, but lives in his old room (B3) when he comes back during school breaks.

The *maison bleue* is a detached, single-family house situated on a plot of land that covers 440m² (20m long by 22m wide). The footprint of the house sits on an outside foundation of 63m² (7m long by 9m wide). The house occupies three levels, composed of a basement (*sous-sol*), ground floor (*rez-de-chaussée*) and upstairs (*1er étage*). There is also a small attic above.

Following are some graphic representations of the different levels of the *maison bleue*, created with the free tool Kozikaza.

Basement (*sous-sol*) underground level of the *maison bleue* includes the

cellar (C1), garage (G1) and driveway (G2) slanted down from the street level.
(figure 1):

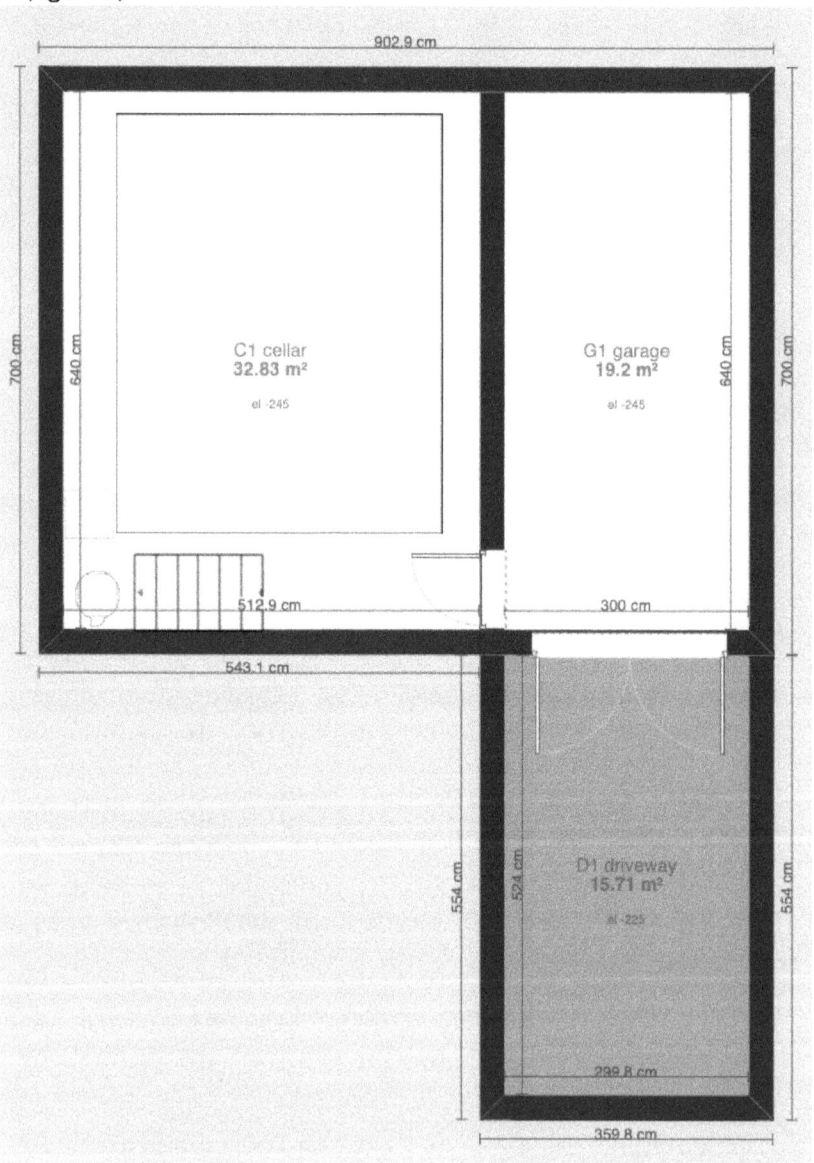

Above-ground, inside the 30cm-thick walls, the interior liveable surface area (*loi Carrez*) is calculated at 104m², which is the main figure used to determine resale value. The Carrez law was created to avoid imprecision in the measurement of real estate. A sanctioned technician (called a '*géomètre*') must be hired to establish the official surface area by taking the interior floor plan, then subtracting partitions/walls, stairs, balconies, terraces and any interior area without at least 1.8m clearance.

Ground floor (*rez-de-chaussée*) level of the *maison bleue* including the living room (L1) and dining area (D1) inside, and the front (Y2) and backyard (Y2), pool (P1), terrace (T1) and shed (SH1) outside.
(figure 2) :

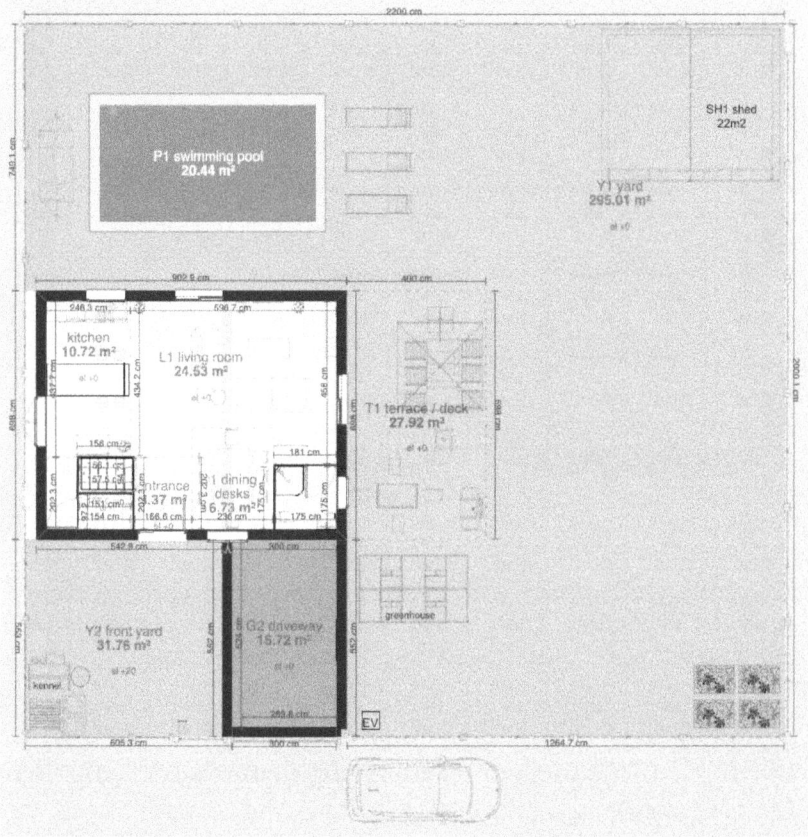

The interior is the size of an average townhouse in the country, but a bit smaller than the average detached house (124m²) in France. It has three bedrooms, each with a double bed, and a convertible sofa in the living room, enabling the whole property to sleep a maximum of eight people. The inhabitants share two full bathrooms.

* * *

Upstairs (*1er étage*) level of the *maison bleue* contains the three bedrooms (B1, B2 & B3), seen here. The attic (A1) which is just above the bedrooms, is unseen on the images.
(figure 3):

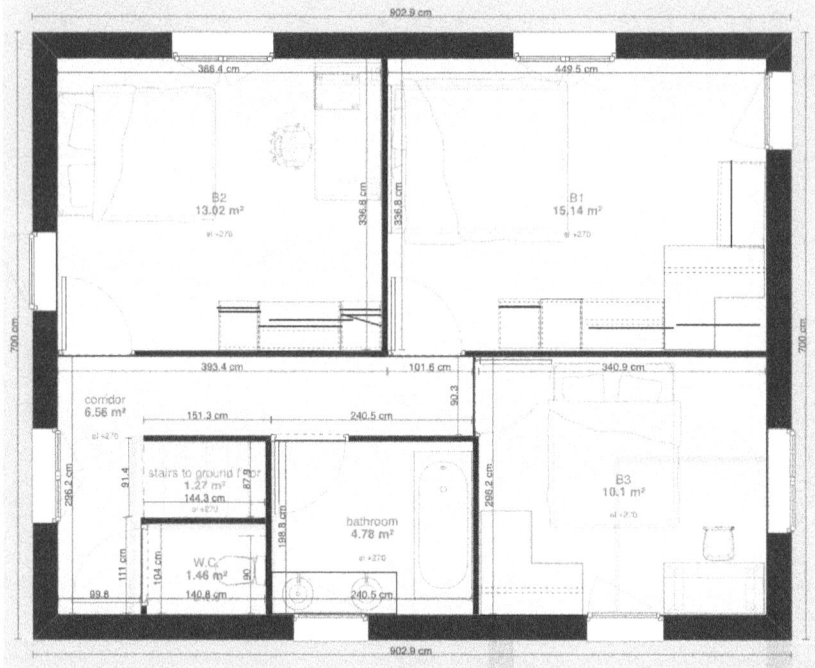

We've broken up the home into 14 distinct 'spaces' which could **each** be rented out separately. There's also the 'whole home' combining all of these spaces in a traditional fashion. Here's the breakdown of these attributes:

Whole home
- (H1), entire property of house, 104m², and surrounding land, 295m² (includes all listed below)

Spaces which could be rented separately:
- (A1), attic, 30m², or 30m³ total (available year-round but practical for boxes only)
- (B1), master bedroom, 15m²; (available separately only if residents move into one of the other rooms, B2 or B3; unlikely to rent each room to three different sets of travelers on unrelated bookings)

- (B2), second bedroom, 13m²; (16m² if paired with downstairs shower)
- (B3), third bedroom, 10m²; (13m² if coupled with downstairs shower)
- (C1), cellar / basement, 33m² (20m² usable for activity); or 50m³ total
- (D1), dining / desk study, 7m²; seats available: 8 sold separately by hour/day
- (G1), parking garage / box, 19m²; or 38m³; accessible from G2 or from the interior via C1
- (G2), driveway parking spot, 16m²; an awning above provides shade and rain protection
- (L1), living room / salon, 25m²
- (P1), swimming pool, 20m²
- (SH1), shed, 22m², or 44m³; accessible for vehicles through side gate going over lawn;
- (T1), outdoor terrace / deck, 28m²
- (Y1), yard / lawn, 295m²; including P1, SH1 and T1 within its perimeter
- (Y2), front yard, 32m²

Dependent spaces which cannot be rented separately
- Kitchen, cupboards, bathrooms, showers, closets, stairs, corridors, etc.

The surface areas are listed to establish the value, and also see what's possible in each space. Estimating value will be covered in the chapter 'Money: Meters Matter Most.'

Some of the spaces of the *maison bleue* are not dependent, per se, but they are tightly connected. The yard (Y1), for example, is not likely to be rented to retired campers, while at the same time college kids rent the pool (P1), and 30-somethings hold a baby shower on the deck (T1). It could conceivably happen, but the groups might not appreciate the others' presence, badly affecting ratings.

The Forestiers have decided that it's probably best to open the yard (Y1), pool (P1), and deck (T1) on all listings simultaneously, but when they get a booking for one of them, they block the calendars of the other two. Decisions like these will be discussed in the 'Preferences' chapter. You'll get to anticipate 'what if?' scenarios and gauge your comfort-level (and that of your housemates), so you can make choices best adapted to your situation.

The family has also decided on the availability of each space. This has allowed them to create the following calendar for the different spaces of

the *maison bleue*.
(figure 4):

Maison Bleue availability calendar Year: 2023												total available days
space	JAN	FEB	MAR	APR	MAY	JUN	JUL	AUG	SEP	OCT	NOV	DEC	
H1	1	X	X	X	X	X	X	1-31	X	X	X	16-31	48
A1	1-31	1-28	1-31	1-30	1-31	1-30	1-31	1-31	1-30	1-31	1-30	1-31	365
B1	X	X	X	X	X	X	X	X	X	X	X	X	0
B2	2-31	1-28	1-31	1-30	1-31	1-30	1-31	X	1-30	1-31	1-30	1-15	318
B3	2-31	1-24	13-31	1-21	9-31	X	X	X	5-30	1-21	2-30	1-15	269
C1	2-31	1-28	1-31	1-30	1-31	1-30	1-31	X	1-30	1-31	1-30	1-15	318
D1	2-31	1-28	1-31	1-30	1-31	1-30	1-31	X	1-30	1-31	1-30	1-15	318
G1	1-31	1-28	1-31	1-30	1-31	1-30	1-31	1-31	1-30	1-31	1-30	1-31	365
G2	2-31	1-24	13-31	1-21	9-31	X	X	X	5-30	1-21	2-30	1-15	269
L1	2-31	1-28	1-31	1-30	1-31	1-30	1-31	X	1-30	1-31	1-30	1-15	318
P1	X	X	X	1-30	1-31	1-30	1-31	X	1-30	1-31	X	X	184
SH1	1-31	1-28	1-31	1-30	1-31	1-30	1-31	1-31	1-30	1-31	1-30	1-31	365
T1	X	X	X	1-30	1-31	1-30	1-31	X	1-30	1-31	X	X	184
Y1	X	X	X	1-30	1-31	1-30	1-31	X	1-30	1-31	X	X	184
Y2	2-31	1-28	1-31	1-30	1-31	1-30	1-31	X	1-30	1-31	1-30	1-15	318

Reading this calendar, you see that -
- The attic (A1) is available year-round (until it becomes filled with renters' boxes). Same with the garage (G1) and shed (SH1), which can be rented to individuals for parking and storage, but are off limits to other renters.
- The master bedroom (B1) is never available separately, but only as a part of the Whole home (H1)
- The third bedroom (B3) is only occupied when Richard returns on break from school, as he'll do February 25-March 12, for example. B3 is available for rental March 13 to 31, when Richard is at university.
- Calendars for the pool (P1), terrace (T1) and yard (Y1) are tightly aligned. They could be rented collectively, or solely, but it's unlikely to have two different renters for two of these simultaneously.
- All spaces apart from the attic (A1), garage (G1) and shed (SH1) have their calendars blocked for the month of August, and the end of December. This is when the Forestiers go together on their family vacations, leaving the whole home (H1) available for

rental.

Adding up the available days in the far-right column will be useful in determining the rental value potential of each space. In the subsequent chapters of this Evaluate section, we'll create hypotheses by entering the number of days into a simplified formula, multiplying by the expected daily revenue from a certain usage of that space. This will allow us to compare different usages, and how much could be generated from each.

Location
Your property is set in a certain locale, which gives it a set of attributes. These run from the value of real estate in that area, to the strength of demand from tourists, to the number of college students, to the level of urban density, to the local regulation and taxation. Each city has its own proper regulations and taxation, as does the country overall.

Let's imagine the *maison bleue* is located in a desirable area of Toulon, postal code 83000, within 4km of the city center, near easy transport links to office buildings and schools. Therefore, the summer 2022 purchase valuation would be around €3 500/m² (€364 000), and the long-term unfurnished rental value around €14/m²/mo. for the whole property.

Using the example of Toulon will allow you to extrapolate for your particular city, and compare with others. In terms of tourism, cost-of-living, local economy, size, rental demand, student population, etc., Toulon is pretty middle-of-the-road. However, it's among the cities in France with the highest property tax. This makes it less desirable for a new investment, an idea we'll explore later. For now, the Forestiers already live there, so they'll make do with what they have.

Toulon's population is under 200 000, which gives property owners more liberty to rent how they want, however, not as much as if the population was under 50 000. These distinctions will be covered in the 'Regulation' chapter.

The property tax rate for Toulon is 43% (21st most expensive city in France), which is not as bad as it seems. The '43%' is simply a base number in the overly-complex calculation. The annual property tax bill for the *maison bleue* is €1 878. If it was a pure investment property, this tax would need to be factored in to calculate the net return. However, the *maison bleue* is the Forestier's main residence, so we're going to leave out property tax in our simulations.

Space / Assets
Let's now turn our attention away from the '*maison bleue*' and to your property. Here is a list of the many different kinds of spaces you may

own, which could each be an asset that is rented separately-

Dwelling (entire): Villa | Chalet | Whole Home | House | Apartment | Condominium | Loft | Studio

Shared accommodation: Room | Bedroom | GuestRoom | BonusRoom

Detached dwelling: ADU | Tiny house | Mother-in-law unit | Treehouse | MobileHome | Campsite | RV/Campervan

Outdoor Event/Activity/Dayuse space: Terrace | Rooftop | Pool | Garden | Open Air Location | Sports Location | Spa & Wellness | Lawn | Unusual venue

Indoor Event/Activity/Dayuse space: Lounge | HomeCinema | Bar | Workshop/Atelier

Storage: Parking spot | Garage/Box | Barn | Store room | Attic | Basement | Shed | Warehouse | unused spare room

Amenity: EV Charging Station | Kennel | Farm

Other asset which could be rented (not all are covered in this book): Waterside Location | Boat | Car | Power tool | Appliance

This list is meant to be as complete as possible. If we've missed anything, please let us know at info@mypropertypayday.com so we may include in future editions.

Now that you know what you've got, the next chapter will help you establish what it's worth.

CHAPTER FIVE
Money: meters matter mostly

Since many new platforms have sprung up, creating the sharing economy, a few have chosen to also invent a new pricing basis for rentals.

Some have the number of beds determine the price. Thus, a smaller place with more beds will be priced higher than a bigger place with fewer beds.

Other platforms price based upon time used. A pool can accommodate a dozen swimmers at once, but the platform charges per person per hour, instead of a figure based on max capacity.

Serviced apartments charge more for amenities such as an in-room kitchenette. Co-work offices charge per seat. Parking spaces are per month. Storage is often per box.

None of these convert easily from one to another.

With all of these disparate methods, how does one arrive at a price which is both attractive to renters and profitable to property owners? The basis that we advocate at My Property Payday is by settling on the same unit of measure used in the real-estate profession for decades: **the square meter** m^2 (equivalent of the square foot f^2 in the US and the UK).

Both residential and commercial real estate sales prices in France are expressed in euro per square meter, or €/m^2. Home and room **rental** prices are expressed in €/m^2/mo. So why shouldn't it be the same for short-term accommodations? Or parking? Or storage? Or any other use of that same space.

In France, nationwide limits are placed on how much you can charge to student lodgers per m^2 per month in two different zones. Further long-term rent controls are in place in certain municipalities, regulating the maximum increase in €/m^2/mo. from year to year.

The unit of measure in all cases is the square meter.

* * *

Size matters (small is worth more :-)

That square meter isn't alone, of course, it's a part of a whole. It could be a m² in a cow pasture, or a m² in a studio apartment. It's a market principle that the **bigger** the whole, the **smaller** the value of one m² within that property. The inverse is also true. The **smaller** the whole, the **bigger** the value of one m² within.

Take two apartments of similar condition, on the same floor, in the same building, in the same city. One has a surface area of 50m² and is called a T3 in France, because it has two bedrooms (don't ask). The other has a surface area of 18m² and is called a studio. The T3 will have a lower sale price/m² and lower rent/m²/mo. than the studio. This logic follows in **all** the listings you see to buy or rent property, and in the calculator provided by the city of Paris to figure rent (because of rent control - more on that later).

STR platform search results list sleeping capacity only. They never tell you how big is the accommodation. This runs contrary to everything we know about valuation. A 20m² youth hostel room with four bunk beds is not worth more than a 50m² hotel suite with a California kingsize bed.

Most hosts also omit to put the surface area in their listing description. We feel this is not only an error, as adding m² helps tourists better evaluate what they're getting, but also without m², you as a fellow host don't know what you're competing against.

You sleep four and so do they, but their rate is €40 less. You may be tempted to match it. In most cases you'd do better to stick to your guns. If your method is sound, and you respect your goals, you should do fine in STR. We're not saying to completely ignore comp rates, but they shouldn't be given outsize weight versus all other factors.

Just because your competitors are cramming in guests like sardines in a can doesn't mean you should follow suit. Sure, you could better outfit your place for the occasional party which has one or, *à la limite*, two more guests than you normally host comfortably. The Optimize section will present nifty ideas to do this in a clever way. You should get better reviews by respecting common norms on space allotted per person.

Time matters (less is worth more :-)

What changes from instances of sales or rentals for the same exact space is the amount of **time** those square meters are allocated to the buyer/renter. **More** time (a permanent purchase) costs **less** per unit (€/m²/mo.). **Less** time (a 3-year lease) costs **more** per unit (€/m²/mo.).

It stands to reason, then, that **even less** time (a one-month lease) should cost **even more** per unit (€/m²/mo.). A two-day rental should cost more per day than a one-week rental. This is why platforms like Airbnb and Booking allow hosts to put both a nightly rate, and an overall discount for extended stays. Instead of a volume discount, they enable a time discount; the more time you rent that space, the less you pay per day/night.

Here is a chart which illustrates how time can affect the value of a particular property. In all cases, we're referring to the same property. The only thing that changes is the amount of time it's used. The chart goes from a 25-year mortgage on the far left, to a 3-day rental on the far right.

As you can see on the bottom line, the less time it's used, the higher the cost per day. The longer it's used, the less the cost per day.

(figure 5):

Comparing theoretical value of real estate based on amount of time used

Property: apartment in Paris Size in m2: 60
Sale value/m2: €10,000 Sale value total: €600,000
Rental value €/m2/mo.: €34 (note: avg. across Paris in 08/2022, unfurnished incl. charges)
Usage: accommodation

Transaction type:	Purchase	Rental	Rental	Rental	Rental	Rental
Contract type:	mortgage	standard lease, unfurnished	standard lease, furnished	mobility lease, furnished	short-term via ecommerce platform	short-term via ecommerce platform
Term (years):	25	3	1	0.75	0.04	0.01
Value per Year	€24,000	€24,480	€28,152	€36,598	€55,506	€56,360
Term (months):	300	36	12	9	0.5	0.1
Value per Month	€2,000	€2,040	€2,346	€3,050	€4,270	€4,697
Term (weeks):	1300	156	52	39	2	0.43
Value per Week	€462	€471	€541	€704	€985	€1,084
Term (days):	9125	1095	365	274	14	3
Value per Day	**€66**	**€67**	**€77**	**€100**	**€141**	**€155**

The time effect economic phenomenon is borne out by observing the correlation which happens in the real market. We encourage you to employ the same basic time logic to your pricing.

Of course, you'd benefit from a finer exploration of the ratios between one column and another. Should a mobility lease be 20% or 40% higher than a 1-year lease? For the shortest terms you'd do best to consider seasonality, and play with daily rates to see how that affects occupancy, to find which balance delivers the highest overall return.

The 'Value per year' line assumes 100% occupancy year-round, which is unrealistic for the last three columns. However, the last line is absolutely realistic, averaged out over the course of a year of rental bookings.

For now, it's good enough to acknowledge that less time rented should equal a higher daily rate. If you're charging the same per day for a 2-week rental that you'd charge for a 3-month rental, there's something wrong, and you should revise accordingly.

This effect is further accentuated for the spaces **inside** a property.

Imagine inside the 60m² apartment listed previously there's a bedroom of 12m². The value of the bedroom rented on a student lease should be higher per month per m² than the price/m²/mo. of renting the entire apartment to university goers.

A common and valid way used by real estate agents to estimate the value of space in the case of a home sale is the following... Interior which meets *loi Carrez* should be valued at a ratio of 1/1; Interior lower than loi Carrez (<1m80): 1/2; Exterior liveable area (like an outdoor terrace): 1/3.

So, if the standard interior is valued at €6 000/m² on the resale market, then the part of the inside which is less than 180cm high because it's under the slanted roof could logically said to be worth €4 000/m². An exterior veranda could be said to be worth €2 000/m².

About 20% of apartments in Paris have a balcony or terrace. Less than 5% of those are large enough or attractive enough to cater to event coordinators.

Location and other Factors

Of course, many other factors can influence the price, such as condition, amenities, decoration/style, view, etc. The most important of these is the location of the property. The price per m² of your property will be very similar to that of your neighbors. The variation between the very best and worst properties on the same block is almost always slight compared on a price/m² basis. However, price per m² between properties located in geographical areas far apart will vary greatly.

Location influences price per m² for both the sale market and the rental market in lockstep. Looking at the 20 arrondissements in Paris, we compared sale price €/m² with rent €/m²/mo. from highest to lowest. There is a **90% correlation** between the sale and rental prices, with five neighborhoods sharing the exact same ranking on both lists, and the others predominantly within a spot or two.

Thus, the average sale price per square meter in a town can be used as a fairly reliable measure for both resale and rental, for any property in that town. For any particular sale, the variance from the mean €/m² differs, but not greatly.

In some big cities, regulation is a factor which topples the natural balance of space/time. Rent control artificially lowers long-term lease rates (columns 3 and 4 in the previous table) without affecting short-term rentals (columns 5, 6 & 7). Legislation restricting the number of Airbnbs in a town drives up the nightly rates of the ones remaining with the authorization to operate.

While you must comply with laws in place, your space/time ratios should not be bent down, nor up, too far from where they would be without government intervention.

Amenities

Owners who rent their entire dwelling to holiday makers, can earn an 80% premium on their rental rate per week, if the property includes a swimming pool.

Other amenities similarly drive up demand (a lot) or the amount you can charge (a little) per time used. For now, you'll make do with what you have. The 'Make it Better' chapter in the Optimize section will detail amenities you may consider adding, and estimate the impact those extras will have on your bottom line.

Revenue management

Hotels, airlines, theatres and other temporary 'space-sellers' have a product which is limited in quantity, and perishable. The opportunity to sell what they have disappears each day, just like expired milk. Either they get a booking for room 307 on July 14th 2024 or they don't. On July 15th 2024, they can never again sell room 307 for July 14th 2024.

These companies operate by a set of pricing principles and methods designed to maximise overall yield. A full in-flight economy cabin would show wild variations between the price paid by the person in 10C and the person in 23D. That's because they bought at different times, in varying conditions from two distinct points of sale, and other factors.

Revenue managers work their inventory like the stock market, ratcheting prices up or down by the minute depending on demand, and reacting quickly to what the competition is doing. Their goal is the greatest overall ticket take from fares of passengers on that flight, or theatergoers on that night, or room renters in their hotel.

Similarly, homeowners can apply some of the key principles of revenue management to your rentals, mostly on the STR segment:

Occupancy vs. Rate

Before you look at your rates, first look at occupancy. Are you where you expect to be, at this time of year? Realistic occupancy expectations for STR should be around 35% in low season, 55% in mid-season (or year-round average) and 75% in high season. If you're below these levels, you may consider lowering your prices, especially if you're just starting out. Try a -5 to -10% decrease for a month and observe.

If you're fully booked, you should absolutely consider raising your prices. You're almost certainly leaving money on the table. If you're hesitant, try a small incremental strategy, say a 2 to 4% increase for a month, and see what happens. If you're still fully booked, repeat for another month with another 2 to 4% increase.

***

Key days/dates

Special events: On holidays, major cultural festivals and sports match days, you can and should charge more than you usually do. During the 2024 Olympic games, Airbnb predicts the average host in France will earn €2 000 gross total, for an ADR of €200, or 70% above the ADR generated on the platform in summer 2022. The average host in the Paris region should achieve an ADR of €221, or 85% above the €119/night garnered on Airbnb in IDF in 2022. An 85% increase in ADR is what hoteliers were able to get during the 2012 London games.

Weekend vs weekday: Friday and Saturday nights will be the most popular, and warrant a higher rate.

In one month, you could have a dozen different rates if you're fully optimizing daily tariffs. Ask your region's tourist office, or your city hall which upcoming events are the most attended by people from out-of-town.

Minimum stay threshold

Unless you have little demand, or lots of competition, a two-night minimum would be our lowest recommendation. More, and you'll miss out on weekenders who don't want to pay for Sunday. Less, and you'll risk being empty on a Friday night, one of your most lucrative days.

If, one month out, you see your calendar has holes, like an unbooked Wednesday here, or an empty space on a Tuesday, you can temporarily lower your minimum stay threshold. Of course, you should also gauge your capacity to deliver a quality customer experience on such a quick turnaround. If your outgoing guests check out late at noon, and your incoming guests arrive at 4 p.m. will you have enough time to get the space ready?

Seasonality

Your property will have greater demand at certain periods of the year, and less demand at other periods. What is the premium you could ask for? Which reduction should you employ for the thin months?

Keep in mind high and low seasons can differ per region. February, during the Winter school break would be low season in Nantes, but high season in the *Pyrenées* for peak skiing conditions, and in Nice, because that's when they hold their well-attended annual *Carnaval* parade.

Long-stay discounts

You're more likely to generate more revenue by slightly discounting for a 7-day request, rather than counting on getting two separate bookings for 5-days and 2-days at regular rates. It takes a lot more effort to get that second booking than it would to accept the reduced-rate 7-day stay.

Operationally, it's also more work for you and your team. In some areas, there's a lack of cleaning staff available midweek. Do you want to do that yourself? Will you risk that the space is less than pristine when the guests arrive?

Everybody does it, including hotels, so volume discounts are widely considered a good idea, and expected by guests. The questions are, how many days and what percentage?

Referencing the example above, if your average ADR is €150 normally, then a 5-day booking would bring you €750 gross. Even if you discounted your 7-day stay by 25%, you'd still make more money for that week, €787.50 gross, than accepting the 5-day plus having two empty days. A good compromise, which is probably still attractive to tourists, would be a 15% discount for a 7-day stay, generating €892.50 gross.

Revenue managers are true professionals who earn their money. The hotels, airlines and other companies they work for can't afford to leave money on the table. Proof that they don't comes from hotel industry data company CoStar, who predicted hotel transactions to increase by 15% in 2023.

While the bar has been raised significantly in the sharing economy in recent years, the vast majority of hosts (and even property managers) don't have a clue how to price their space. They remain amateurs, far below the level of professionalism shown by revenue managers. They have no plan, no methodology, nor any system of putting it in place.

Worse, if they are using tools tracking what others are charging on Airbnb, they reassure themselves with the illusion of using science. Examples of these bits of software include Airbtics, AirDNA, Key Data, Beyond Pricing, PriceLabs, RateGenie, Wheelhouse. They are covered thoroughly in the 'Toolset tack-ons' chapter in the Optimize section.

Case in point: According to Inside Airbnb's data, there were 75 241 listings in London on 14 March 2023, of which 45 714 (61%) were for entire homes rather than rooms within a home. Airbnb does not endorse the data published by Inside Airbnb. It has argued Inside Airbnb's data does not properly identify active listings and does not account for the fact that multiple listings might be for the same property.

The worst solution of all is when hosts hand over control to Airbnb by activating that platform's so-called 'Smart' pricing. The platform inevitably selects rates which are far below market value, and may not even cover your expenses and labor.

Now, we're not saying don't use these tools. They are useful, when consulted in context. But you should not consider them the 'be-all, end-all' basis to go by. There's a more useful North Star to guide you, one that's been used successfully for decades.

Rental valuation the My Property Payday way

In our philosophy, we believe the Resale market informs the LTR market for accommodation. Subsequently, the LTR market informs the STR market.

Fluctuations are rampant at the end of the spectrum with the shortest time usage for accommodation. Frequently, these data points are out of whack for a spell. However, they almost always fall back in line when observed over a period of several years. Annual average ratios from type to type are fairly constant from year to year.

In our methodology and algorithms at My Property Payday, we deploy the following:
- Multiple data sources- not scraping Airbnb alone
- Weighting m^2 as the most important factor
- Standard ratios between rate types- like Low season vs. High season
- Space elements- as explained earlier in this chapter
- Time elements- as explained earlier in this chapter
- Base rates- so you can add platform fees on top
- Usage components- the same space could be used for lodging or an activity or storage, but although the space and time are identical, rates are different for each usage

The same basic rule of thumb works, albeit crudely, in comparing different uses for the same space. Let's imagine you had a $14m^2$ box/garage space and were allowed to put anyone or anything inside. The price you could charge for rent to a person will be about double what you could charge for parking.

The price you could charge for storage would be about 20% more per unit (m^2/m^3) than for parking. However, renting parking you'll use up all the space, and recoup all the value, whereas you're unlikely to do so with storage. Taking into account occupancy per unit, your rental income potential for storage will be about half as much as parking.

So, these uses follow fairly consistently on the lines of, "the higher value the contents, the more rent you can charge." With activities, it's the value of the show being put on which determines rental income. For the same space and time, a movie production crew will pay thousands, while an art class will generate '*des clopinettes*,' or peanuts.

This book advocates looking at each of your spaces as a distinct asset in your portfolio. All asset managers encourage diversification for both good returns and hedging your bets against volatility.

Those who trade stocks and bonds already have one data point which allows them to compare different products and their performance over time: the share price. In order to attempt the same within the sharing economy for real estate, we need to settle on one data point. We have chosen the **Resale cost/m²** in a given area as the reference. This is the jump off point from which we calculate all rental prices.

From that one data point, all the rest of our estimations flow. We can continue to refer to it even when our usage changes. If we stop renting short-term (or are forced to abandon due to new legislation), we needn't scrap our calculations and go back to the drawing board. We can maintain our methodology, which will be reinforced, because we now have real data from both the resale market, and the short-term rental market.

We do not fully reveal our proprietary formula in these pages, for several reasons. Foremost, because it requires constant adjustment, and we want this book to hold information which will be relevant for a long time. Also, while it works for us, it may be overly complex for clients to maintain themselves, requiring live digital feeds from the source data, and chain-reaction calculations.

That's why we've chosen to promote guiding principles, rather than refer to a spreadsheet which would be out-of-date the moment it's published. If you follow these principles, you should do fine with your pricing. Should you wish to optimize, My Property Payday is happy to consult with you on an ad-hoc basis.

We're building out our toolset so members may complete their simulations online. Meanwhile, contact us for custom reports estimating the earnings potential and suggesting pricing for different uses of your property throughout the year.

CHAPTER SIX
Uses best adapted to each space

Some spaces just naturally lend themselves to a certain usage. Bedrooms for accommodations, of course. Terraces for events. Attics for storage. Living rooms for activities. Garages for parking, etc.

You could follow the logic, and use your space the way most other people do. This is certainly a good first step.

To truly maximize the potential of your space, though, you could look at it in a different way. This begins by seeing each of your spaces through the eyes of others. They will attribute a value to your space when used in a certain way that you may not have thought of.

Also, one of your spaces doesn't always have to be the same thing. A loft could hold morning yoga classes, then host nomadic independents for co-working during the day, and finally tango instruction at night.

Try opening your mind before settling on what each of your spaces is meant for.

Diversify usage

What will any good investment advisor tell you is the number one thing you should do with your asset portfolio? Diversify.

Want to best manage the return on your stocks? Diversify.

Prefer to hedge your bets against radically changing taxation and regulation? Diversify.

Experiencing wild swings in demand from high season to low season in your business? Diversify.

Competition driving your prices lower and lower? Diversify.

With real estate, diversification hasn't been possible. Until now.

During the March 2020 lockdown in Paris, there was a 100% increase in the number of furnished long-term rentals advertised, as owners switched from offering their space on STR platforms like Booking.com.

As laid out in chapter three, we'd highly recommend treating each one of your available spaces as a separate asset. Each asset will become either more, or less attractive for different uses throughout the year. Position your space so that it's ready to meet higher demand, when that demand arises.

In January, everybody's looking to store away their Christmas decorations, but fewer people are looking for a room to rent, unless it's near a ski resort. The French Alps saw an 80% occupation rate for ski resort properties for the December 2019 holidays. In July, people are travelling for vacation, usually in larger groups, looking for a place to swim and barbecue, maybe to camp.

Festivals, conventions, major sports matches and other events drive up demand for short-term lodging. Look ahead in your town's calendar to anticipate booking requests.

Categories of Uses

Here is a listing of the 12 main types of usage, and more than 100 sub-categories, which could each be a different reason why someone or a group of people might wish to rent your space-

Accommodation, STR: motivations and populations can include Tourism | Bed&Breakfast | Festival attendees | Business Travellers | Training | Seeing family/friends | Hospital visits | Event attendance | Divorcees | Job loss rebounders | undergoing Renovations at primary residence | Campers | Gîte breaks | Retreats

Accommodation, LTR: Student housing | Reassignment | Relocation | Research/sabbatical | new Main residence | Roommates | Co-living (prefer shared living to the solitude of own space) | Intergenerrational

Activity (recurring): Yoga | Dance | Book club | Poetry reading | Language exchange | Jam session music in rehearsal studio | Practice Sports/Exercise/Fitness gymnastics martial arts | Painting lessons | Hobbyists | Cinephiles | Scouts | Cultural | Sewing circle | Toastmasters public speaking | Rehearsal stage | Podcast recording | Association discussion | Political civic get-together | Neighborhood watch organizing | Pré-natal | Childcare/nursery | Pet Care | Petting zoo

Business function (recurring): Coworking space | Office space | Workspace | Office desk | Board meeting | Business center | Consultation (therapy, massage, makeover) | ChildCare

Corporate/Teambuilding (one-off): MICE (for "Meetings, Incentives, Corporate Events) | Meeting clients | Networking | startup Pitches | Conference Day office | Corporate event spaces | Dark store | Offsite | Presentations | Awards | Conference rooms | Training sessions | Seminar breakout

Creative endeavors (one-off): Film studio shoot | Cinema preview | Photostudio | Ad spot | Production | Wrap party

Celebration/Party (one-off): Birthday | Anniversary of marriage | Baby shower | Bachelorette/Bachelor party (*EVJF - EVG enterrement de vie de jeune fille* or the *enterrement de vie de garçon*) | Wedding or Reception | other private Function

Dining/Drinking (occasional): Restaurant | Banquet hall | Kitchen studio recipe lessons | Beer Garden | Wine tasting | Bar/Cafe | Club | BBQ

Experience/Entertainment: Standup comedy | Theater play | Immersive | private Concert |

Launch (one-off): Gallery art exhibition | Showroom products | Venue press conference | Offsite demonstration | Trade show hall | Mobile Location | Pop-up shop

Parking (daily access): Car | Motorcycle | Trailer | RV | larger items

Storage (long-term): Boxes | Furniture | Container | Appliances | Seasonal | smaller items transportable by hand

Other: Bag storage by the hour | Winterizing boat/car/motorcycle/RV campervan | Church religious service | Recording Studio with equipment | Carpentry/Textile Workshop with machines | Hobby meetup with material left onsite | etc.

This list of more than 101 uses is meant to be as comprehensive as possible. If we've missed anything, please let us know at info@mypropertypayday.com so we may include in future editions.

Matching usage with space

Here is a list of the 17 main types of spaces that folks commonly have in France. This is an expanded version from the 'Which Assets?' chapter appearing at the beginning of this Evaluate section.

Next to each type you'll find the broad categories of usage which would probably present a match. That's to say the usage would likely be accepted in that space and adapted to it.

Spaces which could be rented separately, and categories of usage which you could consider:

1. (H1), **Home** 1: complete property of house, and surrounding land; entire apartment/condominium; whole loft
    - Accommodation, STR; Accommodation, LTR; Corporate/Teambuilding; Creative endeavors; Celebration/Party; Experience/Entertainment; Launch
2. (H2), **Home** 2: standalone structure which can be inhabited on shared land (guest house / cabin / cottage / ADU / tiny house / '*roulotte*' or camper or trailer / mother-in-law unit / yurt or tipi / treehouse, etc.)
    - Accommodation, STR; Accommodation, LTR; Activity;

Celebration/Party; Dining/Drinking
3. (A1), **Attic**
    - Storage
4. (B1, B2, B3…), **Bedrooms**
    - Accommodation, STR; Accommodation, LTR; Storage
5. (C1), **Cellar** / basement
    - Activity; Storage
6. (D1), **Dining room** / desk(s)
    - Activity; Business function; Dining/Drinking
7. (E1), **Exceptional space**: hobby room / children's playroom / home cinema / private bar, lounge / adult gameroom / home gym, etc.
    - Activity; Business function; Celebration/Party; Experience/Entertainment; Launch
8. (G1), **Garage** / box
    - Activity; Parking; Storage
9. (G2), **Driveway** off-street
    - Parking
10. (L1), **Living room** / salon / family room / den
    - Activity; Business function; Celebration/Party; Experience/Entertainment; Launch
11. (O1), **Office** / spare room / guest room
    - Accommodation, STR; Storage
12. (P1), swimming **Pool** / jacuzzi / pond
    - Activity; Corporate/Teambuilding; Celebration/Party
13. (R1), **Reception room** / parlor / sunroom / study / library
    - Activity; Business function; Celebration/Party; Experience/Entertainment; Launch
14. (SH1), **Shed** / barn / detached workshop or garage
    - Storage
15. (T1), outdoor **Terrace** / deck / veranda / rooftop / pergola
    - Activity; Corporate/Teambuilding; Celebration/Party; Dining/Drinking; Experience/Entertainment; Launch
16. (Y1), **Yard** 1: backyard / lawn / pasture / farm
    - Activity; Corporate/Teambuilding; Celebration/Party; Dining/Drinking; Experience/Entertainment; Launch
17. (Y2), **Yard** 2: front yard, enclosed
    - Activity

Look at your own list of spaces you made after reading the 'Which assets?' chapter. Start to match which uses you would like to explore for each of your spaces.

The next chapter, 'Preferences' will help you further narrow down.

CHAPTER SEVEN
Preferences

Who are you?

Be honest with yourself. There are situations you love, and others you hate.

You may not like meeting strangers in their pyjamas. Or their swimsuits. Or have tent-dwellers open your sliding glass door at 2 a.m. to heed nature's call.

Or maybe you love those quirky things. You could be an extrovert who thrives on meeting new people, the more different the better. You're free and easy with your personal space and love entertaining a regular flow of new folks.

Whatever your personality traits and your state of mind, there's a way the sharing economy can gybe with you and your preferences.

And let's be clear, this is YOUR home. The sharing economy must adapt to YOU.

Let's start by asking a few questions

It's assumed that if you rent the place where you live when you are away, that you are OK with most of the following uses and populations. Otherwise, the sharing economy may not be for you. Obviously, some part of it **is** for you, because you're reading this book ;-)

Where your preferences really come into play is when a certain usage happens at the same time as you're occupying your personal space. Inevitably, you'll have interactions, so you must be ready to deal with queries and complaints, be patient while you wait for guests to finish in an area before you can use it, tolerate different behaviors, noises and smells.

House rules only go so far, post acceptance. Once you've opened a possibility, guest expectations take over. If you don't meet them, your ratings will suffer. It won't matter that you were upfront and transparent on your listing, and clear in your communications. The majority of other hosts are allowing something that you're unwilling to. Will you take the risk of disappointing guests? Or will you join the crowd? Or will you choose to not play that game, while remaining active in other parts of the sharing economy?

Here are the questions to ask yourself, which will help you determine the uses which align with your lifestyle:

While you are home, will you accept the following? Let this list guide you to determine your Preferences:

- Overnight use?
    - Weekdays (Mon-Thu)? Weekends (Fri-Sun)?
    - Short-term (from 1 to 29 days)?
    - Long-term (from 30-365 days)?
    - By Foreign tourists? By Students/Teenagers? Children / toddlers (2+) in group? by Business travelers?
    - Sharing your personal bathroom with guests?
    - Simultaneous usage from unrelated guests?*
- Day use?
    - Outdoor guest access to toilet/shower?**
        - Campers/caravans or tents pitched on your land? Swimmers?
    - Parties? BBQ/meals? Events where alcohol is served?
    - Yoga/Fitness studio? Music practice?
    - Photography/publicity/filming?
    - Corporate training? Co-working?
    - Bag storage by the hour?
    - Storage boxes long-term?
    - Parking with daily access?
    - Daycare / infants?
    - Pet-sitting?

*From renters who don't know one another. Each one would be in a different bedroom, but they may share a bathroom.
**If you do not have toilet/shower outside your home, are you OK providing a house key or code so outdoor guests may use the facilities indoors?

Answer honestly if you're willing to accept each activity or scenario in your home. Set aside maybes, or circumstances or qualifiers like 'only if...' You must choose Yes or No.

Consider that you'll be in the home at the time of the activity, or that you are there with the person described. Be honest, and invite your fellow home dwellers (spouse, children, lodger, etc.) to chime in with their opinions.

Here is how the Forestier family of the *maison bleue* answered these

questions.
(figure 6):

Acceptable	While you are home, will you accept the following:	Not acceptable
X	Overnight use?	
X	Weekdays (Mon-Thu)?	
X	Weekends (Fri-Sun)?	
X	Short-term (from 1 to 29 days)?	
X	Long-term (from 30-365 days)?	
X	by Foreign tourists?	
X	by Students/Teenagers?	
X	Children / toddlers (2+) in group?	
X	by Business travelers?	
	Sharing your personal bathroom with guests?	X
	Simultaneous guest usage?	X
X	Day use?	
X	Outdoor guest access to toilet/shower?	
X	Campers/caravans or tents?	
X	Swimmers?	
X	BBQ/meals with alcohol?	
	Parties?	X
X	Yoga/Fitness studio?	
X	Photography/publicity/filming?	
	Music practice?	X
X	Corporate training?	
X	Co-working?	
	Bag storage by the hour?	X
X	Parking with daily access?	
X	Storage boxes long-term?	
	Daycare / infants?	X
X	Pet-sitting?	

Here is an explanation for some of their choices: the Forestier family is fortunate the *maison bleue* has two full bathrooms, allowing them the luxury of maintaining the upstairs bathroom for family when they have guests staying in the house at the same time. They don't want to take the risk of parties, even youth birthdays, getting out of hand.

Since Nina works from home, and they go to bed early, they've chosen to forego clients who are musicians, which is odd, given their professions, but OK. They'll keep suitcases of guests just before checkin, or after checkout the same day, but don't think the peanuts they'll earn is worth the trouble for tourists who aren't staying there. Finally, they'll tolerate toddlers as part of a family rental, or as members of a group enjoying the yard and pool, but they don't want babies staying regularly in childcare.

You'll have your own reasons, which are perfectly valid for you. It's your home and personal space, after all, and that of the other members of your household.

The better you anticipate situations before they happen, the happier everyone involved will be.

Skill set

Similarly, there may be things you like to do, and others you hate to do. You have things you do well, and others you do less well. Here are some skills and tasks to think about. Are you willing/able to call upon them?

Languages spoken: both Lille and La Rochelle attract many tourists. However, most visiting Lille are foreigners, likely speaking English. The vast majority visiting La Rochelle are from France. If you're hosting them in the region *Rochelloise*, you will be expected to address guests in French. If speaking French is either not something you can do or like to do, it's best not to attract tourists, or to do STR at a different location instead. Speaking Italian is rare in France, and emphasizing this in your listing could please a part of the tourist population and get you more bookings to boot!

Handyman: Campers might want access to an outlet or extension cord, or a water hose, or worse, a sceptic tank to unload their black water. The terrace umbrella or lounge chairs might need to be repaired. Improvements you think of could be realized without calling in an expensive specialist.

Tech support: co-working people want to print occasionally. Sometimes the Wifi goes out inexplicably. Coffee makers and kettles go on the fritz. Can you help business travelers with these issues? Better yet, can you optimize so that each workstation for digital nomads has power and USB outlets at their fingertips?

Heavy lifting: Folks who want to store their belongings *chez vous* might not be able to lift them into the space you've allotted. Or, you may not want them to, for fear of them injuring themselves or damaging your walls during the move. If so, will you offer to lift their items for them? Will you get the boxes or furniture to carry out to their van when they pick up?

Gardener: Sure, you could have a service maintain the lawn, and a pool boy for the *piscine*. However, it's a good idea to have some knowledge in this area before you welcome outdoor guests. Do you know how to test the chlorine levels? Can you raise/lower the water temperature? Will you identify and remove plants which are irritants to the skin or create allergies or worse- poisonous? Are your tomatoes protected from a wayward soccer ball?

Decorator: This is less about a guest who doesn't like the color yellow asking you to repaint. It's more a guest who can't sleep with sunlight asking for blockout drapes. Or installing a bar or wardrobe for hanging clothes. Or a small desk workspace in their rented room. Or an outdoor cove with a protected awning for taking their meals, because you've decided your kitchen and dining table are off-limits. Handling these little touches yourself can save money, and lead to greater customer satisfaction.

Great! Now that you know exactly what you're willing and able to do, let's look at what you are allowed to do, in the next chapter on Regulation.

CHAPTER EIGHT
Regulation

It's your property, but you can't do whatever you want with it. Numerous regulations (*reglementations*) exist, some overlapping. This chapter outlines what is permitted by law in France (as to our knowledge at the time of publication).

First, we must reiterate the obligatory disclaimer that the following does not constitute legal advice. Before undertaking any of these practices, it's best that you consult with appropriate professionals for guidance.

Accommodation purposes

Let's look first at the space usage of having someone pay to stay in your property. Sounds simple enough, doesn't it? Well, believe it or not, there are at least **a dozen different legal frameworks** we can think of which allows this to happen at your home in France.

Before we start deriding France for an overly complex system, let's first give thanks that these structures exist. Without them, we couldn't reliably operate, not knowing where we stood, nor where we should concentrate our efforts or how to invest for the future. Limbo is no place to run a business.

With frameworks, we know precisely what we can and can't do, who we owe money to and for what. Most importantly, we can predict and project outcomes, which allows us to create appropriate strategies, pricing and objectives.

Set aside for now any space which is **not** part of your primary residence, like secondary residences, investment property, undeveloped land, etc. There are at least another dozen legal frameworks for these.

Also, for the moment forget about subleases, coliving arrangements and anything else out of the ordinary. For the majority of you, it's easy to set aside these exceptions, because they don't apply to you.

Only about 10% of the population in France owns a secondary residence, and 67% of second-home owners are 60 years old or over. However, 60% of people in France are homeowners. Remember the first two thirds of this book is aimed at this majority covering all ages which owns but one property.

What we have left are scenarios of a person (or persons) staying in your primary residence. The first question to ask is "For how long are they staying?" There are distinct statutes for stays 'up to 30 days' and 'more than 30 days.' Note, we're talking about any **single** stay here, not the total accumulation of nights rented to all guests.

Up to 30 days (STR)
Whole home renting
Short-term rentals go by many names in France... *la location courte durée* or *LCD*, *la location saisonnière*, *la location chez l'habitant*, and *la location d'une chambre chez l'habitant*. The legal term in France that covers all of them is '*meublés de tourisme*.' We'll cover *gîtes* in the section on secondary residences.

There are few grey areas remaining, but still a lot of confusion about what the regulations actually say. For example, we hear all the time "you can't do Airbnb for more than 120 days," or "it's illegal to sub-lease." Neither is true in all cases.

If your property is in a multi-unit dwelling, you must first verify that the by-laws of the building do not expressly prohibit short-term rental. See if the *règles de copropriété* includes a clause of '*habitation bourgeoise*' forbidding all commercial activity inside the dwellings of the building. If not, and there's nothing expressly denying short-term rentals, then you may in all likelihood conduct that activity legally in that building if the town also permits it.

One lawyer, Dimitri Bougeard, who has looked into this matter extensively, reading all rulings up through November 2022, interprets the law in favor of STR (*LCD*) practitioners. Three things, he claims, should help owners who do STR in apartment buildings remain *tranquille* or rest easy:

1) That STR is not defined as a 'commercial' activity, in the way that hotels or '*parahôtellerie*' is. As long as you don't personally provide 'services' with your rental (breakfast, airport shuttle, etc.), you should be OK.
2) That a *Bourgeoise* simple clause is not sufficient to ban STR. If the building OK's the practice of *professions libérales* such as psychologists, lawyers, doctors, dentists, massage therapists, etc. within their walls, then they **must allow STR** also.
3) That if the building's *règles de copropriété* do not expressly forbid

STR, you should be OK. The building would need to specifically stipulate with a *Bourgeoise* exclusive clause, banning every other usage, including by *professions libérales* in order to truly ban STR. Such lock-tight legal language is extremely rare, especially as bylaws were often established decades before STR was even thought of, and they're hard to modify.

Maître Bougeard reminds us that the basis of French law is *'liberté,'* meaning all which is not forbidden is authorized. If no law or jurisprudence prevents a certain practice, then it may be permitted to continue. In this case, the city or region may have specific regulations which override the building's bylaws, so check there first.

To change the building statutes typically requires an unanimous vote by all residents, which is hard to achieve. If you start this kind of business, and you remain a conscientious neighbor, it's unlikely the building will successfully shut you down. Being able to accurately predict what the future holds should make you more comfortable about investing your time and energy to set it up properly.

Info gathering

For vacation rentals in France, there is an obligation to collect renter information so they may be identified by immigration authorities. If you accept a reservation through a platform, like Booking, normally they should take care of this for you. If not, or you get a guest directly, you'll be expected to know their first and last names, their date and place of birth, nationality, home address, e-mail and telephone.

Extras may = reclassification

There are dangers of including food/drink or other services with the accommodations you offer. If you do, the *fisc* may consider that you should have charged 20% VAT for the **entire** rental. STR Example: €100/night +VAT = €120; LTR Example: €1 000/mo. +VAT = €1 200.

If you didn't charge your guest/tenant VAT, the *gouvernement* still considers that it is owed. That means your gross income after paying VAT in the STR example becomes €80/night (or €800/mo. in the LTR example).

Room renting

On Airbnb in Paris, 20% of ads are for a room in the host's main residence. This may be due to the fact that the availability of this asset (365 days/year) is three times that of the whole home (120 days/year). It's also less expensive than a studio or 1-bedroom apartment, and doesn't require any registration with the city.

When the lodging is in a room in a house the owner occupies, and breakfast is included, it's called a *chambre d'hôte* (anglo-saxons would call it a 'bed and breakfast' or 'B&B'). A *chambre d'hôte* requires pre-registration for this classification from the chamber of commerce and industry. Although limited to five rooms and 15 total guests, it's subject to harsher restrictions than even hotels need to meet.

When someone rents a room without breakfast in an owner-occupied home, no specific registration is required. Guests can stay for one, or 31, or 301 or any number of days without any restriction. That means you can do STR anytime, as much as you want, in one or several rooms while you, the owner, are on the premises.

The new offer 'Airbnb Rooms' specifically addresses this type of rental. It's a return to the roots of the platform, which started out with hosts and guests sharing the same space at the same time. The founders didn't know if owners would accept strangers in their personal space when they weren't there. They did, and were even willing to hand over cash for an 'air-bed' or blow-up mattress, hence the genus of the brand's name.

Camping

Camping has a number of regulations all their own, under the *'parahôtellerie'* umbrella. However, you should be OK if your town's *PLU* (*plan local d'urbanisme*) doesn't expressly prohibit the activity in your yard, and you don't go over six campsites or 20 people total, and only operate occasionally. The main things to watch out for are disturbing the neighbors, and ensuring safety and security, especially keeping campers away from public waterways.

Some urban areas prohibit camping on residential property, and others require you to declare your activity to the city hall. Minimum obligatory amenities include a source of potable water, a sink and a toilet.

Please note, where most of us come from, camping is associated with nature, peace, a slower simpler pace of life and exploring the outdoors. This isn't necessarily the case in France.

Clients are often inner-city people looking for cheap digs, and a different setting to express their urban lifestyle. Most of your competing French campsites will have loudspeakers with noisy singalongs, acts soliciting group participation set to flashing lights every day from early morning into the night. It's a raunchy party environment in close proximity with barely 50cm between tents and hundreds of people sharing the land which is mostly asphalt with nary a tree nor critter in sight.

Think of the films *Les Bronzés*, or *Camping* 1, 2 and 3. That's what many locals expect, and if they don't get it *chez vous* they're prone to creating that rude atmosphere themselves.

RVs in France are unfortunately sometimes associated with migratory tribes with a bad reputation. Locally called '*gens de voyage*,' they travel in packs of multiple campervans. Typically, they take over public property like an abandoned lot, unused field or parking lot.

The idea is to not pay for the space they inhabit, so it's unlikely they'll look to reserve a paid plot like yours. Also, platforms verify payment means before accepting reservations, which is another assurance of getting paid by going through them. However, it's your responsibility to ensure the travelers pull up sticks by the agreed-to departure time.

To avoid trouble, you must set very clear expectations and boundaries from the start. Don't hesitate to thoroughly screen folks and uncover their motivations before accepting reservations.

Beware Overstays

If you allow anybody to stay more than 30 days consecutively in your property, their status automatically changes to one of a long-term renter living there full-time. This has drastic implications on your rights, obligations and earnings potential, which are covered later in this chapter.

Squatters are a genuine problem in France. Although new laws better protect homeowners, and you can get out of trouble if you act quickly, it is by no means an easy or inexpensive process to rid yourself of someone who overstays their welcome.

In the case of renting out your whole home while you are on vacation (or having people surreptitiously take over your premises while you're gone), you could be **denied access to your own residence** upon your return. Building concierges, property managers, outdoor cameras and other electronics with notifications (like an alarm), or at the least trusted neighbors should be employed to provide you with immediate notification. Check out providers like Minut and Roommonitor to keep tabs on your space.

In addition to precautions and screening, you should keep your original deed and property title secure someplace else than your main residence and hold an electronic copy in the cloud which you can access in a moment's notice. Law enforcement, judges and bailiffs (*huissiers*) will require proof before aiding you.

More than 30 days (LTR)

Long-term rentals, or *la location longue durée (LDD)*, can take many forms.

LTR has completely different regulation than short-term. This begins with a number of elements which must appear in the listing offering a traditional lease. There's also a standard of decency which must be met, such as a minimum size requirement, as nothing smaller than 9m² and 20m³ per person may be rented long-term. This is about the same size as the Japanese shoebox apartments marketed under the Ququri brand, at 95 square feet (or three tatami mats).

Every stay greater than 30 days must have a lease agreement (*bail de location*) signed by the landlord (or their representative) and renter. You can also have a lease for 30 days or under, but it's not an obligation.

Leases used to be one of two kinds, either furnished (*bail d'une location meublée*) or unfurnished (*bail non-meublée*). Furnished leases are for a minimum of one year. Unfurnished leases are for a minimum of three years. It's the furnished leases for under a year which carry new possibilities.

The mobility lease (*bail mobilité*), introduced with the *loi ELAN* in 2018, finally filled the grey area in-between '30 days' and '1 year'. It can be from one month, two months, three… all the way up to 10 months. The mobility lease is not renewable, however it can be extended, provided the total length of occupation is 10 months or less.

If the renter wishes to stay on after the 10 months are up, the landlord must agree to a new traditional lease, which not only carries a 1-year minimum (if furnished), but is subject to additional inspections, restrictions, and constraints, most likely including a rent reduction.

Unlike the traditional 1-year and 3-year leases, the mobility lease is **not** subject to rent control. The landlord is completely free to charge what the market will bear for a 1 to 10-month period.

If the mobility lease is so flexible, and allows owners to charge more, why aren't all landlords switching? The main reason is that most prefer to 'set it and forget it' with a stable tenant for a fixed period. Another reason is because they can't. You see, the mobility lease is only applicable in certain cases.

Firstly, the unit must be rented furnished, and there's a list of minimum items required in order to classify it as such. These include a not only a water supply, toilet, shower and heating, but also a bed, blanket, shutters or window coverings, closets or shelves, lights, a stove with at least two burners, a table and chairs enough for occupants as well as the required dishes, silverware, glasses and such to serve all tenants, an oven or microwave, a refrigerator and freezer or combo, and enough cleaning supplies.

Secondly, the renter must be 'displaced,' or temporarily staying in a new area, which is not their permanent residence. They could be a business traveller or in the process of relocating for work. They could be a student or otherwise in training sessions. They could be doing volunteer work or an internship. Since these temporary states are open to interpretation, and difficult for an owner to verify, it's best to get the renter to sign a declaration that they are in one of the qualifying conditions. That declaration should cover you, the landlord.

Limiting who you can rent to reduces the pool of candidates. Qualifying tenants may not be looking for your type of residence. For example, if your place is a 2-bedroom, and all they need is a studio or 1-bedroom.

Thirdly, even though there's nothing in the text of the loi ELAN that expressly says so, the mobility lease may be intended for renting only entire dwellings. If you have a 3-bedroom flat, you may not be able to have a separate mobility lease for each tenant of each bedroom, if they share common areas. This may be OK in towns with populations under 200 000, and outside of dense 'zones tendues,' which require a change of usage for this setup. Jurisprudence in Paris ruled on February 16, 2023 that a configuration with multiple mobility leases requires the habitation status to go from residential to commercial.

Again, startups and established providers can help you with the legal and administrative side. Le Bon Bail for lease contracts. Bellman, ChouetteCopro, Matera, or MeilleureCopro if you own the whole building and must establish a *syndic de copropriété* for management.

Lease term and possibility of changes

If a dwelling hasn't been rented previously, or has remained empty for 18 months (and there are no other local price restrictions in place like rent control), the owner is free to offer the term period they choose (among the three mentioned previously), and to set whatever rental price the market will bear (barring any local rent controls). If you've inherited a renter from the previous owner, or the dwelling was rented less than 18 months ago, you're stuck with continuing the previous deal, under the same terms.

If you're coming from the US or the UK, you may feel handcuffed by the French regulations limiting rent increases on long-term leases. Median rent in the top 50 US metropolitan markets hit a record $1 849 in May 2022, up 15.5% from a year earlier, according to Realtor.com. In some US cities in 2021, landlords upped asking prices 30%, leading to rejections of prospective tenants of 1-bedroom flats in Manhattan making less than $150K. Similarly 10-15% rent rises were seen in 2021 across the UK.

What goes up, must come down. ApartmentList released rent information showing continued deceleration in the US in March 2022. The report stated "Year-over-year rent growth stands at 2.6%, down significantly from a peak of 18% in late-2021." These volatile rental market corrections don't exist in France.

Clameur records an average rent hike of 1.3% across the whole of

France, every year, for the past five years. Inventory of properties for rent dropped 10% in the past six months ending 2023 Q1, according to Bien'ici.

You may say to yourself, "There's no way landlords in France can make money on LTR." But they do. **A lot** of money. This is mainly due to tax advantages, which we'll start to cover in the next chapter.

Once a lease is signed in France, consider it set in stone for you, the landlord. You cannot make any changes to the lease, and notably cannot raise the rent. If the term is three years, the monthly rent must remain the same for the whole period, regardless if inflation goes up, property taxes increase, or you've made substantial improvements to the property. You must wait until the three years are complete if you want to up the rent.

The same rent increase restriction applies if the lease term is 1-year, 9-months or 1-3 months. The landlord must wait until the period around the lease renewal date if they want to raise the rent. Because the rent is practically unchangeable for a long time, the landlord has extra incentive to get the price right, and use a sustainable methodology to arrive at their number.

Notice period

The landlord is committed for the length of the lease, but the renter is not. The tenant may leave with 90-days' notice on a 3-year lease, or 1-month notice on a 1-year (or shorter) lease. Renters in high-density areas (*zone tendu*) are allowed to give 1 month's notice, regardless of the length of the lease.

Renewal periods just before the 3-year or 1-year lease anniversary are your only window of opportunity to revise the rent. If the property is in a rent-controlled city, you'll have to follow the barometer from the *mairie*. If not, you're still beholden to the government's national consumer price index, "*l'indice de référence des loyers (IRL) de l'Institut national de la statistique et des études économiques (Insee)*."

Each year, the federal state provides new guidance, based on inflation and other factors. Usually, landlords are granted no more than around 1% rent increases. However, after the pandemic, with inflation running rampant and nearing 10%, the government allowed landlords to raise rent up to 3.5% until June 2023.

This index holds even when you change renters. A landlord cannot charge more to the incoming renter than they charged to the outgoing, unless they made major improvements in the interim. To do so puts the landlord in high-density areas at risk for significant fines, if the tenant files a complaint. The tenant has three years to challenge the general rent, but only three months to challenge an increase to the supplemental rent (*complément de loyer*) for better amenities and such.

Roommates or colocations

There's specific legislation (from 1989) which covers when people who are unrelated share the same roof.

The lease must be a traditional type (1-year minimum). It will be collective, without mention of who gets which room, and how much each pays. That's for the roommates to figure out for themselves.

If one leaves, it's the responsibility of those who remain to pay the difference or find a new roommate. Once they agree, the new tenant is presented to the landlord for their approval, and added as an addendum to the joint lease agreement.

Like in many other countries, the lease payment responsibility is shared (*clause de solidarité*). If there are three roommates, and one leaves, the remaining two are responsible for paying the entire rent amount.

Renters may have access to aid (from the CAF), but the landlord should always be paid directly from the tenant, without concern for where the money comes from. You'd be surprised how big the lodging subsidies can be. Students routinely have more than 50% of their rent bill picked up by the State.

Mix your ideal cocktail

Properties in seasonal areas with varying demand would be well to mix short-term rentals in high-season with the mobility lease in low-season. You'll hear our mantra of diversification repeated several times in this book, and seasonality is a big reason why you should consider the practice.

Type of residence
  Primary residence
  STR in main residence

First of all, in France, your main residence is designated at the time of purchase, and subsequently when filing taxes. There's a new requirement (first deadline was July 1, 2023) to declare all property you own, whether it's your main or secondary residence, and who lives or rents there.

When it comes to administrative procedures in France which benefit the individual, like obtaining your permit to drive (see the book French License), or voting in elections, documents, forms, websites and even representatives are only French-speaking. However, when something benefits the state, like paying speeding fines, suddenly the fonctionnaires translate into several languages to better accept your money. So, it's unsurprising that the *fiscal immobilier déclaration* is available in English.

If it's the home where you live, in most cases, you don't need to register with your city hall to begin renting on a short-term basis. If your main home is in a city which has restrictions in place, you are limited to 120 days of this kind of activity, and you must register with the city hall beforehand. In all other towns, there is neither a day, nor a declaration restriction. You may rent short-term all year around, and don't need to register with your city hall. This may change soon, as the federal government in November 2023 gave municipalities the ability to go farther, including reducing the limit to 90 days for primary residences.

There are some detractors, like Le Bon Coin, who advise their users to a more strict interpretation, meaning 120-day limit for primary residences across the land. However, neither article L 324-1-1 nor article L 324-2-1 of the *Code du tourisme* mentions a 120-day limit. It certainly applies in municipalities and zones with specific legislation, but may not outside these areas. Check with your local city hall (*mairie*) to be sure.

LTR in main residence

If you're doing LTR in your primary residence, it's likely you're renting out one or several rooms to lodgers, each unit on a separate lease. It's unlikely (or impossible) you share a common lease with all lodgers as in a roommate or coliving arrangement. It's also unlikely any of the rooms you rent are unfurnished.

Thus that leaves us with the following possibilities: a Mobility lease, a Student lease or a traditional Furnished lease. All of these LTR arrangements are commonly done in secondary residences.

Secondary residence

This covers doing STR in a holiday home or investment property, which could be a villa, chalet, or a *gîte*. We will cover investments in the Expand section.

To be called a *gîte*, the dwelling must be completely separate from the owner's main dwelling, and autonomous (own kitchen, bathroom, etc.). Breakfast is not provided in a *gîte*. Although they're mostly found in rural areas, there's no restriction on where one can be set up.

Gîtes have their own specific status, and a declaration must be made to the city hall at the time of establishment. Every stay in a *gîte*, no matter how long from 1 to 30 days, must have a rental contract (separate from platform terms and conditions). If you make more than €23 000 gross in a year, you're obligated to create a business.

You are not limited by the 120-day rule for doing STR in a secondary residence. However, Jedeclaremonmeuble.com recommends you declare your *location meublée* to the INPI and get a Siret number prior to commencing your STR activity. You'll also need to register with the city hall (*mairie*), the same way you would for a main residence. This is done by filling out Cerfa form 14004*04. At this point, you may discover that your town has more restrictive laws in place than the nation at large. See the section 'Regional specifications' further on in this chapter.

Owners may need to get approval from the city for a change of purpose (*destination*) or of usage. Purpose (*destination*) deals with structures, like an apartment building becoming a hotel. Usage (*usage*) deals with how the owner is allowed to exploit their property, ie lodging (*logement*) or tourism (*tourisme*).

You may also need to complete a certain additional requirement before renting. For example, in Paris and the little crown (*petite couronne*) plus Lyon and Marseille, a secondary residence must first have its purpose changed to a commercial unit (*local commercial*) agreed to by the city hall. Second, in compensation, an existing commercial unit of equal size, and likely in the same *arrondissement*, must be purchased and converted to long-term housing. This rule is so the total square meters in each city neighbourhood allocated to be primary residences of inhabitants never decreases. In some cases (Paris notably), you'll have to convert double or triple the STR space into LTR space before being granted the right to operate short-term rentals in a secondary residence. Nobody does this in Paris because it doesn't make economic sense.

Purpose change with compensation is a very complicated and expensive procedure, making it unaccessible for all but those with extremely deep pockets. If this is you, luckily there are organisations like Usecom Conseil specifically designed to assist you with a *changement de destination* or *d'usage*. A combination of notary public (*notaire*), real estate agent (*agent immobilier*) and possibly lawyer (*avocat*) specialising in the property sector could also be gathered to accomplish the change. It's virtually impossible to do this by yourself.

One way around this restriction is if you transform a unit into accommodation which **already** has the status for commercial usage. This could be a former office (dentist, psychologist, etc.), shop (keys, shoe repair, florist, etc.) or service (café, boutique hotel, etc.) that you transform into a residence which can be rented out to tourists. Renovating one shop to add a shower, kitchen and bedroom, with a complete set of furniture, is much cheaper than buying two or three places, only one of which can be used for short-term rental.

For example, a shoe store in the 4th arrondissement could be retrofitted to become an apartment, rented out 365 days a year and the city hall couldn't do anything to prevent this new commercial activity.

Refurbishing would certainly cost lower and be less hassle than buying two equally-sized dwellings in the same neighborhood in Paris, where the average purchase price per square meter is €10 000 or more.

Some big cities are more lenient. For example, in Lyon, the change of purpose need only apply to dwellings greater than 100m² in the center. In Marseille, Nice, Strasbourg and Versailles, the municipalities have decided to allow a 'temporary' usage change, from three to nine years, with a simple registration. There is no financial compensation required for the initial secondary residence. The same owner can only have one or a handful of such properties, depending on the rules of the city.

All cities of 200 000 people or more can have such compensation requirements for secondary residences. Some smaller villages which are near these metropolitan areas are also subject to such regulations, as they are considered to be inside the same density zone.

Outside of the cities mentioned above in this section, and the restriction zones, if the building doesn't prohibit STR, it's fair game for your secondary residence to be used year-'round for short-term rental. You read that right, outside a handful of cities/zones, you can do STR 365 days per year in your holiday home in France. No compensation is required of you either, except to collect the tourist tax and transfer it to your town's coffers.

In nearly all cases, registration with the city hall is required, and the registration number must be displayed on all your listings. The procedure is a mere formality, and you're likely to get authorised in under a month without any background check, inspection or other vetting.

The laws are constantly changing, so it's best to double-check with your city hall to be on the safe side.

LTR in a secondary / holiday home / investment property
   Unfurnished LTR
   Traditional lease, three (3) years minimum, main residence for tenant

If you rent unfurnished, you'll still need to provide a minimum of furnishings, such as heating and hot water, electricity, a bathroom with a shower, a private toilet, a kitchen with potable water, stove and oven or microwave. Anything in the dwelling at move-in which subsequently breaks must be repaired or replaced at the owner's expense.

Furnished LTR
   Mobility lease, one (1) to 10 months maximum, temporary residence for tenant
   Traditional lease, one (1) year minimum, main residence for tenant
   Roommate leases or *colocations* (HMOs in the UK), one (1) year

minimum, main residence for tenant

You could offer your property to several housemates as unfurnished, but it's much more common to do so in a furnished dwelling. To qualify as furnished, you are obliged to provide a number of amenities. If you're doing coliving, an expanded list is highly recommended.

Renters are more likely to be young, without many belongings, and unrooted, meaning they're only interested in staying there as long as their studies or internship lasts.

DPE and AER

The new energy efficiency regulations mainly affect investment property, which is rented out entirely and year-round. The subjects of DPE and AER will be covered at greater length in the Expand section.

Regional specifications

Where is your rental located? Certain municipalities and high-density areas carry restrictions which go beyond the national regulations mentioned above.

STR regionally

All cities of 200 000 residents and greater require pre-authorization and getting a registration number before commencing STR activity in a secondary residence. Some cities of more than 50 000 inhabitants located in dense zones also carry these pre-requisites.

In France, 100 municipalities have voted texts restricting STRs. While that's a far cry from the total of more than 40 000 towns in the country, it's a growing trend. Be thankful this is handled on a city-by-city basis in France, and mixing STR and LTR in the same property is authorised, which leaves you room to manoeuvre. The federal government in the UK is ready to prevent **all** LTR landlords across the country from converting to STR. Dublin has a minimum 21 consecutive day stay requirement. New York banned STRs for all intents and purposes in 2023. France is more flexible in this respect.

Some communities go farther than requiring a registration number. Saint-Malo, for example, instituted a limit of 12.5% of STRs in the historic city center. If your application/authorisation comes after they've already reached that limit, you'll have to wait until someone before you stops their activity before you can begin yours. Annecy now has 2 800 STRs, but instituted a cap of 2 200 registered landlords allowed to operate a *meublé de tourisme*, and a waiting list.

La Rochelle proposed further limits to their 6 000 STRs beginning in September 2022. These were actually quite clever, aimed at satisfying the demand for student housing for their 15 000 university attendees. If an owner rents to students for nine months, they'll be allowed to rent to tourists for the remainder of the year. Apartments smaller than 35m² in the city-center wouldn't be allowed to do STR under any circumstances. STR operators and community leaders appealed, and the limits were not enacted as of December 2023.

Biarritz is putting in similar legislation as La Rochelle where owners need to rent up to a student nine months of the year in order to do STR in the summer. This, following an increase from 8.5% of all lodgings doing STR to 13.2% in the past three years. Nearby Bayonne is preparing measures, as are other popular destinations in the Basque country like Saint-Jean-de-Luz. These are likely to stick.

In the Paris region, aka *Ile-de-France* or *IDF*, the number of days you can rent your secondary residence is restricted for four interior counties or départements, and unrestricted in four others at the periphery of *IDF*. You'll really want to respect the rules in Paris, which has the legal authority to fine an individual owner €50 000 for breaking the rules, and they've exercised this right in the courts. Paris has 40 full-time agents investigating illegal STR activity. This brigade issued more than €2 million in fines in 2018, their first year of operation, and €8.6 million in fines to 555 illegal hosts since then. Concierges have also been dinged by the long arm of the law, considering them complicit and liable when they help owners operate illegally.

Many owners appealed the penalties, and the majority of them got off on a technicality. The city of Paris needed to prove that each apartment in question had documentation specifically designating the space for habitation... before January 1, 1970! The *mairie* couldn't come up with the papers in most cases, or the files contradicted their cause, as in one document which expressly stated there was no running water, eliminating designation as a living space *de facto*. Although most fines weren't collected, you might not want to press your luck, as the mayor is likely to pursue appeals and workaround ordinances.

You must request authorisation and be issued a permit number in la *petite couronne* or 'small crown' covering Paris (75), Hauts-de-Seine (92), Seine-Saint-Denis (93) and Val-de-Marne (94). This means that it's easier to commence a short-term rental activity in the *grande couronne* or 'big crown' including Essonne (91), Seine-et-Marne (77), Val d'Oise (95) and the Yvelines (78).

The latter three all have major attractions in their own right, respectively Disneyland (#1 attraction in all of France with 14.6 million visitors in 2019), Auvers-sur-Oise where Van Gogh is buried, and the domain of the Palace of Versailles (#3 with 7.3 million, more than the Eiffel Tower at #4). Plus, they have many lovely towns only a 30-40 minute train ride to the center of Paris. It's quicker to go from Le Vésinet to Châtelet than from Boulogne-Billancourt to Châtelet on public transportation, and Le Vésinet is a much more pleasant place in which to stay!

In the town centers of Serris and Chessy, both bordering Disneyland Paris, 20% of all properties were dedicated to STR. No longer. Mayors are using a mandatory change of usage declaration (*changement d'usage*) to lower that to 2% maximum among secondary residences downtown. In the wider zone the municipalities will only except 1% of STR's operating year-round. Primary residences can still be rented on a short-term basis up to 120 days per year.

The change of usage declaration is a game-changer, as permits are awarded on a first-come, first-served basis. New players who apply quickly can supplant owners who have conducted STR activity for years without complaint from neighbors. Some homeowners associations are banding together to fight a losing battle. Their loss could be your gain if you comply more quickly.

Although many similarities are shared on home sharing trends, each market is unique, especially as it relates to taxation and regulation. You may be used to doing STR outside France, which works well for you without issues. Or you may have had problems elsewhere and have written off that possibility for your French home.

The best choice of usage for identical properties in different cities might be radically different. Doing Airbnb at your primary residence in Paris is currently limited to 120 days. While restricted, Paris allows much greater availability than in other major European tourist destinations. In London, short-term rentals are limited to 90 days a year. In Amsterdam it's 60 days. In Berlin, it's 0 days if you're not staying there at the same time as the guest.

Since April 2022, Amsterdam forbids renting out houses worth more than €533 000 for the first four years following the acquisition. This goes for new builds and existing homes. Six owners have already been dinged, each for an average of €22 000.

So, it may be that doing STR in Paris is less lucrative than it once was, but still very much worthwhile; in London and Amsterdam not so much, and in Berlin not at all.

LTR regionally

Dense zones or *zones tendues* are cities with at least 50 000 inhabitants, or are located in a wider metropolitan area bordering a county or département which is considered densely populated. The government has a website you may visit to learn whether or not your space is in such a zone.

In dense zones, some laws are altered to offer advantages to renters. For example, normally a tenant on a long-term lease needs to give several months' notice prior to vacating: 1 month for a one-year, and 3 months for a three-year. However, in dense zones, the notice period allowed is shorter: 1mo. no matter which type of lease they signed.

Little by little, nearly every major city in France (200 000+ inhabitants), and sometimes bordering communities, will have rolled out rent control (*encadrement des loyers*). These include Paris, Lille, Lyon, Bordeaux, Montpellier and some towns bordering these cities.

The laws now include the obligation of publishing the official rent-controlled figure in the listing. This is not as straightforward as it seems, because the rent controlled number is not the same throughout the city, and it's also not one number, but two. Actually, it's a range, from the minimum (-30% of mean) to the maximum (+20%).

However, they've given more leeway than unfurnished flats on the amount of supplement they can charge. You could say the amenities are 'exceptional' and charge 20% above. The poorly written law allows great leeway in what justifies higher rent, notably in the categories of location and comfort.

It's your judgement versus the local authorities, and they're highly unlikely to do a check (*contrôle*) unless your tenant vehemently asks them to. Even so, the renter only has 90 days from signing the lease to file a complaint to the commission, and then that body must decide in their favor. If they do, an individual landlord could be fined up to €5 000.

The city of Paris has developed a calculator to help landlords figure out how much they can charge and stay out of trouble. The Paris mayor has also recently been granted the authority to check and enforce rent controls, which is the jurisdiction of federal agents elsewhere.

The entire region has an IDF calculator (including Paris) to determine the 'loyer de référence' for the locality of your property.

There is a bit of tolerance above the maximum plus possibilities to add amenities or bundle charges for a higher rent.

Uses other than habitation

We know of no restrictions on how much you can charge, nor how many days you may conduct rental of your space for storage, parking, amenities, activities or events. That is, if it's authorized in the first place.

If your property is in a collective dwelling, like an apartment building, the by-laws (*règlement de copropriété*) may prevent commercial activity, or restrict the hours, or the number of people, or whether or not alcohol can be served. Common sense should be your first guide.

For the rest of the legal contours, look to the following information as a primer (but by no means fully comprehensive).

***

Activity (recurring): There are many variables here to consider. First, ensure the activity doesn't cause disorder, is not dangerous, and doesn't infringe local noise ordinances. Basically, if you do it and the neighbors don't complain, you should be OK, especially if one of the neighbors has been doing something similar without any trouble. Commercial license may be required in some cases.

Here's what you're looking at under different *quatres figures* (scenarios):

- No Clients visiting: The widespread adoption of working from home (and government encouragement to do so) has made *télétravail* widely accepted. Provided it doesn't infringe on other ordinances in the town or if in a collective building (like excessive noise at certain hours) this activity should be fine. Endeavors such as Podcast recording can fall into this area.
- Welcoming adult clients: Whether the independent worker (*profession libérale*) is you, or a pro who's renting your space, the conditions are similar. They are also treated the same whether or not the space is the registered place of business (*domiciliation*) or not.

    If your place is in a town of 200K+ people, or in the Hauts-de-Seine (92), Seine-Saint-Denis (93) and Val-de-Marne (94), you'll need to request permission for mixed use (*dérogation pour usage mixte*) from your city hall. If your space is on the ground floor of a multi-resident building, you might not need the city's approval. If you're in a collective building (*copropriété*), you'll need that body's blessing as well. A dedicated insurance policy (*assurance spécifique*) for the activity may be required.

    Spaces which are classified as those which 'welcome the public' (*établissements qui reçoivent du public*, or *ERP*) are subject to further requirements for accessibility and safety. These can be onerous, and are to be avoided in a property rental business. Strategies which typically get around the ERP classification include hosting the activity in the same space (such as a living room or basement) which is also used for family/resident purposes. Health services, like those provided by a psychologist, require a separate waiting area, which could also be a foyer or sitting room used by residents.

    A separate entrance to the activity room could raise a red flag to tax inspectors, so it's best to direct visitors to the same entrance used by inhabitants. A detached dwelling

- would almost certainly **not** be considered a space of permanent habitation (*lieu où vous habitez en permanence*) and thus subject to ERP regulations.
- Welcoming youngsters: Includes activities like running a Childcare/nursery (*crèche*). A nanny is typically paid €3-4 per child per hour.
- Welcoming pets: furry friends Pet Care | Petting zoos fall into this category. Owner of premises and any workers must have an appropriate diploma or certificate or attestation (from a *DRAAF*). The kennels must meet certain requirements, and be washed daily. If there are fewer than 10 dogs, a declaration must be made to the *Direction départementale de la protection des populations* or *DDPP*. More animals requires additional installations, like a minimum of 100m distance to the nearest neighbor's habitation (which is a good idea no matter how many animals). A separate receipt must be given for each service provided over €25. A dedicated insurance policy covering pet watching is required.

Business function (recurring): If a liberal professional is conducting their main business on your site, you may require a commercial license, or a change of usage from city hall if you live in a big city, or in three counties on the periphery of Paris. If your property isn't in one of these places, and your local PLU doesn't expressly forbid or regulate this activity in a home, then you and your business partner may be able to proceed without any administrative rigamarole.

Corporate/Teambuilding (one-off): We know of no restrictions for this activity which differ from others mentioning ERP or PMR outlined above which welcome non-resident clients.

Creative endeavors (one-off): Photographers and film crews should already be well-aware of the restrictions in their field, such as having the right insurance if one of the crew is injured on your property, not capturing the image of the neighbors without their permission, parking permits, etc. They're also quite autonomous with their own equipment, including generators, but it would be good to know your electricity output limits if they wish to plug-in, especially if a circuit break could affect the power supply of neighbors.

They'll tell you your possessions will be put back where they were at the end of the shoot. However, it's a good idea to hide valuables, and take pictures before and after if you wish to make a claim.

* * *

Celebration/Party (one-off): Local ordinances? Many accommodation platforms like Airbnb specifically prohibit booking parties.

Private venues are subject to maximum capacity limits (*capacité d'accueil*) for both indoor and outdoor areas. For indoor, they're usually capped at 4m² per person. We'd recommend you set your own threshold at 5m²/person to be on the safe side, meaning maximum 10 people in a 50m² apartment. Also, check the load-bearing capacity of roofs, balconies, decks, terraces and such before allowing a crowd and heavy equipment like ice chests, dozens of bottles, and speakers onto the structure.

Cultural activities: very few regulations govern hosting these kinds of endeavors in your home- Book club, Poetry reading, Language exchange, Painting lessons, Hobbyists, Cinephiles, Scouts, Cultural bonding, Sewing circle, Toastmasters public speaking, Rehearsal stage for drama, Association discussion, Political civic get-together, Neighborhood watch organizing, etc. Dance has a few, but are mostly the responsibility of the instructor.

Dining/Drinking (occasional): Surprisingly, it seems anyone can sell meals in or from their house, or apartment, provided it's on the ground floor, and they've passed HACCP training on food hygiene and security (*formation hygiène et sécurité alimentaire*). The cleanliness of your space must be impeccable, and you can't ever allow a pet to enter the kitchen. The business activity must be declared, and you can be visited by inspectors.

Selling alcohol would require a liquor license (*permis d'exploitation*). Serving free alcohol to those at least 18 years old seems to be fine.

Education: independent teaching, private schooling (*soutien scolaire*) may be subject to ERP or PMR requirements.

Exercise / Sporting activity: this could include practicing Sports/Exercise/Fitness gymnastics martial arts Yoga . The home gym that you rent may be considered by the authorities to be subject to the classification as an 'EAPS' (*établissements d'activités physiques et sportives*). If so, you must have a civil responsability insurance policy and meet *ERP* requirements.

Experience/Entertainment/Show: Concert, Show/spectacle

Many owners host music acts at their home venue ad hoc without doing any pre-admin or qualifications. However, we understand if you hold more than five such solo artists, or eight events from a group of musicians (no idea why this distinction exists) annually, the organizer should have a license (*licence d'entrepreneur de spectacles*).

If the neighbors don't like the noise level from music (or parties, sports, cultural or other activities *chez vous*), and it goes on into the evening (10 p.m. to 7 a.m.), you could be subject to fines for 'night disturbances' (*tapage nocturne*). If direct negotiations with the annoyed neighbor fail, and the authorities are called in, you could risk sanctions from €68 to €450, and possibly more if it goes before a judge (highly unlikely for a first offense). It's a smart move to invite nearby neighbors, or at least inform them.

Health and wellbeing-related: Dietician consultations, Esthetician/beautician, Massage therapy, Pedicures, Pre-natal prep, Psychologist, etc. See ERP or PMR comments above.

Launch (one-off): Art gallery for a day. A Pop-up shop would require a commercial license.

Parking (daily access):

Platforms, management companies and startups are all clamoring to assist you in monetising your parking investment. However, they **do not** usually offer a *'cadre'* or legal framework binding you and your renter. No, the platforms are for the most part intermediaries to bring both parties together, but it's up to you to formalize the agreement, collect payment directly, and handle any disputes. They have handy forms to establish contracts, but it's unusual for them to provide additional services or representation.

Monsieur Parking is one standout which offers to find and secure a long-term renter for a €150 agency fee. Lease terms, payment means, access times, notice periods and such are freely decided between the parties without strict government oversight. Subleasing and renting the same space to different customers at different times are authorised, if you can manage the complexity.

Owners have much more liberty with parking rentals than for accommodations. If the space is rented separately from a dwelling (not part of a tenancy), the law of July 6, 1989 doesn't apply, meaning you can charge what you want (no rent control), for how long you want. It's up to you and the renter to decide together. If the renter ever fails to pay, or is late, you have the legal right to evict them immediately and end the lease.

In addition to the price, there are many things to work out between the owner and the renter. Hours of access and whether they must notify you or not. Whether the driver can put their own lock on the door. If the car is an EV, whether electricity is included or limits on usage, or how much charging costs. If they are allowed to store anything else in the garage, and if you, the owner, can keep anything else in the space.

Renting a space where a paying customer is parking their car **is** an activity which is subject to VAT. However, you don't need to include 20% for the government in your listings, unless you earn more than €32 600 annually from parking rental alone.

Storage (long-term):

We recommend that with their belongings, your renter provides you with a comprehensive list of the items in your care, along with an estimation of the value of each.

In most cases, it is forbidden to stock merchandise in a residence, that is, inventory that a shopkeeper intends to sell.

If your garage is underground (*sous-sol*) and below habitations (including your own) it's against the law to store 'material' there. The term '*matériel*' isn't defined, however the wording continues to expressly allow parking of a vehicle. If some damage, like a fire or leak, starts underground, and it's caused by something other than a car, the insurance company might not cover it.

To cover your heinie, inform prospective space renters that you disallow holding any contraband, dangerous items, weapons, chemicals, liquids or sensitive documents to be stored on your premises. Also, you should get a civil insurance policy, if you don't already have one (most homeowners do).

Renting an unfurnished space where a paying customer is storing their stuff (other than a car) is **not** an activity which is subject to VAT.

Swimming: Your backyard pool that you rent may be considered by the authorities to be subject to the classification as a 'paid watering hole' (*établissements de baignade d'accès payant*). If so, you're obliged to have a civil responsability insurance policy, which is a good idea anyways. To follow the law to a 'T' you should meet *ERP* requirements and have a certified lifeguard (*personne diplômée ayant le titre de maître-nageur sauveteur*) on watch.

Grey areas
  Coliving
  While there is clear legislation on *colocations* or roommate arrangements, coliving in France exists in a grey area in-between this and hotel regulation.

Communal Living complexes (*habitat participatif*) are extremely rare, but they do exist. They, too, have their own legal framework (*loi* ALUR).

Coliving does not.

Given the number of companies in this space, and the expanding number of dwellings, there is widespread enthusiasm for coliving, and faith it'll be worked out in due time. As-is, the practice is tolerated, and there have been no high-profile moves by the government, nor challenges in court to dampen spirits. The Lyon area has been grumbling about coliving because it sidesteps rent controls, but no new legislation has yet been proposed or voted on.

As there's nothing on the books specifically prohibiting coliving, the practice should be de facto allowed under French law. The biggest risks are likely to be if the authorities re-qualify your coliving establishment as something else. For example, if the government decides that providing Netflix and cleaning with the rent are 'services,' then they may consider you're running a hotel or quasi-hotel under the *'parahôtellerie'* classification. Or, if your renter overstays their welcome and moans that their tenancy should be re-classified as a roommate situation, or other one- to three-year lease.

Colocataires, or roommates, can call the space they rent from you their main residence from day one of the lease. Under a coliving arrangement, after the eight-month mark, your lodger will acquire this status as well, which you may consider prohibitive.

Co-living is all about flexibility, harmony and pay-as-you-go. Tenants and landlords both get benefits from the arrangement, if everyone's on the same page. If any co-liver overstays his welcome, the whole atmosphere can change, and the community can fall apart.

No matter what kind of contract you sign with a tenant, once they've lived there for eight consecutive and complete months, that space becomes their primary residence. A person's main home carries a number of protections, as it's considered if they lose their primary residence, they have nowhere else to go, and it may be the landlord's responsibility to find a housing solution for them. Terminating in the wrong way can expose the landlord to a wrongful eviction judgement. On a month-to-month arrangement, no such liability is assumed.

A primary residence in a furnished dwelling becomes *de facto* a minimum 1-year lease. The landlord can only break that lease with at least a month's notice just before the anniversary date, and only for certain reasons, such as moving into the space themselves (or lodging a close family member). The monthly rent cannot be increased during that year, and might actually have to be decreased if the space is located in a rent-controlled zone.

If the other co-livers no longer feel comfortable sharing their space with the protected renter, there's very little the landlord can do. The likely result is that the existing co-livers move out the next month, and prospective co-livers become harder to find as the home gets a bad reputation. You could end up with a big empty space, with one protected renter you can't get rid of, and a shortfall on your balance sheet. The protected renter becomes ecstatic as they now have the whole place to themselves for peanuts. They have zero incentive to cooperate to accept new intruders into their vast private domain.

Some coliving providers have their renters sign a different kind of lease, called a *'contrat de bail en logement-foyer.'* This lease elects their space as their main residence from day one. Old-age homes (EHPAD) and other similar collective residences often use the *logement-foyer* lease. We're unsure of the legality or the implications on notice period, renewals and possible rent increases, all of which makes this agreement riskier than the mobility lease.

Serviced apartments go by *Aparthôtel* in France. Basically, if you have at least a kitchenette, a washer, a workspace and wifi, you have the amenities longer-term business travellers seek.

If your property is a part of a building of serviced apartments, then you already have a property manager, likely on-site and providing a conciergerie. These dwellings are regulated differently than individual furnished rentals.

Size: no minimum, unless it's the renter's primary residence.

Miscellaneous
SACEM may have the right to claim money from owners who provide a way to access media in the homes they rent. If you receive a notice from them, take it seriously.

What the future holds
Proposed changes are being discussed in the Assembly which could affect the number of days and tax treatment of STRs. Votes are expected to happen in January or February 2024.

It's no use to speculate, as it's a common occurrence in France for populist politicians and candidates to spew about what they're going to do. A radical speech turns into a tepid proposal, which is watered-down when it finally passes, and set to be enacted in several months or the following year. Sometimes there's a successful appeal, or a group of Sage administrators which strikes down the text, or you need to wait for the first court case to happen to see if the new law has any teeth.

The best thing for you to do is to act now to exploit your property by all legal means, and prepare yourself to diversify at any moment. Create multiple revenue streams this instant, ensuring you're always making money no matter which way the wind blows.

You can't fight city hall. Industry associations like the CLF and SPLM in STR, and the UNPI and FNAIM in LTR have proven to be weak and unsuccessful in their attempts to lobby on behalf of their numerous constituents. Save your energy, and use it to make your space the most attractive for all kinds of rentals.

Laws change often. So signup for updates at MyPropertyPayday.com and check your city hall for alterations.

CHAPTER NINE
Taxation

It may appear incongruous to broach the subject of taxation before talking income. We know you'd prefer to get to the good stuff first, like how much money you could make. That's coming, starting with the very next chapter.

Well, in France, the *fisc* (tax authority) often asks you to declare what you're going to do **before** you start doing it. Failing to declare, or declaring the wrong thing, can have dire consequences. This can affect not only how much of your revenue you get to keep, but your status as a person or entity having the right to engage in that activity in the first place.

Some of these choices can be changed in the future. Others can't, or only in one direction. Backtracking or downgrading your regime is usually impossible. Better get good advice from an expert in order to make the right selection from the get-go.

France taxes real estate in an assortment of ways, and at a high rate compared to many countries. From building materials, to labor, to land, to renovations, to rental income and property tax. France has the second-highest ratio of property tax vs. GDP (4%), according to the OECD. This is mostly due to the 7-8% 'notary public' fees (about 6% goes to the government) assessed to the buyer at purchase, the equivalent of Stamp duty in the UK, which can be just as onerous.

Real estate developers are cautious. Although the *gouvernement* dangles incentives, they are not considered attractive enough for supply to meet demand. In most metropolitan areas, there are not enough houses, apartments, rooms, garages, etc. to satisfy the buyers, renters, and users.

One of the perverse effects of this tax situation is that those who already possess property have an advantage over those that don't. It's a perpetual sellers' market, where owners and landlords have the upper-hand, at least in finance. This is not likely to change any time soon.

Municipalities try to combat this by establishing rent control. Regardless of debates on its effectiveness, owners must factor rent control in their plans if they live in a zone where it applies.

Property Taxes

France has two annual taxes on property, one for possession- *taxe foncière*, and another for usage- *taxe d'habitation*. In most communes they each end up costing about the same amount. The average amount paid per household in 2019 for the *taxe foncière* was €827, according to the *DGFiP*.

The usage tax, *taxe d'habitation*, was discontinued by président Macron, and will disappear completely in 2023… for owner-occupiers. It will still be due for secondary residences and investment property.

If a secondary residence is not rented out, the local authorities can automatically increase the *taxe d'habitation* by up to 60%. Even if you use the property often, but not enough that it becomes your primary residence, you can get hit with the 60% *majoration*. Each town treats this differently. Versailles only taxes the secondary residences 20% more, where other nearby towns like Orgeval apply the maximum supplement of 60%. This extra tax is an incentive pushing owners to engage in rental activity for their second home, which sidesteps the supplement.

Thankfully, it is common practice to pass the *taxe d'habitation* on to the tenants, when there is someone occupying the property. It is legal to do so, if the lease includes a provision that the tenant pays this tax.

Both taxes are collected by local authorities- the city and the *département*. As they form a major part of local revenues, and one is going away, there's widespread belief that the other which remains will be hiked significantly. Already, the *taxe foncière* increased 28% in the past decade, according to the UNPI (*l'Union nationale des propriétaires immobiliers*). That's precisely what happened in Paris, which recently raised their *taxe foncière* by 50%.

The way that the *taxe foncière* is calculated is a bit convoluted, so we'll try to walk you through a simplified version. First, you take the government's estimated rental value of the dwelling (*référence de loyer*), expressed in €/m²/mo. and multiply that by the number of square meters they think you have. Let's use €14/m²/mo. times 100m², giving us €1 400. Then multiply that by 12 months to get €16 800 of estimated rental value in a year. Multiply that by 50% (*abattement valeur locative du bien*) taking advantage of the first standard deduction to get €8 400. Then, once again multiply that by 50% (*abattement forfaitaire de revenu cadastral*) for the second standard deduction to get €4 200. It's **this** number that you finally multiply with the overall percentage applied that year by the local authorities. There are several fingers in the pie, but all you care about is the total. Let's say it adds up to 30%, which when multiplied by €4 200 gives us that year's property tax bill of €1 260.

Comparatively speaking, the property taxes in France are not that bad in the long run. Certainly, they discourage going for short-term gain, like house-flipping. However, if you stay in the home past five years, you'll likely be better-off tax-wise than in some other places.

Let's compare two cities which both have one of the highest property tax rates in their respective countries: Austin, Texas and Bordeaux. Looking at a purchase as a primary residence of an identical 500K property in each city in the year 2023, here's what the owners would pay in property taxes after one, five, 10 and 20 years.
(figure 7):

Property tax comparison

Purchase price	Size	Price per m2
500000	110m2	4500

Comparison	Austin	Bordeaux
One-time Property Tax at purchase		
in Percentage (%)	0%	7%
in Currency ($,€)	0	35 000
Annual Recurring Property Tax*		
effective Percentage %	1.95%	0.50%
1Y ($,€)	9750	2602
5Y ($,€)	48750	13010
10Y ($,€)	97500	26020
Total Property Tax		
5Y ($,€)	48750	48010
10Y ($,€)	97500	61020
20Y ($,€)	195000	87040

*includes waste removal in France

Income Taxes

Choosing your *Régime*

It's a good idea to choose your tax scheme, or *régime*, prior to commencing your activity, if it involves accommodation rentals. A lot of administrative hassles can be nipped in the bud, fines avoided, and you'll likely keep more of the money you earn.

Your choices start with the *formulaire P0i* or P0i form, also known as the Cerfa 11921*05 for LMNP or LMP. On the form, you'll need to list the date you begin/began renting out, the tax regime you choose (this can be changed in subsequent years) and how you plan to apply VAT (*TVA*).

The first thing this form does is declare and register your business. *entreprise individuelle* (EI) or an *entreprise individuelle à responsabilité limitée* (EIRL). The EIRL disappeared in 2022.

LTR almost never comes with extra services, so you'll likely want to choose the base (*franchise en base*) in the majority of cases. However, you may want to make this same choice even if you're running a B&B or *gîte* short-term. You may think it's harmless to serve coffee and a croissant to your guests. After all, what's €5 to the host when they're making €100/night on their holiday rental? Well, that pétit déjeuner, didn't change your gross earnings from €100 to €95 (€100 - €5), it lowered earnings to €75 (€100 - €5 - €20 for VAT).

If you provide a service, however small, you must collect 20% VAT, and forward that to the *fisc* (French tax authorities). When that service is bundled (*compris*) with the rest of your rental, you must collect 20% VAT on the **entire amount**. This is what hotels must do. Failure to do so could leave the property owner on the hook for the 20%, drastically reducing your profit margin. You could also raise your prices 20%, but that's not likely to bring you back to even-Steven.

Your occupancy rate would almost certainly go down, as your prices become less competitive versus the surrounding options. Also, your ratings could take a hit, as your guests were expecting so many extra services for their 20% premium, but all they got was a pastry and a cup of Joe. It's not worth the risk, unless the services you provide are so wonderful they become a big differentiator, and justification for charging more.

Instead, why not strike a deal with local businesses to provide services to your guests. You're off the hook for the VAT, and your guests are probably getting a lot more than you could provide yourself. Plus, the surrounding community of *commerçants* could become allies in promoting your business, or at least stop seeing you as a competitor.

You have five months from the form completion to sign up with a certified management center or *Centre de Gestion Agréé* (CGA). Also, after your 2nd year in business, you must subscribe to the CFE (*cotisation foncière des entreprises*).

My Property Payday strongly suggests you get a qualified accountant and fiscal advisor on your team to reduce your tax burden. There are many simple things you could be doing from the start to lessen your exposure. Here are some of the golden areas to explore.

Tourism tax

Municipalities want their cut of the short-term accommodation market. Just like they add a tourism tax (*taxe de séjour*) for hotels, they expect you as an STR business to collect this for them. Luckily, both Airbnb and Abritel do this on your behalf. I don't know of any other platform operating in France which collects the tourism tax for every municipality in the country. However, all platforms operating in France have an obligation since 2020 to report on the STR activity going through them which concerns your address.

I say luckily two platforms collect on your behalf because it can be quite complex. Some cities charge differently for day 2 versus day 1. Some charge less for children. Some charge one rate for high season and another for low season. Of course, some parties who reserve throw a wrench in the whole works by showing up with more people than were on the original reservation. Ask your local city hall (*mairie*) how you should be charging and how often payment should be made.

If you use other platforms than the two above, or accept direct bookings, this means you must make a plan of how you're going to handle this, from collection to reporting to payment. Will you ask for it from guests upon arrival? It's not the best way to greet people, but you might need to get other things from them anyway, like a passport number or a form required by customs. Will you simply increase your prices a couple euro to cover this expense? This may make your listing appear slightly less competitive on price. Will you eat the fees for all but the largest groups? Whatever you decide to do, we recommend you stick to that process consistently to better keep track and avoid discrepancies with your local *mairie*.

Income Taxes on rental revenue or Income tax (*impôts sur les revenus*)

Conceivably, the *fisc* considers all rental income (above a certain threshold) to be taxable. This should cover every kind from STR, to LTR, to parking to storage to activities. In practice, only certain platforms (like Airbnb) report income, and not every owner reports all of theirs from the sharing economy.

Like with any STR in France, if you earn less than €760 in a year, you needn't pay taxes on rental income. However, unlike other STR regimes, if you make more than €5 000 gross in a year, you're obliged to create a business (with the associated costs and reporting burdens). A separate receipt must be given for each service provided over €25.

Furnished over Non-furnished

"I'll let you in on a little secret..." So many gurus in France spout breathlessly about their exclusive inside information into making a killing in property investment in the country. They'll only reveal it with a paid membership to their VIP club, or a fee-based subscription to their courses, or their book which is simply a 90-page autobiography of someone in their early 20s who was driving a bus before discovering this loophole.

But every accountant in the land knows the trick. So do many landlords. Here's the formula: **Meublé** plus **LMNP** plus **régime Réel**. Let's go into a bit more detail about what each of these terms means, and the implications on profitability.

Meublé means furnished. The opposite would be *non-meublé* or unfurnished. You must explicitly claim to be doing one or the other in France. Even if you choose unfurnished, there's still a minimum amount of furnishings and appliances which the landlord must supply. There's a longer list to qualify as furnished. We're mostly talking LTR here, as it's assumed and in most cases required for any lease or stay under 1 year (and possibly anything under 3 years) to be supplied with all mod cons (modern conveniences).

LMNP for *Loueur Meublé Non-Professionnel* means you're acting as an amateur, or not professional landlord of residential property as defined in the French tax code. The alternative as a pro would be *LMP* for *Loueur Meublé Professionnel* and we'll get into that a bit further on.

Régime Réel means you're subtracting the real cost of **all** expenses, rather than taking the standard deduction for French tax purposes, called the *micro-BIC*. At first glance, the *micro-BIC* looks great, as it allows you to deduct 50% of your rents to cover expenses, even if you didn't spend anywhere near that. (Renting unfurnished under *micro-BIC* only allows you to deduct 30%.) Closer inspection shows that's not the half of what you **could be** deducting. Further details in a couple paragraphs.

All three are fiscal plays (*optimisation fiscale*) for owners to keep more of their rental income. Worked in combination, there's a cumulative effect of deploying *Meublé* and *LMNP* and *Régime Réel*. The first, *meublé*, also offers the benefits of increased revenues and greater flexibility. You can usually charge 15-30% more for a furnished dwelling than for an unfurnished one. It's quite easy to fill a flat with new furnishings for less than that extra 15-30% would bring you in the first year. Your ROI is already on the plus side in Y1, and the furnishings should last for many years beyond. You'll continue to rake in more per year with the odd broken glass or torn sheet replacement as your only additional expenses here.

The monthly rent for a furnished residential accommodation must still comply with the local rent control (*encadrement des loyers*) laws in place (if applicable).

LMNP distinguishes from LMP, which is much more onerous. You won't go 'pro' until your revenues in a year surpass €23 000 **and** they represent more than 50% of your total household income.

Régime Réel is where the real (pun intended) fun starts. That's because in France, you can deduct far more things than you can in the UK and most other countries. It's not simply deducting the price of materials, renovations, charges and fees from the town and your property manager, if you deploy such a *conciergerie* or *gestionnaire*. You can deduct mortgage interest (*intérêts d'emprunt*) payments on a rental property, which bizarrely you can't do for a primary residence, as you can in the USA. Annual property taxes can be written off. The deductions don't stop there.

You can also amortize (*amortir*) not only the contents, but also the entire property itself! Even though property prices have inevitably risen in France over the long term for decades (regardless of if they've been renovated), the *fisc* will allow you to treat your rental real estate as an asset which is losing value over time (usually 35 years). Any unused portion of losses from amortising can be carried forward into future tax returns indefinitely, until the last *centime* is written off. The powerful lever for profitability that is amortisation can only be pulled by opting for the real expenses (*régime réel*) tax scheme.

If the property is a purchase (see Expand section at the end of this book) for the expressed purpose of renting out, you can also deduct the costs associated with the acquisition. This includes conveyancing (*frais de notaire*) typically 7-8%, real estate agent fees (*frais d'agence*) typically 5%. On a €100 000 purchase, you've just saved yourself upwards of €12 000.

Furnished renters, pros and non-pros LMP and LMNP fiscal obligations.

Consult with a certified accountant (*expert-comptable*) to decide which structure is right for your situation. Of course, by choosing a complex structure, you're sure to need an accountant to set it up and maintain it for you. These services are surprisingly cheap, costing in some cases no more than €300/year, which is also deductible.

Since the choices of furnished versus unfurnished, pro versus non-pro (LMP vs. LMNP) and real expenses (régime réel) versus the standard deduction all concern investment property or secondary residences (more so than your main residence), these will be covered in detail in the Expand section, Acquisitions: Big budget. There, you will find handy tables for at-a-glance comparisons.

One thing to watch out for, as more and more landlords choose furnished for the tax advantages, the supply could eventually outpace the demand for that kind of rental. Recently, in the downtown area of some major cities like Bordeaux, Rennes or Paris, the oversupply of furnished rentals forced some owners to reduce their furnished rents to attract new tenants. Only 10% of the total rental market in France is for furnished accommodation. While demand is increasing for this kind of turnkey rental, it could reach a saturation point in the future.

While unfurnished rentals don't offer nearly as many tax loopholes, there is one worth considering, and it takes a whole lot less effort than LMNP to exercise it. It's called *'Loc'Avantages'* and the principle is simple: rent your apartment for below market value, and the government will cover the difference in the form of a tax break. There are, of course, a considerable amount of conditions to be met. The renter will be a person on public assistance in great difficulty. This is not a stable population which consistently pays the full amount on time, and causes no damage.

All monies earned from sharing platforms should be declared on your tax return, unless the total is less than €760 for the year. Under that amount, rental income is exempt.

Property management fees are tax deductible

If your *conciergerie* charges you 25% (par for the course in STR), you're not really paying them €0.25 on every Euro you make. By going through a property manager, your taxable income is decreased, and you can stay in a lower tax bracket.

Plus, if you make more than €23 000 in a year, you normally have to pay social charges (*prélèvements sociaux*) of 17.22% on your earnings. This means if you make €22 000, you don't pay these social charges, but if you make €24 000, you must pay €4 133 to the state.

Not so if you go through a property manager (*agence de gestion* or *conciergerie*), which renders your earnings exempt from social charges. If your property is capable of producing upwards of €2 000 per month in short-term rentals, it's wise to consider the services of a property manager. Choose one yourself at MyPropertyPayday.com and ask them what they think is your property's potential.

This significant tax avoidance tip makes it quite tempting to have your property professionally managed. If your concierge is worth their fees, you should expect that you'll make more money with them than without them. Many property managers claim pros earn 30-40% more than individuals. How do they make you more? Scenarios are covered in the 'Optimize' section of this book.

Capital Gains Tax or CGT

Like many places around the world, in France, there are no capital gains taxes when selling your main residence. In the US, if you can prove you lived in your owned home two out of the last five years prior to sale, you can exclude up to $250 000 as an individual ($500 000 for a married couple filing jointly).

The French tax authorities are even more generous. There's no length of stay requirement for the property to be considered your primary residence. You could rent it out for 15 years, then move in for just a few months while your sale completes, and keep all the cash. That's right, **all**, regardless of how much you made, without need of activating an exclusion, without having a married partner to boost your exclusion amount.

The *fisc* took some taxpayers to court in 2013 because the couple claimed to move back in merely four months before their sale went through. The judge sided with the homeowners, and the fiscal authorities appealed. The *gouvernement* lost again in the second court case, as there is no minimum time limit for occupying a main residence defined in the tax code.

It helped that the couple didn't own any other property which was available to them at the time. But that didn't stop the authorities from prodding further into the bowels of the building looking for holes in their story. They actually went so far as comparing water and electricity usage during the four months to gauge if the levels were coherent with full-time occupation by the number of family members claimed. While the electricity bill seemed suspicious, the water works checked out, and that was enough to satisfy the judge. The couple kept 100% of the proceeds from selling their 'main residence' of four months.

Many owners use this late move-in strategy, because they know if they don't, they'll take a big hit. For rental property, the fisc applies punitive capital gains tax or CGT (*impôt sur la plus-value*) on property value increases starting at 36% (see breakdown in next paragraph). They require investors to own the property for 30 years before completely waiving CGT. Since CGT isn't tied to income, you could be jobless and flat broke before the sale, and the *gouvernement* will still apply the same high CGT. *Tant pis.*

Landlords who sell rental dwellings pay capital gains tax of 19%, plus 17.2% for social security contributions. A complete exemption exists after 22 years for the tax on the capital gain and after 30 years for the social contribution.

Thanks to the Brexit provisions, CGT social charges drop to 7.5% (from 17.2%) for British residents selling property bought in France before the break from the EU. This is one of the rare cases where foreigners get a better deal than the locals!

In addition, gains of more than €50 000 from selling a second home (or rental) are subject to a special tax of 2-6% on that surplus amount. It's a sliding scale from 2% (or €1 200) at the €60 000 mark, and 6% (or €15 600) at €260 000 and for any gain above.

There's one neat trick which erases most of the CGT pain for furnished rental property under the LMNP regime. Let's say you bought for €250 000 and sold a decade later for €350 000, realising a capital gain of €100 000 (before deductions). However, during that decade, you amortized, or de-valued your rental property to the tune of €100 000. In pure accounting, the property should have a residual value of €150 000 (the original €250 000, minus the amortized €100 000).

Under any other regime, the government would consider that your capital gain is €200 000 (the resale price of €350 000, minus the €150 000 after amortisation). Not so under LMNP. It's like the €100 000 benefit you got for 10 years never existed.

Other rental income tax

Proceeds from renting a garage/box/basement are considered property income (*revenus fonciers*) and must be reported. Making under €15 000 per year you can choose the tax regime *micro-foncier* for a standard deduction of 30%, or itemise by selecting the *régime réel*. Above €15 000 per year you can deduct a lot more, but most individuals won't reach nearly that amount.

It's unclear if you're renting out property (attic, spare room, shed, etc.) for storage which is **not** one of the types of spaces listed in the previous paragraph, does that represent a loophole? To help you decide, know that all sharing economy platforms, including in the storage sector, must declare revenue earned, and by whom, to the *fisc*.

CHAPTER TEN
Determine Pricing

How much should you charge? You could just as well ask, "What day is it?"

In a completely de-regulated world, the price to rent a particular space would fluctuate much like the stock market. Stocks (*actions*) change by the second. So would property if we let it.

Expect to adjust often. The shorter the term, the more frequent your price changes should be: for accommodation rentals between 1-30 days, adjust at least weekly, or every couple days; for 1-12 month rentals, adjust every month; for 1-year rentals, change every year (if the law permits).

ADR on Airbnb increased 16.4% in France since 2019. Regions within the country which did even better than that include the Atlantic seaboard, PACA (*Provence, Alpes, Côte d'Azure*), Normandy and Paris, with a 61% increase.

The Paris exception

Let's take a deep-dive into Paris, to understand how such an increase became possible. We already know Paris is the top destination for tourists in the world. What you may not know is just how scarce rentable property is in the Capital.

The ordonnance of the 18th of August, 1667 limited the height of buildings in Paris at 15.6 meters tall. This rule hasn't budged in the center and only barely nearer the *Péripherique* ring freeway. The *Périph'* essentially follows the city limits set by the *Enceinte de Thiers*, established in 1860 during the height of Baron Haussmann's public works.

More than half of all buildings still standing in Paris today were built during Haussmann's massive revamp. *Haussmannien* structures are characterized by a 'noble' third floor (*deuxième étage*) with higher ceilings and ornate windows, a sixth floor (*cinquième étage*) with a balcony stretching the width of the building, and a seventh floor (*sixième étage*) at the top for servants, the famous '*chambres de bonne.*'

The size of Paris has remained at 105 km² for 160 years. To give you an idea how small that is for a world-class capital city, the surface area of Paris is the equivalent of 7% of London.

In 1881 at the end of Haussmann's works, the population of Paris was 2 269 023 souls. On the first of January, 2014 the population of Paris was 2 220 445 inhabitants. The amount of people Paris can hold hasn't changed for 140 years.

In today's Paris, you can't build up. You can't build out. There are zero empty lots and very few zones where you can demolish and reconstruct. Paris is full.

The result on the resale market is that Paris property is a sure bet to hold its value. It never falls too fast, nor too far. Houses in Stockholm were selling in the Spring of 2023 for 20% less than their peak. Steep drops are hitting Sydney -14%, San Francisco -15%, Auckland -22%, and Toronto -16%. According to Oxford Economics, UK house prices in 2023 could end up as much as 15% lower than 2022's peak - that's **across the whole country**. Meanwhile, in Paris in late 2023, resale prices are falling... only 0% to -2% and actually rising in the 7th *arrondissement*.

If you own one of those rare squares in Paris, you're one of the select few that has something everyone covets. Regardless of rent control, despite STR restrictions, you're doing yourself a disservice if you don't leverage your Paris flat every day, for all it's worth.

Even with a 61% price increase, it's very likely that hosts doing STR in Paris are leaving money on the table. Owners of rental property practically everywhere in France are missing out. Either they're not choosing the most advantageous ways to rent, or they're not charging what they could. If you're lucky enough to have property to rent in France, you should treat it as the precious commodity that it is, and expect better returns.

Use the median as your North star

Let's remember our grade school math here (or maths if you're from the British Isles) and recall the difference between the mean and the median. The mean is the average. The median is the middle number, or the one which comes up the most often.

Ironically, the mean is used more often. In areas where the things you're comparing are pretty homogenous, the mean is probably your best bet: the average price of a cauliflower, of a movie ticket, of a liter of *essence*, etc. Even real estate prices can effectively use the mean, in a place like the USA, where houses in the same town look alike because they were constructed from the same developer at around the same time, are made from the same stuff and are all pretty suburban, meaning not clustered around a very expensive and sought-after city-center.

However, real estate in France is not like that, as properties side-by-side on the same block can differ wildly. They could have been built 100s of years apart, with radically different materials, styles and heights. Oh, and in a country with around 40 000 *châteaux* or about one per town, not to mention a few *hôtels particuliers* in each centre ville, there's always at least a couple outliers kicking up the averages for the majority.

For space in France, the median would be a more accurate north star to guide you, if you could find it. Most published figures you'll see will be the mean. The median for real estate numbers will typically be somewhat lower.

Unless your space is attached to one of those exceptional properties, our recommendation is to aim for a price which is a bit below the average you've seen posted.

Ask yourself honestly how your space compares with those around you. Is it about the same? Is it better? Or is it a little bit below par?

The pricing tolerance for variance to the median is pretty low in France. If your target is French customers, the recommendation is to not stray too far from the median.

If your target is customers from outside France, or tourists, you could go up to +30% or down to -30% from the median ADR.

For some uses, such as long-term rentals, pricing is heavily regulated, thus mostly decided for you. See the 'Regulation' chapter for details.

National LTR monitor

The French minister of lodging (*logement*) decided in 2020 to share the prices paid by tenants on long-term leases. Data for rents in nearly 35 000 *communes* are compiled on the site www.ecologie.gouv.fr/carte-des-loyers.

Data comes from trusted sources and market leaders SeLoger (17 million visitors monthly), LeBonCoin, pap.fr, and uses pretty solid methodology from OLAP, ANIL, and PriceHubble. It sure beats looking at every listing in your area and doing lots of calculations on a spreadsheet!

To see what LTR prices are practiced in your area, first go to the site and choose to look at either apartments or houses. Then click on the corresponding *carte des loyers* to zoom in on your town. Rental prices are expressed in €/m²/mo. Let's look at Rennes in postal code 35238 to see how best to use this tool.

The first number you see is '11,8€' (the French use a comma ',' instead of a period '.' to separate euros from cents) which means that the average in that part of Rennes is €11.80/m²/mo. So, they're saying the average

35m² flat there rents for €413/mo.

Now look closer by clicking on the little wrench in the bottom-left of the pane. More detailed figures will slide over. Scroll to the bottom of them. Under *"Déterminer les seuils"* click the drop-down menu and select *"Ecarts types"* on the left, and *"5"* on the right. Look at both this section and the very bottom *"Isoler les classes"* section. See how the number 11,8 is on the high extremity of the light red band, which is much thinner than the very fat orange band. Light red only represents 5 437 out of 34 964 rentals, or 15.5%. Orange (between €8 and €9.90/m²/mo.) represents 15 724 or 45% of rentals. There's another big yellow band below that, also more than twice as big as light red. This reading tells us that unless our property in Rennes is exceptional, we'll likely be safer rounding down our pricing closer to €11/m²/mo. and be prepared to accept near €10/m²/mo.

However, that's just one reading. While this is a great new resource, a couple of caveats should be taken into consideration when using these figures to help determine how much you should charge for long-term residential rent of your space.

The data is already several months old by the time it's published. It will only be updated every two years at best (the example above for Rennes is from 2018, and this is being written in 2023). By the time you see them, these average prices could very likely have increased 5-10% in the open market.

Still, this is a useful tool, even if you're not doing LTR. Remember, STR prices flow from LTR, which flow from resale.

Base rates

The concept of using base rates for STR can be a bit tricky to get your head around, if you're unfamiliar. Base rates apply mostly to fast-moving markets, commonly short-term rental for accommodation. A base rate is the first building block you start with in the journey to what becomes the Public rate that the end consumer sees.

The first reason base rates exist is to protect you from the ever-changing world. While acknowledging market effects, they provide grounding and structure for reacting to the market. In a simplified way, you could think of your base rate as your 'net' revenue per night, but there's more to it than that. Your true fiscal net could be higher or lower, depending on your situation.

Used properly, a base rate provides a buffer, and minimum acceptable threshold, guaranteeing each rental is worth your time and effort. Base rates apply upward pressure.

Public rates apply downward pressure. There's only so much guests are willing to pay for your place, in that particular moment. The competitive landscape of alternative inventory available to them either helps or hinders selection of your property for their chosen dates. Above a certain level, your public rate starts to seriously affect your occupancy negatively. So, you should also set a minimum target to guide you, which we recommend as 40% occupancy.

The second reason to use a base rate is to make your calculations easier. Your base rate becomes the starting point, and other elements are added on top. This is the best and most logical way to proceed.

What if we did the opposite instead? What would happen if we didn't have a base rate? We might start by asking ourselves "How much should I charge per night?" Let's say we settled on charging €100 for a night.

We get a reservation through Booking.com for May 8th right away, which should make us wonder if we could've charged more. The guest comes and goes and we soon see €85 in our bank account. We scratch our heads because we were expecting €100, but we hadn't counted on the 15% commissions taken by the platform.

Next, we look around and see the mess the guest left, and the linens that need washing before the next reservation in a little while. Someone's got to tidy this up and we're unavailable. Luckily a cleaning service offers to come by lickety split and do the job for €35. While relieved, something tells us we should have charged the guest that amount.

That crisis was averted, but some time later we get a letter from the city hall. Inside is a bill for the tourist tax that we hadn't planned for, including €5 for the night of May 8th that seems so long ago. It's too late to collect from the guest, so I guess we'll have to eat that cost, too.

A quick calculation tells us the €100 we were expecting from May 8th has turned into €45, and we haven't even paid income tax on that yet. We were working backwards.

We vow to work forwards next time. We'll **start with a base rate** and include all the necessary elements before publishing our prices. In our formula, we should:

- Take into consideration: platform commissions, cleaning fees, additional guests, pet fees, seasonality, holidays and special events in your area, weekends/weekdays, volume discounts, tourist taxes, and when you're nearing legal limits (120 days in a main residence, for example)
- Not consider: concierge/property management fees, income taxes

A year wiser, we're prepared. We've settled on €80 as our base rate (reasoning to be explained later). We now know May 8th is a holiday in France, and in 2024 falls on a Wednesday. While this is as unremarkable a day as there is, the following day is Ascension, another national holiday. Chances are many people will simply take the Friday off to enjoy a long weekend. So, while early May is normally low season, we're confident in applying the 25% premium for mid-season (but not the 50% premium for high season). Thus €80 + 25% becomes €100.

The number we input on the calendar of the platform is €115 to cover their commissions. On top of that we charge €35 for cleaning and €5 for the tourism tax. The total (public rate) seen by the consumer on Booking.com is €155 because that site doesn't charge a separate fee to guests (other platforms do). The amount we see after paying the maid and the *mairie* is €100.

This is more than double what we saw in the first example. The €155 may have been at the higher end of what the market would bear, but we did get a reservation. Also, the cleaning fee did skew that particular night higher than it would have been on a longer reservation.

If we get a request for a discount, because our prospective guest offers to stay four nights, we're ready to knock off 10% without batting an eye. We've already figured our take, and what we're willing (and unwilling) to do before they even ask. In accepting, we've brought their nightly rate down to €117.25 on average (€115-10%discount=€103.50 x4nights=€414 +€5x4=€20tax +€35cleaning=€469 /4nights=€117.25) which is very attractive for them. Our take becomes €87.98 per night (€103.50-15%) or €351.90 total over four nights, for the same level of work on our part.

The third reason to use a base rate is because each platform charges a different commission. These differences are of course widespread between different categories, like storage and LTR, but wide discrepancies exist as well between platforms in the same exact space.

For example, Airbnb is geared to make the most money from travelers. Booking, starting out targeting hotels, makes most of their money from hosts. At the time of writing, it is still possible for Airbnb to charge individual hosts 3% (and guests up to 18%), while Booking charges hosts 15% and is free for travelers.

Platform fees in general
   Events/activities: The platforms take 7-10% commissions
   Parking: 10% to 15%
   Storage: 10% to 20%
   LTR: €25/mo. on PAP (SeLoger is the largest site, but only for pros)
   STR: 3% to 20% for hosts (and a further amount up to 18% for guests)
   On STR platforms, there are wild variations of business models and compensation levels. MediaVacances asks for an annual subscription of €89 to €129 (depends on property size), plus 3% commissions on rent collection. Abritel gives hosts the choice between an annual subscription of €249, or 8% commissions. Vrbo recently scrapped their subscription

model for a straight percentage, aligned with similar OTAs.

The fourth reason to employ a base rate is because the commission rate for a particular platform can change (platform decision) or you may accept a higher percentage (your decision) in exchange for higher visibility and attractiveness.

Without a base rate, you'll make less on Booking than you make on Abritel. Because Booking has more traffic, you could get more reservations, but earn less. If you input the same final amount on each site, regardless of commission rate, you're **competing with yourself**. Smart shoppers will shortlist your space, then look where they can get it for the cheapest price.

If you use the same base rate on all sites, you're **pitting the platforms against one another**. Your space appears less expensive on Vrbo than Airbnb? Fine, you don't care. You're receiving the same net amount from either channel.

If you decide to invest in your own site in an effort to get direct bookings, establishing your base rate means you already know what to charge. You could even add a 5-10% premium, knowing direct will still be less expensive to the traveler than through an ecommerce site. The extra money must also cover the extra labor, risk and systems needed to process direct payments.

Gravy train

If you're just starting out, it's best to begin with the attitude that 'this is all gravy' before worrying about how much money you're 'leaving on the table.' Every €1 you earn is a euro you didn't have before, and it has cost you nothing.

This is not like real estate sales, where you want to protect as much value as possible, knowing the buyer will slowly pull you back to the market level.

No, in STR it's a plausible strategy to start off with a price well under the market. You will get more bookings, and guests will have the impression they got a bargain. Ratings should be high, which is a great way to start a fine reputation. You'll need 5-10 good notations anyway to get decent visibility versus the competition.

From there, you can walk your prices up with each reservation. Future guests won't have any idea how much previous guests paid, so there's really no downside to this approach. Keep raising until either you've reached your target, or occupancy dips near your minimum threshold.

Activate

CHAPTER ELEVEN
Potential Revenue

How much money could you make by renting your space? This chapter could start visions of sugarplums dancing in your head! As well it should, because no matter if you're just getting started, or well on your way, you could be making more.

We know this because most folks have only activated **one** of their assets. What's more they've only turned on **one play**, or usage for that asset. Often that one play is **not optimized**, and only deployed for a **part of the time** that it could be. Both veterans and novices will have their eyes opened to new revenue streams, and turning their existing ones into raging rivers of revenue.

The beginning of this chapter looks at each use **individually**, exploring the revenue-producing potential of deploying that particular method alone, over a one-year period. With such a view, we are able to compare different uses, on a pure monetary basis.

The end of the chapter details scenarios of **combining** methods, a much more powerful income generator. If you have considerations which are just as important as money, solutions are provided to meet those objectives in the subsequent "Social Butterfly" chapter. It all starts with establishing your goal, which is the very next chapter.

A good general way to compare is to choose common data points. For this, the primary one we will select is the average daily rate, or ADR. This will be expressed in a fairly conservative range. You may wish to take a moment to break down ADR and other terms by reading the Glossary at the end of the book.

Average daily rate or ADR for the year = take all the revenues expected over the course of the year (not including cleaning nor tourist taxes nor platform fees) and divide by the actual rented nights for that usage. By averaging, you take away seasonality, which is more complexity than we need at this stage.

Note, all revenue figures are gross, before taxes and expenses.

Individual Plays

Accommodation, STR (short-term rental)

Definition: renting space for **less** than 30 days at a time for lodging purposes

Availability: Primary home limited to 120 days; 2nd home 0 to 365 days; Room in primary residence unlimited

Occupancy expected: 50-60% year-round (from 35% in low-season to 75% in high-season)

ADR- revenue per day: €50 to €500

Considerations: There are far too many variables to list an average for all locations, property types and all seasons. Suffice to say that Airbnb's ADR for Q4 2022 was $153, and Hilton's was $152 according to All The Rooms. It stands to reason as STRs are much, much bigger than hotel rooms. Still, it's a notable milestone for STRs to surpass one of the world's biggest hotel chains.

Configurations: Whole home STR furnished; Room STR, furnished

Luxury

Definition: renting space for **less** than 30 days in a row for lodging purposes at a posh abode

Availability: same as above

Occupancy expected: 40-50% year-round (from 15% in low-season to 65% in high-season)

ADR- revenue per day: €500 to €1000

Considerations: The *Luxe* category stands alone. Owners of villas, *châteaux*, private hideaways and penthouses with spectacular views are extremely selective about how their property is used. Most rent on a very short-term basis through exclusive platforms with bundled concierge services, or have agents working off-market whispering to prospects already known in their little black books.

We're talking €25 000 per week for a pristine villa, up to €650 000 for a month at a Saint-Tropez palace. The hoi-polloi go on trips at three times the rate of other *voyageurs*, on average 14 times per year. At that rate, it's easy to see how the estimate of €325 billion spent annually on luxury travel can be reached.

If you don't quite yet have a space like this in your portfolio, and you're just a bit short of cash to purchase outright, there are new fractional-ownership providers. Examples include Pacaso, Altacasa and Mansio.

You'd have 40 days to make bank in a year, or enjoy for yourself.
Platforms for STR:
Ultraluxe: The Collectionist (22% commissions), OneFineStay
Entertaining: Cookoon
Productions: 20000lieux

Amenities Outdoors & Camping

Owners are free to charge what they want, and on Louer Dehors, the range was from €3-€7 per hour per person. A stone's throw from Paris, a couple in Asnières-sur-Seine rents their garden for €4/hour/person.

Camping may be a victim of its own success. Corporations have scooped up 850 of the Mom and Pop sites. One third of all camping revenues are captured by five groups: Capfun, Sandaya, Huttopia, Siblu and European Camping Group (ECG) which is targeting €700 million revenues in 2023. Camping Paradis, which recently raised €31 million, is one of several franchisees operating in the sector. Huttopia, with 16 000 sites on 100 campgrounds generated 3 million nights sold in 2022 for €95 million in revenues, a 38% year-on-year increase.

If a certain population of campers are turned off by corporate parks, they may be more attracted to green spaces managed by private citizens offering a human touch. In the past 10 years, more than half of the municipal or rural campsites have disappeared. Sites with fewer than 50 lots are especially vulnerable to closure, as it's very difficult to reach profitability with such limited inventory.

Running a boutique campsite on private property, your bar to profits is much lower. You should be in the black from the very first rental, as your activity requires little to no new investment.

Accommodation, LTR (long-term rental)

Definition: renting space for **more** than 30 days at a time for lodging purposes
Availability: unlimited for homes and rooms
Occupancy expected: 85-90%
ADR- revenue per day: €10 to €100
Considerations: Again, there are variables for locations and property types.
Configurations:
Whole home LTR, unfurnished: Traditional, Roommates;
Whole home LTR, furnished: Traditional, Roommates, Coliving, Mobility;
Room LTR: Mobility, Traditional

Whole home, furnished LTR: This option is quite regulated, but it's worth the trouble, because of the numerous tax deductions available, and the fact you can charge a premium for the supplied furnishings, utilities and amenities. Minimum lease is a reasonable 1-year period, which strikes a good balance between flexibility and continuity.

Furnished rentals also attract a clientele which is more sure to pay. It's counterintuitive. You'd think that someone with more possessions would have more money, and have no issues with using some of that money for rent. However, 99% of unpaid rents are from people who've moved in with their own furniture and appliances. Furnished renters represent less than 1% of tenants who haven't paid, and needed to be pursued by their landlords for collection.

This can be a big issue in France. Since Covid-19 hit in March 2020, unpaid rent (*impayés*) situations have increased in the Paris region by 62%, according to Imodirect. Long-term *impayés* of 30 days or more have gone up 300%. Still, the national average for unpaid rent after 30 days is only 3.5%. As a landlord, you can absorb this risk yourself, or take out an insurance policy against it.

Whole home, unfurnished LTR: Note, this option is not covered at length in this book, because it's not recommended. It's the most heavily regulated, least flexible (minimum 3-year lease), deceptively cumbersome administratively, and least profitable owing to the fact that not as many expenses are deductible and income is often rent-controlled. This usage appeals to landlords who like to 'set it and forget it.'

On the renter side, if it is a larger unit, it's more likely to appeal to families. Couples with kids have likely accumulated many furnishings that they want to keep. Also, parents can be picky when it comes to the safety and newness of articles for babies and toddlers. For most, only their own personal stuff will do. If you want their business you'll have to rent unfurnished.

Roommate situation or "*colocation*"

This is the classic situation where all renters are on the same lease, which must run for at least one year (furnished) or three years (unfurnished). The dwelling becomes the main residence for all (see "Regulation" chapter for implications) and if one renter stops paying the others are liable for the full amount.

In France, 7% of all rentals are in HMOs or with roommates. Compare that with 40% in London. Clearly there's potential for more of these in France. However, this traditional arrangement may not be the best option for putting together unrelated renters.

* * *

Coliving

This is a modern setup where each renter has their own lease, typically running from one to 10 months long. While flatsharing roommates are more associated with students and the young, coliving appeals to all ages, for reasons of preference as well as economy.

Coliving is a global phenomenon. Fully 18% of all Americans, 60 million people, live in multi-generational households, with at least two adults in situ, related or not. Such arrangements have quadrupled in the United States since the 1970s. Fully 11% of all adult children live with their parents and almost **half of all young adults** aged 18 to 29 are living with their parents — the highest level since 1940 — according to U.S. Census Bureau data.

Not-so-young people are also being priced out of the rental market in cities around the world. Singles in their 30s, 40s and 50s have tremendous trouble finding a studio or 1-bedroom which meets their budget. A room in a shared dwelling costs 24% less on average nationally, and 46% less in Marseille, -36% in Paris and -34% in Lyon according to Flatlooker. While a landlord can charge more overall for a property by doing coliving, from the renter perspective, it's often a bargain compared to the monthly price of a studio or 1-bedroom.

By Cushman & Wakefield's estimate, there are about 7 820 coliving beds in the United States operated by companies, and more than 54 000 coliving beds in the pipeline or run by individual landlords.

Coliving has caught the eye of real estate investors, attracting nearly €1 billion in Europe over the past year. Coliving and student housing are among the most attractive asset classes for the coming decade, according to Brookfield Asset Management, with $263 billion in real estate held.

Startups and established property companies in France are well aware of the opportunity. Just before the world's biggest B-to-B real estate event, 300 coliving proptechs met in 2023 at the inaugural MIPIM Co-Liv Summit. The annual growth rate of the coliving market in Europe is 20-25% per year, according to Colonies. A study by JLL counts currently 10 000 coliving dwellings in France, a number which should grow beyond 26 000 in 2025. Cohabs claims the demand for Coliving exceeds that of traditional by 10 to 50 times.

Homies opened a single house with 21 shared rooms in Lille. The Babel Community already has 168 young professionals living together in one building in Marseille. Bouygues Immobilier has partnered with a fund by Ares Management to create a platform to launch coliving dwellings with an investment capacity of €450 million.

Outside of students and young professionals, there's another population attracted to shared accommodations: single parents. One in four French households are headed by a single parent. Some coliving complexes, like Commune House, specifically cater to monoparental families. There's even a coworking office called '*Moi et mes enfants*' setup for this.

On the roommate finding site LocService, 1.5% of requests come from a parent housing their offspring either part-time or full-time. More than half of roomies would be happy to share their space with a parent and child, although there's a strong preference for moms over dads, and 4+ year-old kids vs. infants or toddlers.

Entire dwellings in urban areas with a minimum of three bedrooms and two bathrooms can lend themselves to becoming coliving spaces. The most desirable spaces have a private bathroom or at least an in-room sink for each person, lots of secure storage space outside their rooms, a wide open salon/living room, a large kitchen with full dishwasher and refrigerator, an outdoor area, and many nooks where tenants can be alone outside their bedroom. You should have the ability to offer individual locks on each bedroom door, which should be designed for noise insulation, like the rest of the walls.

Coliving in your main residence would be tricky. Maybe you would be comfortable with it, but it changes the power dynamic among tenants. They may not appreciate sharing with their landlord, or feeling that they can't complain when you leave a dirty coffee cup in the sink. Coliving is all about harmony, which is a delicate balance to maintain over many months.

We'll cover coliving more in the Expand section, where we go in-depth on secondary residences.

Activity (recurring)

Definition: activities can take many forms, usually an instructor and their students come to your space for training purposes

Availability: unlimited

Occupancy expected: 10%

ADR- revenue per day: €10 to €40

Considerations: You could just offer your space for activities out of the kindness of your heart. Perhaps you are a proponent of physical fitness, and you simply want to support instructors and encourage people of all income ranges to participate.

A standard yoga mat is 60cm wide and 180cm long. If we figure 80cm between mats laterally and 40cm lengthwise, that means we need a minimum of 2m²/person including at least double that for the instructor and their material.

A *prof de yoga* might typically pay €25 to €35 per hour to rent a space from a commercial establishment or municipality. They must have large class sizes and charge each individual a pretty penny to make the math work for them in those expensive spaces. You could charge less than that, and you both would be content. The instructor could afford to run smaller, more intimate classes where they give more attention to each student.

If you did want to make this a money-making enterprise, a 20% cut seems a reasonable request. A percentage ensures the instructor isn't paying more than they are getting. Also, they'd have to pay a certain amount anyway to a municipality or gym for space rental.

However, a revenue share has some drawbacks. If your class teacher isn't so successful, you may be getting a measly cut from two students per week. A percentage of the take would offer little incentive to maximise that take.

A better solution for the owner is to propose 10% of max capacity. For example, if your space can host 8 students (and 1 teacher) at €15 each, you could charge the instructor €12 per session (€120 x 10% = €12). That way, every student above four is costing them less. Conversely, if they get three or fewer students, the instructor is paying more than the standard 20% rate. It's up to them to attract a wider following.

Resources: We-Peps lets you rent your space for yoga and other exercise activities.

Configurations: Yoga | Dance | Jam session music in rehearsal studio | Practice Sports/Exercise/Fitness gymnastics martial arts | Podcast recording | Pet Care

Business function (recurring)

Definition: an executive and their colleagues, or unrelated digital nomads use your space as their office on a regular basis

Availability: unlimited

Occupancy expected: 10%

ADR- revenue per day: €10 to €40

Considerations: A couple in Clichy-la- Garenne claims earnings of €1 000/mo. renting their apartment to businesses during the day on OfficeRiders. The knowledge workers sharing the space could be from the same company, or different ones. They could be habituals at the spot, or execs just passing through. A number of service pros (*professions libérales*) don't have a set place of business, and might prefer cutting hair, repairing bicycles, helping with homework (*soutien scolaire*) or otherwise consulting with their clients *chez vous* (where regulations permit).

Rent can vary widely depending on the type of activity, demand in your area, how successful your pros are, and the revenue model you agree to with them. To give you an idea, here's what one business is charging- Anticafé coworking space: €4/seat/hr.

On the expense side, you may be expected to have superior Wifi, provide coffee/tea and snacks, clean and comfortable shared desks or tables, possibly one or several breakout/meeting rooms, an atmosphere that's well insulated from noise and an isolated area from which to make video and vocal calls.

Configurations: Coworking space | Office space | Workspace | Office desk | Board meeting | Business center | Consultation (therapy, massage, makeover) | ChildCare

Dining/Drinking (occasional)

Definition: a social gathering mixing food and/or beverages
Availability: only limited by regulations
Occupancy expected: less than 1%
ADR- revenue per day: €50 to €500

Considerations: Organizations like Eau de Vigne will do all the animation for 10 invitees, and give you a cut of their proceeds from sales of bottles (*dégustation vente à domicile*).

Configurations: Restaurant | Banquet hall | Kitchen studio recipe lessons | Beer Garden | Wine tasting | Bar/Cafe | Club | BBQ

Activity (one-off)

Host gourmet meals in your fabulous demeure with Cookoon. The startup claims you could conceivably earn €40 000 in a year from dining and cocktail events (at €800 per evening, four times a month). Seems far-fetched, and only applies to the chic-est of settings. If this describes your space, why not tempt adding it to the 'mix' (pun intended). They claim 40 private homes in their 'Collection' and only members of their 'Club' can organise or get invited to these exclusive evenings. Who knows what the rich get up to, so it could be possible.

A more middle-class version exists called Eatwith. They purport to hand-pick locals from more than 130 countries to host dinner parties, food tours, and cooking classes. Presumably, you'd do this in your own space, instead of them sending you a chef. If you have a talent in this area, you could invite folks to sample the cuisine in your *cuisine*.

Corporate/Teambuilding (one-off)

Definition: you host all employees of one company for at least a half-day for training or celebration
Availability: unlimited
Occupancy expected: 1%
ADR- revenue per day: €300 to €3 000

Considerations: Your place should have that something special which makes it a unique experience to be remembered. Most companies like to change the area for each kickoff, so you shouldn't expect repeat business from the same customers.

Creative endeavors (one-off)

Definition: you host the crew and talent creating content with your space as the backdrop

Availability: unlimited

Occupancy expected: less than 1%

ADR- revenue per day: €900 to €3 000

Considerations: This is really hit-or-miss. Either you've got what the creative director is looking for in that particular moment, or you don't. There's no prospecting or selling involved.

If you're lucky enough to be selected one time, that may be the entirety of your 15 minutes of fame. Creative people want something unique for each project. If your living room is already out there in a movie, TV spot, magazine exposé or billboard, the new director will likely look elsewhere.

The ultimate jackpot is being chosen as the home of one of the main characters on a TV series. That could mean multiple shoots over several years. We wouldn't recommend holding out for this, and denying the one-off inquiries until you get it. It may never come, so take the short-term money and run.

Configurations: Advertising Photo Shoot | Commercial Ad | Music video | Film and TV | Influencer Post

Celebration/Party (one-off)

Definition: a one-time event for a special occasion

Availability: only limited by the holding capacity, how many people your property can host, respecting fire codes and regulations

Occupancy expected: less than 1%

ADR- revenue per day: €100 to €900

Considerations: The less often this special date occurs, the more you should be able to charge for it. A wedding should cost more than a family reunion, which should cost more than a birthday party.

Note, certain platforms like Airbnb have recently forbidden parties. That's OK, other platforms like Mynöx are better anyways at attracting the right crowd for mingling and *tching-tching* which doesn't expect a sleepover.

Configurations: Birthday | Bachelorette/Bachelor party | Wedding or Reception

Experience/Entertainment (one-off)

Definition: any performance you'd go to a night club, music hall, theatre or cinema to see, could also be shown from the comfort of your home

Availability: only limited by regulations

Occupancy expected: less than 1%

ADR- revenue per day: €30 to €300

Considerations: There are a multitude of pro venues out there, but none as intimate as your living room, none as convivial as your barn and prairie, none which breaks down the 4th wall as well as your home stage.

Configurations: Standup comedy | Theater play | Immersive art | Book reading | private Concert | Show | Circus act | Spectacle

Launch ceremony (one-off)

Definition: Event for the day or by the hour

Availability: unlimited

Occupancy expected: 50%

ADR- revenue per day: €300 to €1 000

Considerations: Before you look askance at your place, thinking there's no way anybody would want to rent it for this purpose, remember Rudy Guiliani's team organized a press conference in front of a Four Seasons Total Landscaping store!

In the USA, Home Studio List and Peerspace are among two startup platforms catering to this usage, where they claim that $150 an hour is the standard fee. The latter is trying to break into France. We know of at least six local French platforms operating in this sector.

Configurations: Gallery art exhibition | Showroom products | Venue press conference | Political campaign announcement | Offsite demonstration | Trade show hall | Mobile Location | Pop-up shop

Parking (daily access)

Definition: one or several spaces you make available for others to place their motorized vehicle, whether two, four or more wheels

Availability: unlimited

Occupancy expected: 30-90%

ADR- revenue per day: €2 to €8 rented on a monthly basis

Considerations: Ten years ago, the European Parking Operators association estimated the annual rental generation of spaces on the continent at €6 billion.

For many Americans, this enormous figure can seem hard to fathom. The US has upwards of seven spaces for each and every registered car in the country. Los Angeles makes churches allocate a parking space for every five seats in the congregation, and hospitals set aside two parking spaces for every hospital bed. Up to 1998, 1.7 spots per dwelling was the rule for building developers, resulting in 14% of L.A. County's surface area dedicated to parking. How can something so plentiful be worth so much?

Well, parking is much more scarce in Europe, acutely so in France, and on the road to extinction in dense urban areas like Paris. Today, the City of Light counts one parking space for every eight headlights. Tomorrow, the number of spaces will be reduced by half.

Already, since the pandemic, 3 700 Parisian restaurants were allowed to build outdoor terraces right on the street parking spots outside their doors. Valued up to €392/m² a spot transformed into a terrace can earn €5 000/mo. for the mayor, which is about double what she'd get for €6/hour street parking. These supposedly temporary wooden structures are now all but grandfathered permanently.

Most private parking spots in France are from 12m² to 15m² in ground surface area, or 24m³ to 30m³ by volume if enclosed. One of the top platforms for renting a parking spot calls itself '12 point 5' referencing the 12.5m² typical size. For the most part, they are rented or leased on a monthly basis.

The center of urban areas are where the demand and rental charges are the highest. In Paris, you can charge from €100 to €250 per month. In Lyon or Marseille €75 to 135/mo. In Bordeaux, Biarritz, or Cannes, €80/mo. In Nantes €65/mo. In Normandy, Brittany and the Loire Valley around €50/mo.

Depending on the location of your spot, your annual gross potential could be from €600 to €3 000 per year. If you live within walking distance of a major sports stadium, convention center, airport and such, you may be able to charge more on an ad hoc basis.

One company, Carsup, specializes in caring for luxury vehicles. Ferraris, Aston-Martins, Porches, Bugattis and the like have a space on the *huppé* Avenue Foch in Paris, plus get treated to concierge services like detailing, oil changes and fill-ups. The company claims more than 1 000 autos in their garages, and more locations coming across chic European capitals. There's a huge market for this, and even rich people don't necessarily want to pay top dollar. You could take advantage, offering your own space to this audience, and as the French say, "*tirer ton épingle de jeu.*"

By the way, there is no word in French for 'driveway.' You can describe your spot as inside a garage/box which can be locked (*fermé à clef*), in a collective parking garage/carpark (*dans un parking, place de stationnement*), underground (*sous-sol*), in a shed/barn (*grange*), in front of the house (*devant de la maison*), behind a gate (*portail*), and/or covered (*abrité*).

Configurations may include: one car or several motorcycles/scooters; dozens of bicycles or e-scooters.

***

Storage (recurring, with occasional access)

Definition: someone else's boxes, furniture or other belongings stored on your premises

Availability: unlimited

Occupancy expected: 20%

ADR- revenue per day: €2 to €8

Considerations: Americans value their garage space, even if one-third of them only use it for storage. Even then, that's usually not enough. Around one in every 11 Americans pay nearly $100 each month for self-storage.

If the need is proportionate in France, where living spaces are smaller, then we're talking 6 million people and $7.2 billion spent annually. Professional owners of logistics facilities (depot, warehouse, etc.) in France earn between 3.5% and 4.5% gross yield annually, and raised their rents by 15% in 2022.

Self-storage is a $40B a year industry. Public Storage made an unsolicited offer to buy rival Life Storage for around $11 billion in stock. Stuf, a New York-based self-storage startup, raised $11M in 2022. US startup Neighbor claims some owners make $50 000 a year on their peer-to-peer platform. Thanks to Amazon, warehouse rents have never been higher.

French startup Costockage claims you can make €2 000 a year doing this, which seems more realistic. The going rates in Paris are €20-25/m³/mo., in the suburbs and big cities €10-20/m³/mo. and in rural zones €5-10/m³/mo. Costockage publishes the average going rates for storage in different geographies in France on their platform.

Is your property in an area with significant demand? Storebox, a Vienna-based self-storage, warehousing and logistics startup which raised €52 million in 2021, primarily targets cities with populations of 30 000 or more. If your place is in, or borders such a town, you could be in luck.

Do you have the kind(s) of space(s) that would attract folks who want to store their stuff? Here are the criteria of the most sought-after spaces:

- Dry: the ground is not susceptible to collect water, or at least things are up on pallets off the ground. The area should not attract humidity or condensation.
- Accessible: few steps and easy turns to carry items to their quarters. Ground floor or street-level spaces will be more attractive than basements or attics.
- Voluminous: for items like couches, beds, armoires *et al*.
- Secure: a lock on the entrance or a door which requires a key or

code for entry.

Storage space is measured in cubic meters, or m³, meaning one unit is 1 meter long by 1 meter wide by 1 meter high. People will want to store voluminous items in your space like beds, couches, armoires, sporting equipment like skis, musical instruments and recording equipment, paintings and sculptures.

To figure the total rental income potential of one of your spaces, first measure the surface area. Let's say your target space is an extra room in your home. Start by the footprint, or square meters on the floor. If the bottom of one wall is 2.5 meter long, and the other is 4 meter long, you multiply those two figures to get 10m² for that room. To get cubic meters, you then multiply the m² figure by how high the ceiling is.

The average ceiling height inside residential property in France is 2.5 meters, and the minimum is 2.2 meters. There is no minimum for home garages, detached boxes for flats, so if you don't know for sure, simply figure at least 2 meters high for these spaces.

If the extra room is standard height, then it has 25m³ of space for storage. When figuring realistic income potential, you will rarely, if ever have each and every single m³ filled by renters. It's harder than a game of tetris to get the items in there without wasted space, because they're not all going to be rectangular with right angles. Plus, you'll need some way to get to a particular box without having to move every other item. Figure 60% max. capacity as a realistic rule of thumb. Thus, the 25m³ of potential in the extra room becomes 15m³ of realistic space used continuously for storage.

If you have a tall barn or hangar on your premises, your best bet would be focus on renters with enormous items like boats, light aircraft, collector cars and motorcycles, farm machinery and annual festivals (think of the floats at the *carnival de Nice*, your town's voting billboards or Christmas decorations). It's a benefit to them, because they have very few options to choose from to get their items out of the weather. It's a benefit to you because you earn a lot of revenue in one go, from one renter. It would be much more complicated to earn as much from multiple renters.

Also, even if your space is 8 meters high, it will be rare than you can monetize any of your space above 4 meters high. This is because you can only stack so many boxes on top of one another before they are unstable at the top, and the bottom box can't resist the weight above. To go higher, you'd have to invest in sturdy warehouse shelves like you see in a lumber yard, and maybe a forklift.

A Southern US-based startup called RecNation does nothing but storage for recreational vehicles and boats. The fact that they manage thousands of enclosed units in several states gives you some indication of the huge market potential for such a venture. France is just behind Germany in European RV marketshare. StockOn is a French company in this market, allowing private property owners to place ads to store caravans on their lot, or winterize boats under the BoatOn brand.

The more densely populated the area around your space, the more demand there is for storage, and the more you can charge for it. While your space may reside in the suburbs or a rural area, and there may be less demand, commercial storage spaces may be far away, and very expensive, making your space more attractive by proximity.

The platforms take 10-20% commissions, which typically includes insurance for the space renter. Renters have a 15-day notice period to stop, but the platforms will expect you to honor a two-month period from the time you wish to cancel and have the renter pick up their stuff.

You'll need to specify which items are acceptable and those you won't take. It's best to rule out the same kinds of items that an airline would deny in their cabin, like flammables, corrosives, weapons and so on. Suggest hermetically sealed plastic containers instead of cardboard boxes to your renters.

Others

Space+Services

Pet-sitting: According to Yoopies, one of the many platforms matching fur babies with caregivers and accommodations, a pet-sitter can charge from €10-€20 per day per pet. There's a lot of competition, as 230 000 people claim this activity in France. Only the top rated hosts with fantastic amenities are able to charge in the higher range.

This activity could help your other activities. More travelers seek dwellings which accept pets. While their expectation is that they can have their pet with them everywhere inside the house, they're also far from home, and probably came there to explore. It could be seen as an advantage to be able to leave Fluffy during the day while they go out and play *la touriste*.

Combining Plays

Each one of the methods detailed previously are lucrative enough in their own right. But what happens when you deploy them in combination? Let's look at an example of doing just that in a property we're already familiar with.

The Forestiers, owners of the *maison bleue,* have chosen a unique mix of the plays listed in this chapter. They've taken measure of their assets on a space-by-space basis, checked the availability of each space on their family calendar, honestly assessed their preferences, verified what is allowed, and analyzed the going rates by season for the uses they wish to deploy.

Consulting with My Property Payday, their data was mixed with market figures and proprietary formulas to arrive at an estimation. This study not only assessed the potential revenue, but also recommended which usage would most likely happen where, the predicted occupancy rate of the space for that usage and referred to the appropriate platforms and providers who could partner with the family to realize these gains.

Here's what they decided to do.

(figure 8):

Maison Bleue uses, platforms and providers

Year: 2023

space name	space	usage	which type?	1	2	3	4	5	6	7	8	9	10	11	12	13	14	15	1	2	3	4
whole home	H1	STR	tourism	X	X																	
attic	A1	storage	boxes					X	X													
master bedroom	B1	none	X																			
daughter's room	B2	LTR	student							X	X											
son's room	B3	STR	tourism	X	X																	
cellar	C1	activities	exercise									X						X				
dining room / study	D1	co-working	office										X									
garage	G1	storage	furniture				X	X														
driveway covered	G2	parking	car											X								
living room / salon	L1	activities	wellbeing												X				X			
pool	P1	swimming	recreation													X						
shed	SH1	storage	boat winterizing														X					
terrace	T1	events	corporate															X				
back yard	Y1	activities	outdoor & sports														X			X		
front yard	Y2	activities	pet-sitting															X				X

Platform columns (1–15): Airbnb, Booking, Homebox, Jestocke, Locaviz, StudyLease, Kiwiiz, Ubiq, Parkadom, YogMee, Swimmy, Allovoisins, Kactus, OhMygarden, Holidog

Provider columns (1–4): M Goodbody, Mme Namaste, Mlle Pilates, neighbor kid

They've used a total of 15 platforms, and partnered with four service providers for the different uses happening in their home. For the rental uses which are expected to generate the most revenue, STR, LTR, storage and activities, from two to four platforms are being used, to better fill the calendar. For the other uses, only one platform is activated for each. Nina could post listings on more platforms, but she thinks this will only bring diminishing returns.

If this seems like a lot of work, then you may wish to get help from property managers and other professionals, which will be introduced in the Outsource chapter.

For Nina Forestier, it's doable as a self-run affair, because she works from home. Most of the plays are set-it and forget it, like storage, parking and the student on a long-term rental. What takes up the bulk of her time is coordinating the short-term rentals, co-working musical chairs, swimming reservations and corporate events. Luckily, for the enterprise offsites, there's always a member of the company team who wants to run the event, so Nina doesn't have to be involved.

She's also partnered with providers. At first, it took some time to find the right ones and agree to a profit share. Now, Monsieur Goodbody coordinates his exercise class schedule, and deals with the students himself, without Nina's intervention. She just makes sure the cellar is clean and aired out in-between sessions.

Same with Madame Namaste's yoga classes, from 8 a.m. to 9 a.m. twice a week, before the co-workers arrive at the dining room table. Nina likes to partake in the sessions herself. The living room is always immaculate anyway, as the maid passes often, and the cleaning costs are deducted making their taxable earnings from renting less.

Mademoiselle Pilates only conducts her outdoor training when the weather permits. For the rest of the time, the backyard (Y1), terrace (T1) and pool (P1) are rented together.

Nina bought the kennels, food, toys, cleaning supplies and accessories for pet-sitting, and she deals with the owners and reservations. A neighbor kid, however, walks the dogs before and after school, helping also with feeding and cleaning. At lunchtime, Nina will either let the dogs out for a bit, or walk them, depending on her schedule.

The trickiest part is handling the agenda. No channel manager exists to block dates on platform G when you get a reservation on platform K. No current solution treats each space separately. Platforms are designed for one use only. My Property Payday is working on a universal solution, accessible online to members who self-manage. Until that is live, you may consult with us on an ad-hoc basis, or purchase the offline tools we've created which are illustrated in these pages.

While the hypotheses of the estimation from My Property Payday are quite conservative, the results are simply astonishing. Take a look at the table for yourself, and then we will make some comments afterwards.

(figure 9):

* * *

My Property Payday: Turn your Spaces into Rental Income, France edition

Maison Bleue rental revenue potential
Year: 2023

space	m2	m3	usage	days (avail.)	hours/day (avail.)	occupancy expected (mid)	total time rented (days)	time rented (hours)	cost/ unit (base)	ADR or cost/ day (base)	total revs (base-low)	cost/ unit (mid)	ADR or cost/ day (mid)	total revs (mid)	cost/ unit (high)	ADR or cost/ day (high)	total revs (high)	total gross revs YR (mix)
H1	104		STR	48		56%	27		€1.06	€110	€0	€1.33	€138	€1,222	€1.66	€172	€3,102	**€4,324**
A1	30	30	storage	365		20%	73		€0.27	€8	€0	€0.33	€10	€725	€0.41	€12	€0	**€725**
B1	15		none	0	0	0%												
B2	13		LTR	318		85%	270		€0.80	€10	€0	€0.99	€13	€3,492	€1.24	€16	€0	**€3,492**
B3	10		STR	269		30%	81		€1.70	€17	€456	€2.12	€21	€570	€2.65	€27	€712	**€1,738**
C1	20	50	activities	318	6	10%	32	191	€4		€254	€5		€318	€6		€382	**€954**
D1	7		co-working	318	9	10%	32	286	€3		€286	€4		€382	€5		€477	**€1,145**
G1	19	38	storage	365		20%	73		€0.27	€10	€0	€0.33	€13	€919	€0.41	€16	€0	**€919**
G2	16		parking	269		25%	67		€0.21	€3	€0	€0.27	€4	€285	€0.32	€5	€0	**€285**
L1	25		activities	318	2	10%	32	64	€4		€85	€5		€106	€6		€127	**€318**
P1	20		swimming	184	8	5%	14	110	€10		€0	€15		€0	€25		€2,760	**€2,760**
SH1	22	44	storage	365		6%	22		€0.27	€12	€0	€0.33	€15	€319	€0.41	€18	€0	**€319**
T1	28		events	184	9	6%	11	99	€10		€331	€15		€497	€25		€828	**€1,656**
Y1	295		activities	184	10	5%	9	92	€5		€153	€8		€230	€13		€383	**€767**
Y2	32		activities	318	9	2%	6	57	€10		€183	€12		€229	€14		€275	**€687**

Grand Total: **€19,402**

If your eyes shot straight to the bottom-right and the grand total, you're not alone. Nineteen freaking thousand, four hundred and two euros! Taking the roughest of calculations used by investors to determine ROI- purchase price divided by annual revenue, we get a gross yield of 5.3%.

This is staggering, considering the owners have hardly invested any new money. They are simply leveraging their initial outlay, which they didn't even think of as an investment. The Forestier family just wanted a nice place to live and enjoy for themselves. Then, the sharing economy opened the door to possibilities unbeknownst to them.

Did you ever imagine so much rental income could be produced from a Primary Residence? Let's remind ourselves this family is living here practically year-round. They only leave the house to go on vacation 48 days in the year. This is for the five weeks of legal *congés*, given to every worker in the land, plus weekends and holidays surrounding their time off. We're not even counting possible *RTT* or *réduction de temps de travail*, which many people get in addition, sometimes as many as 20 days a year. Both heads of household have full-time occupations. Nina does work from home, but *télétravail* is commonplace these days in nearly all fields.

The size of the property, 104m^2, is below-average for a house in France (125m^2). Their living space is nice, but nothing exceptional. It wouldn't be found in an issue of Dwell, or a write-up about notable, unusual or *insolite* places for a getaway. The location of their property, near the outskirts of Toulon, is middle-of-the-road, both in terms of attractiveness and demand. This is far from the status of the *croisette* in

Cannes.

Formulas and figures chosen are truly conservative. Many STR hosts experience better than 56% occupancy, especially if they are only renting during high season. Listings of the same size and area of Toulon are plentiful above €138 per night for a whole home. Toulon doesn't have rent control, but if it did, €21.66/m²/mo. for an LTR including furnishings and charges would likely be under the legal limit for a small bedroom and bathroom access. The storage and parking spaces are empty 75%+ of the time. Activities and events are going on less than 10% of all possible hours. When they are, it's far from capacity, and at reasonable rates.

We're not going crazy here with different groups constantly bumping into one another at all hours. Only one renter stays overnight six months out of the year, and two guests stay overnight a little less than three months out of the year. The owners have their parental suite and bathroom all to themselves when they are home.

The *maison bleue* is active, but not really being run like a resort. Most of what's going on is passive (storage, parking) or transitory (activities, events) for 1-2 hours at a time. It's busier at high season of course, but that's the choice of the owners, who could just as easily shut that part of the property business down at any moment if it gets to be too much.

Suffice to say, this simulation is by no means a stretch of the imagination, or beyond the capacities of two resourceful, 50-something folks of middling energy and modest skills, most of the time occupied with their day jobs.

Again, it ain't all Airbnb

A deeper dive into the figures dispels misconceptions and the disproportionate attention given to some uses. This is unfortunately to the detriment of others, which are quite interesting, monetarily.

For example, everybody talks about Airbnb, and certainly STR usage is the #1 producer here. But only 31% of the rental income at this home is derived from STR (from H1 and B3). If the Forestiers do what everybody advocates, renting their entire *maison bleue* only when they are away on vacation (H1), and nothing else, they would leave €15 078 on the table. Instead, they are activating their unused assets, at the same time as they enjoy the rest for themselves.

In fact, of the two bedrooms being rented, the LTR one (B2) generates twice the revenue of the STR one (B3). Overall in the ranking of money made per usage, LTR comes in 3rd. Clearly the sharing economy is not only about Airbnb. Even if you could do STR year-round, which is illegal in a lot of places in France, you may not want to, preferring to diversify for richer reward. And less headaches. STR is by far the hardest way to earn rental income.

Bundling activities and events, which are very similar, we get a total of €4 382, which takes the 2nd spot. This is more than what's generated by renting the whole home (H1), but less than all STR usage (H1 and B3). The activities subtotal (from C1, L1, Y1, Y2) is €2 726 and the events subtotal (from T1) is €1 656.

In terms of individual spaces, the terrace (T1) is the #4 money-making asset, catering mainly to corporates. The cellar (C1) generates more income than the backyard (Y1), despite having only 7% of the surface area. However, it's available nearly twice as often, in all weather, and it's expected to draw more exercisers than the yard attracts merry-makers, campers and people doing outdoor cookouts.

Swimming (P1), at a whopping €2 760 takes the 4th spot in total revenue generated by usage over the year, which you may find surprising. After all, how many folks are there really who are willing to pay to plunge in another's pond? Even if there are a lot of people, surely this is limited to the very few hottest days of summer, right?

Well, we've already seen that public supply is shrinking, with no lessening of demand for pools. Near the *Côte d'Azur*, where the *maison bleue* is located in Toulon, there are more swimmable days than elsewhere. Still, we're limiting the calendar to six months of the year. Then, we're only expecting three to eight percent occupancy in an 8-hour day, when many days have 16 hours of sunshine. It only takes 2-4 bathers at a time with reasonable hourly rates to amass quite a sum. The veritable income from swimming could be much higher if they really worked it.

Storage produces the 5th most usage revenue, from three spaces. The attic (A1) holds boxes, the garage (G1) stores more voluminous items like furniture, bicycles, and decorative holiday displays. The shed (SH1) houses a 5.5-meter boat, which normally zips around the nearby Mediterranean Sea, but is here ashore for winterizing.

Co-working cranks out the 6th most usage cash. Nina tickles her laptop keyboard from her makeshift desk at the dining table, so it's nice to have others join her, to create an office environment that she finds more productive. All she needs to worry about is broadband uptime, power supply, fully-stocked coffee/tea/snacks and navigating the noise level when someone's on a call or videoconference.

The final slot goes to parking in 7th place. This is due to low demand in their area. In Paris, a slot in an open parking structure can easily generate €100/mo. (€1 200/year), and an enclosed, lockable garage €200/mo. (€2 400/year), which is about ten times what we're expecting here. There's also the fact that the Toulon spot (G2) is outside, on the driveway. Sure, it's off-street, behind a locked gate, and covered, so out of the rain, but it is maybe not as attractive as underground, or fully-enclosed. They could make more parking income if they rented the garage (G1) for this purpose. Instead, they think, perhaps rightly, that storage will pay off better for the garage in their neighborhood.

We didn't count the income from EVs charging at the public station they've installed on their property facing the street in front of the house, because it's so new, accurate assumptions are hard to make. Perhaps they could choose to bundle charging with the driveway parking spot (G2), if their client has an EV. That would up the income potential.

Overall, there's nothing on this list which isn't worth doing. The lowest earners, storage and parking, are practically labor-free. Time spent managing year-round vs. money made likely has the owner earning €50/hour from this pursuit alone.

This is of course, an example. Your property may present greater or fewer assets to activate. It may be bigger or smaller; in a high-rent or low-rent district. Whatever you start with, it's up to you what you do, and how far you choose to go.

Now that you know how much could be earned, let's set your personal goal.

CHAPTER TWELVE
Set your goal

By now, you're certain there's a ton of cash to be made in renting your property. The total earnings are greatly enhanced by activating several assets, opening multiple revenue streams. The ways you use each asset, the availability you grant and how much you charge all have repercussions on your property portfolio's performance.

There are tradeoffs, however. Accepting a full-time LTR lodger means always sharing your space when you're home. The more nights you offer up your primary residence for STR, the more laundry, cleaning and other turnover chores will be necessary.

Different combinations produce different results. Some are more in line with your goals and lifestyle. Others, not so much. This, and the following four chapters juxtapose markedly distinct pairings. Which one is right for you?

Availability vs. Calendar
Up to now, we've used the term 'availability' in its most general sense, answering the question "When **can** it be used?" For the available space to meet our goals, we'll now answer the questions "When **should** it be used?" and "How do I want to **bundle dates**?"

Most owners in France still offer their properties up in a very old-school fashion. It's sold for one week at a time, minimum 7-day stay, Saturday PM to the next Saturday AM. High season, low season, rain or shine, year-after-year. They'll set their prices for each season months ahead of time, and then not change a thing whether they're overbooked or underbooked.

This archaic *mode opératoire* is obviously not optimized for revenue production. Properties routinely sit empty for seven or 14 or 21 days in a row. They get reserved in advance for bargain rates, at a time when desperate travelers are beating down doors for a spot, wads of cash in hand.

Examples of combinations:
Maximize Yield- this will appeal to active investors wanting to generate the greatest return.
Minimize Workload- this combo is for passive investors, who expect their money to work for them, and not the inverse.
Social Butterfly- this is for those who want to have it all, who marry their past-time with their vocation, who value human interaction as much as revenue.
Tranquility- if your home is your castle, if alone time or the family circle is precious, and should remain undisturbed.

CHAPTER THIRTEEN
Maximize Yield

Maximize Yield- this will appeal to active investors wanting to generate the greatest return.

Accommodation, STR:

As seen in the Potential Revenue chapter (and others in the Expand section), STR for your whole home clearly has the highest money-making possibilites. So, how can you work the STR angle in your primary residence? You've got three main levers in an STR business: Inventory, Occupancy and Pricing.

More STR than LTR: Since STR produces the highest ADR for accommodation, you should do as much of this as possible. The exceptions could be if you've already reached the 120-day limit, or in low-season, where STR rates and occupancy will be their lowest of the year. For these months, you could consider the most flexible of LTR options.

Rent one or several rooms: Renting a smaller space will net you more revenue per square meter. Renting each room individually also brings more per square meter than renting them together, or as a part of renting the entire property. What's more, the 120-day restriction doesn't apply to rooms. That's correct, homeowners can rent a room in their primary residence on an STR basis 365 days a year.

You could mix renting rooms on STR while you're living there, and STR the entire home at other periods. Accept instant bookings with a flexible cancellation policy. You'll find you get more reservations, and people don't change their plans that often. Also, a full calendar does amazing things to attract more bookings, similar to the sight of a line outside a restaurant.

***

Charge less: Yes, this does seem counter-intuitive. But if you're just starting out, you won't have a lot of ratings. The top thing you can do to improve the ranking of your listing on Airbnb is to increase the number of reviews. This is even more important than the rating.

Showing a lower price than surrounding alternatives will make more people consider your listing. If guests think they got good value for the money, they'll give you good ratings. It's not automatic, and it's common to have only half of the people who stay provide a rating. You need to chase them, remind them, and pre-empt by showing them you've given them a 5-star rating, in the hopes they'll do likewise. Ratings are also important to guests.

The more 4*+ ratings you get, the more people will reserve your place. When you get at least a dozen satisfied customers, you can inch-up your prices.

Let's put on our revenue manager hats and look at a comparison. Example A) charges €120 per night and gets 50% occupancy. Example B) charges €90 per night and gets 80% occupancy. Which gives a better yield? Well, A) produces €1 800 in a month, while B) produces €2 160 in a month. Reducing your daily rate may actually improve your overall yield.

Allow shorter stays: Leveraging the time element, you can charge a higher ADR for 1-2 day stays. Whether this is your standard policy, or you're just using these to plug holes in-between your longer stays, adding this strategy to the mix will benefit your yield.

Also, each stay should produce a rating. You'll need to chase people, and perhaps incentivize them to get half the people to rate, but this effort is worth it. The more ratings, the more popular your place appears. It's also likely the platform will give properties with more ratings higher placement in search results.

Easy policies: Having a fairly flexible cancellation and refund policy can give tourists the reassurance to reserve without thinking twice.

Instant booking: Turning this on, while having easy policies should fill up your calendar faster. It also creates the same effect as a line out the door of a popular restaurant. When browsers see there's very little room left on your calendar, they're more likely to take a chance on reserving.

DIY: Charge for cleaning, then do it yourself. You've just made yourself an additional 10-15% per stay. You must admit you look good in a French maid's outfit.

Get yourself a direct booking site. This will help you pocket 15-20% more than you would with a reservation through the OTAs. If you're a risk-taker, you could find a means to speak directly with your prospective guest by phone. Offer them a slight discount if they cancel the OTA reservation and re-book directly with you. *Ni vu, ni connu.*

Activate channels like Le Bon Coin which don't charge any fees.

What if you can't do more STR? That depends on the reason holding you back.

120-day rule: Your place is going gangbusters, and you've rented your whole space for 120 nights well before the year ends. The first thing we'd recommend is to raise your prices. If you already have strong demand, that will likely continue even if your tariffs increase.

No place to go: If you don't have friends/family nearby, you may well consider a hotel or another STR. If you're renting out your whole place while reserving a smaller room elsewhere, on pure m² you should be ahead on the deal. Set a goal as to what kind of margin is worth putting you out of your home. We'd recommend a 50% margin as a bare minimum. The net you get from renting your whole place as an STR (after platform fees, cleaning, etc.) should be at least double what your paid-for reservations cost you.

Accommodation, LTR:

For greatest yield, you could do LTR, but only on a mobility lease: The mobility lease will generate the highest ADR of all LTR plays that you can exercise in your primary residence.

It also allows the greatest amount of flexibility. If you did a student lease in an available room, it would be tricky to rent your whole home on STR during the school year. By timing your mobility leases in-between popular periods, you could STR your whole home during holidays, long weekends and *vacances scolaires*.

Activity (recurring):

Choose the activity with the highest price tag. Bypass yoga classes for fitness coaches at €40/hour. Forget furry friend watching for expensive art instructors.

If you have a pool, rent it out as much as you can for a reasonably high scale while you're occupying the residence. This is probably the best plan, as all the revenues come to you, rather than sharing with someone leading an activity.

Business function (recurring):

Co-working would be nice, if popular and regular, but renting out space to highly paid consultants and therapists would be more lucrative. You'll have to find those who'd be willing to close down their practice during your vacations, when you'll be renting out our whole home.

Corporate/Teambuilding (one-off):
Why not, if this doesn't tread on your other plays. Choose an afterwork instead of daytime or several day training which may interrupt your co-working, activity and consultations.

Creative endeavors (one-off):
Gamble only for high-stakes movie or series shoots, which pay the most. Forget about lower-paying photography and such.

Celebration/Party (one-off):
Unless someone wants to rent your place for a wedding or other high-ticket affair, don't bother.

Dining/Drinking (occasional):
This is not likely to bring in much revenue, so skip it.

Experience/Entertainment:
Ditto. This is a nice little addition, but it's better to focus on other uses.

Launch (one-off):
Another roll of the dice, so bet big. Target companies with high-value products like perfume, bags or shoes, who are used to spending more than half of their revenues on marketing.

Parking:
If you've only got one space to sell, try to sell it to the highest bidder. Seek out the owner of a luxury automobile or a collector car. Reinforce security at your space to attract a *clientèle* willing to pay more.

Or, divide and conquer. If one driver is willing to pay €100 per month, then four motorcycle riders should be willing to pay €50 each. Doing so will double your intake to €200 per month.

Or, open your space for shorter periods, like special events or airport parking. It only takes five occasions, charging €20 per night when a nearby concert or sports match is on, to earn the same as a long-term monthly rental would in the above example. You should undercut what the local venue or parking garage charges, which isn't hard to do, considering how much they gouge the customer. Space renters would also appreciate coming back to a cleaner, nicer smelling, more secure spot they can actually get into and out-of easier than those obstacle courses they call parking garages, which were built for the original mini, and not for today's SUVs.

Storage (long-term):
   As this isn't a big money-maker, only do this if you have a dedicated space that can't be used for anything else. Such as an attic or shed, or a room too small for a bed (less than 9m² can't be rented out for accommodation).

Other:
   Combinations to make the most money: STR in the high season, plus…
   Coliving the rest of the year, or…
   Roommates during the school year.

Uses which carry the greatest tax deductions: LTR, then STR, which are both eligible for the LMNP regime.

There are ways to boost your rental income through acquisition, investment and other strategies. Regardless of what the gurus tell you, these all carry a higher degree of risk, and all require much more of your time to pilot effectively. Large capital outlay projects and complex financial structured plans are touched upon in the Expand section of this book.

CHAPTER FOURTEEN
Minimize Workload

This combo is for passive investors, who expect their money to work for them, and not the inverse. In France, these folks are called *'rentiers,'* and many are jealous of them. It's said their money multiplies while they sleep.

Yes, the techniques used by well-to-do people in their secondary residences could also work for little ol' you in your humble primary residence.

Avoid turnover.

Set it and forget it.

Get someone else to do the dirty work. This is discussed at length in the Outsourcing chapter in the Optimize section.

If your time is precious, this may be the path you choose to pursue. But make no mistake about it, if you're using your primary residence to generate rental income, you're earning it.

Accommodation, STR:

You'll want to make guests request a reservation, and evaluate them to avoid troublemakers, rather than accept bookings automatically. You should also have a strict cancellation policy to avoid holding an empty space, or scrambling frantically to try to fill it at the last minute. This will lessen the number of confirmed reservations, but at least when you get one, it'll be a sure thing.

Rent your entire property only during the *grandes vacances*, when you're away for several weeks. Try to secure a party which will stay for a week or more. Failing this, you'll have to account for turnover in-between traveling parties. Who will handle that if you don't have a property management company? Will a *conciergerie* accept your property which is only available six to eight weeks out of the year?

You may find that having a high minimum stay requirement

dramatically lessens the demand for your property. If you don't get any inquiries, or don't find a property manager, or end up doing the turnover in-between guests yourself, STR might not be the play which best aligns with your goals.

Accommodation, LTR:
Rent one or several rooms at least nine months of the year. This means you're almost certainly looking for a student, or displaced worker. Remain firm on the minimum stay. Any change of tenant will create twice the amount of work for you.

Activity (recurring):
This should be turned off, in most cases. If you possess a space which the activity coordinator can get into and out of with their students independently, which requires no upkeep on your part, then this might work out for you. Otherwise, if it requires you to control access, or prep the area, or run interference in a common space, it won't suit your goal of minimizing your workload.

Business function, Corporate/Teambuilding, Creative endeavors, Celebration/Party, Dining/Drinking, Experience/Entertainment, Launch (one-off):
Do not activate these uses. They'll all require heavy lifting on your part to attract renters, serve them and clean up after.

Parking:
Favor year-round renters. Failing that, make your contract a six-month minimum. Offer a special deal if they pay upfront for the whole period.
Make sure they have independent access, so you don't have to be there to let them in or out.

Storage:
Prefer long-term renters. Again, you could set a minimum period, and ask for pre-payment. Restrict access to but a few days a month.

Other:
In general, make the payment processing systems you use as simple, guaranteed and automated as possible. Direct debit, or *prélèvement* is the most popular, and least expensive way to get paid in France. It's not just for LTR, but can also be setup for parking, storage, and many other uses.

CHAPTER FIFTEEN
Social butterfly

This goal is for those who want to have it all, who marry their past-time with their vocation, who value human interaction as much as revenue.

Making money is nice, but you can't take it with you. So, the aim of some people is to accumulate friendships, moments and experiences. For these rare souls, a rich life has nothing to do with money.

Empty nesters or widowers may wish to fill the void with new acquaintances. Folks who work at home may have the luxury of availability on the premises at a moment's notice. Homebodies who've made their domain into a castle of sorts might think there's no better place to go on vacation, and they'd get an ego boost out of showing other holidaymakers all the efforts they've put into making their space a little bit of heaven on Earth.

All those who take the social butterfly approach can enjoy the higher margins from self-management. An option to them could be to accept slightly lower nightly rates, thus driving up occupancy close to 100%, and ensuring a steady flow of new visitors. Keep in mind that the higher the occupancy rate, the more check in/out, room cleaning, laundry and prepping need to be done in a faster turnaround time with no margin for error.

This chapter suggests ways you can increase social interactions while generating revenues.

Two universal truths about the rental business are that

1) the more comfortable you are with sharing your private space with strangers, the more potential money you can make. And...

2) the more fleeting your encounters, the more money you can make.

It's just human nature that most of us are attracted to the new. Striking up a conversation with a person you just met opens up so many more possibilities for dialogue than with an old acquaintance. If you're someone who thrives on discovering all about your guests, and likes to share details about your life, then you'll do well with hosting.

A bonus is that curiosity, and an eagerness to please naturally lead to good reviews. And good reviews lead to higher occupancy rates, and the ability to charge more, if you so choose.

Of course, the population you attract should be just as inclined to interact as you are. Matches are made with the following groups:
- Tourists wanting to discover about the people and way of life in your region
- Locals looking for an experience
- Nomadic workers who want to marry income-generation with exploration

However, these folks are less likely to be receptive:
- Business travelers
- Corporate event attendees
- Coworking by the hour or day

Accommodation, STR:

As you'll be staying there, you'll almost never rent out your whole home on the short-term platforms. Rather, you'll look to rent out each room or space separately. You'll need to make it very clear what they should expect in your listing, and you'll attract folks who are into that vibe.

Offer breakfast, and even afternoon tea as part of the rate to encourage interaction. Invite them to join in the other activities going on at the premises for free.

Allow short stays to have a steady flow of newcomers. You could even set a maximum stay to ensure turnover.

To make it all work, you'll need almost daily cleaning, or at least four sets of linens per space. Get someone else to do this so you can enjoy your company.

Accommodation, LTR:

Unless you really get along, there's no advantage to a long-term lodger for making acquaintances. You'd probably be happier using all of your spaces for STR.

Activity (recurring):

Here, you're only limited by your dreams. Think about which crowd you most like to hang with. If sporty types, there's no end to exercise sessions you could host. If artsy-fartsy folks, there's painting, sculpture, pottery and such. For all walks of life, there's Toastmasters. For charities, there's the Lion's club, which attracts an older demographic which might be right for you.

Think of what your STR guests might want to do, and offer that. It could be cooking classes, or poetry readings, or language exchange, or learning crafts. Ask travelers for ideas, and your cup will runneth over.

Business function (recurring):
Max out this usage, unless white-collar executives aren't your jam.

Corporate/Teambuilding (one-off):
Even if this ain't your crowd, they're likely there for another reason than their day jobs. Offsites often work on soft-skills, or bonding, or getting out of their comfort zone. They might do brainstorming, or games instead of powerpoint.

It could be fun to be around, but don't expect much interaction, unless it's something you propose with their *séjour*.

Creative endeavors (one-off):
While at first glance, this would seem in line with the goals of this chapter, look again through the viewfinder. These pros are interested in your space, not in you. They'd prefer it if you weren't there while they setup for their shot. They don't want witnesses to say what that model or actor is really like. Resist temptation, and give this play a pass.

Celebration/Party (one-off):
Keep it lively with tent campers and swimmers outside to go with the indoors visitors.

Dining/Drinking (occasional):
We can think of no better activity for our social butterfly to host.

Experience/Entertainment:
It's not Live from Daryl's House, it's live from your living room! You could have a standing gig weekly.

Launch (one-off):
There's a ton of buzz associated with new products, new movies and such. How fun to attract excited creative people to your place!

Parking:
Favor using garages to store several people's articles instead of parking one car. This could take the form of housing the bikes of a *vélo* club, or a mobility platform's e-scooters, or a catering company's serving supplies.

If it is a car, why not a touring van? Or a food truck? If it's a good-time jalopy, chances are you'll be invited along for the ride.

Storage:
Only store items in places which are not practical for accommodation or activities. Try to select renters which have some association with events or good times: like *carnaval* once a year, or for musical or theater groups, or festivals. Invite the groups who play at your concerts to your in-home studio for midweek practice sessions.

Other:
Let your imagination run wild. Think of everything which draws a following and makes you happy.

CHAPTER SIXTEEN
Tranquility

If your home is your castle, if alone time or the family circle is precious, and should remain undisturbed, this way of using your property may best match your goal.

This chapter is the polar opposite of the previous one. For maximum tranquility, we're looking to limit lodgers during the same time when you occupy the property. You could go so far as an outright ban of renters whenever you're home. It's up to you. Whatever level of sharing you choose, there's still a way to leverage your space and make money.

This method doesn't preclude you from making as much bank as the previous ones. In fact, Sabine, the social butterfly, wants to create interactions, increasing the time she is on site, and decreasing the availability of the space where she sleeps. However, tranquil Teresa prefers to get out of Dodge, leaving her entire dwelling more often, creating greater potential by renting her whole home.

One big thing the tranquility approach has going for it is the fact that you don't need to work as hard for your money. Endless conversations and multiple interactions can be exhausting, or uncomfortable, or interrupting your concentration, and they're definitely a time-waster. If you believe time is money, then a minute with a guest is taking away a minute you could be using to make more money, or spend the money you've already made on your own vacation, on your terms.

This personality type either anticipates every possible need a guest could have and provides for it ahead of time, or happily delegates communications, advice and troubleshooting to a service managing the property.

Accommodation, STR:
By changing the settings of your listings, you'll sleep easy while continuing to earn. Here are some *pistes* to explore-

* * *

Open your calendar: Peace of mind can come from planning the time you're away well in-advance. Sure, you'll miss out on some last-minute bookings from folks who are desperate to reserve at any price. Instead, you'll gain in predictability both for your operations and income. Some hosts open their booking window six to 12 months in advance, up to the maximum that the platforms will accept.

According to KeyData, the average advanced booking window used by the majority of travelers is 1.5mo. out. You can get good occupancy more than six months out if you have a unique property and play your cards right.

When Olympics tickets went on sale May 11, 2023, demand for lodgings spiked 688% versus the previous week. In October 2023, nine months ahead of the start of the Olympic Games of Paris, occupancy rates for the two weeks of the event were already between 18-25%, according to Beyond. Half of bookings are for seven nights. Demand has already surged 40% in the weeks just before and after the games as well. Tourists want to enjoy France before attending the games, and staff needs to be there for setup and take-down. Smart hosts look at the events calendar a year in advance and plan their pricing strategy accordingly.

Charge more: If guests want to kick you out of your home, they better make it worth your while. If price prevents a booking from happening, fine, you can just enjoy your home yourself.

Strict policies: "What's booked is booked." If you deploy a strict cancellation and refund policy, then every reservation is like having money in the bank. This may turn off some people, or make them hesitant to reserve. Fine by you if your goal is tranquility. You don't want to deal with the hemming and hawing anyway. You want folks who know what they want and will stick to it.

Instant booking: This can help or hinder your tranquility. It may help reduce the back-and-forth messages with prospects before they turn into paying clients, or not. To increase your chances of booking without bantering, put the maximum amount of information in your listing, so your answering most questions before they're asked.

This will also let anybody book without any oversight on your part. Travelers with zero ratings, who are complete wildcards. Guests with poor ratings, who might disturb you by making a racket when you're trying to relax elsewhere.

* * *

Accommodation, LTR:
This usage is not compatible with tranquility in your main residence. However, it could work if your property has an annex with its own entrance and facilities (kitchen and bathroom). Tenants could come and go as they please, preferably without disturbing you.

Activity (recurring):
Nope. You'll likely pass on this opportunity, which most certainly would disturb the peace.

Business function (recurring):
You won't want this going on while you're there.

Corporate/Teambuilding (one-off):
This could be employed if it happens while you're away. Why not, if you're off scot-free after the reservation is made. Our experience is this is unlikely to happen. Company representatives may want to visit before, interact with you during setup and take-down, plus lock-up upon departure.

Creative endeavors (one-off):
This seems an ideal use. It's better daily money than STR, and they don't want you around anyway. Be opportunistic and keep your listing available year-round for this use.

Celebration/Party (one-off):
A possibility if you can slip out before the big day. This may be tricky, as weddings, birthdays and such are important enough to the participants that they'll want a tour of the grounds before committing. They'll also want to access the space for setup and take-down. This is alright if it increases the payday, but not if they have endless special requests.

Dining/Drinking (occasional):
An obvious one to avoid.

Experience/Entertainment:
Incompatible.

Launch (one-off):
Again, if you're not needed, why not.

Parking:

A fantastic use to exploit. It must be easy-in, easy-out for your renter, and require no interaction with you. Establish clear opening and closing hours so you're not disturbed.

Make your space available only on a long-term basis, so you don't have to deal with endless back-and-forth communications. Get monthly payment upfront, preferably through some automated means.

Storage:

This could work for you, if there's no need to cross your living space to access the storage area. Imagine a basement with a digicode from the exterior, and a door you can lock towards the interior dwelling. Or, perhaps you have a shed or annex. If you have a gate on the street entrance, renters will need some way to unlock that to gain access. Again, have strict opening and closing hours.

Other:

EV charging station- You could setup a street-level 'borne de recharge' next to your private parking spot. This will likely be through another supplier like Wallbox that will take care of payment processing and maintenance. Publish it on popular apps like Chargepoint, Chargemap, Blink Volta, Charge my EV, Bump-Charge.com and Plugsurfing to attract folks to your spot.

Delegate- get somebody else to do the dirty work. This will be covered in the Outsource chapter in the next section, entitled Optimize.

Optimize

CHAPTER SEVENTEEN
Make it better

Now that your terrain train is chugging along nicely, let's grease the wheels. You can do this by focusing on the sizzle, or the steak, or both.

Sizzle

The sizzle means better listings, publicity, decoration and such. More than keeping up appearances, this can improve the perception that someone has about what you have.

Listings

Here are some areas you could give attention to which could make your property ad stand out:
- Staging
  - Arrange your property so newcomers feel most welcome. Guested offers this service, but only in the US. In France, look for folks who do this for real estate transactions, who could also perform the service for you. See the Outsource chapter for links.
- Photos
  - Get a pro photographer, perhaps by browsing Meero. Failing a pro service, you could at least use the Exposio app on the latest smartphone with multiple camera eyes.
- SEO
  - Use the most appropriate keywords in your listings. Let Ahrefs or Semrush tell you what people are already searching for, and include those specific words in your *annonce*.
- Descriptions
  - Deploy the tactics of successful copywriters, using

emotive adjectives and action verbs make your place more attractive.
- Change settings to improve ranking
  - When you first list, drag the pin on your map ever so slightly toward the touristy area most folks are going to want to visit. Don't abuse of this, but give your location a nudge, so you're on the zoomed version of the map.
  - Keep your acceptance rate high for those who wish to reserve, and avoid cancellations at all costs. Ask the platform to cancel for you, if possible.
  - Allowing instant bookings and having a flexible cancellation policy when guests reserve both improve your ranking. Appearing higher in the search results will mean being selected for more reservations.
  - Resources: OptimizeMyBnb
- Direct bookings:
  - Avoiding platform fees, so you make 15-20% more per booking sounds like nirvana for those seeking maximum profits. But it ain't easy attracting folks to an unknown site that only has one thing to sell. Once you do, you'll still need to pay 3% to Stripe or some other merchant service to process the payment.
  - Many PMS' can provide you your own site for a nominal fee of around €4 to €10 per property per month. Sometimes they'll even let you host this on your own domain, if you've paid the registrar yourself. RentalReady is one which will publish your site on the no-commission Google Travel portal for free.
  - Resources: Boostly is a vendor of direct booking websites which also has a popular podcast, blog and social channels touting going your own way.
- Advertising
  - Here's a pro tip: Rather than make the GAFAs richer, hand out flyers to local businesses. If they have workers coming in from other branches, tell them you'll strike a deal to lodge their employees while they attend internal meetings and training. Make sure your neighbors and local community knows about your activity. If you're out in the open, you'll be surprized how accepting people are, and willing to send guests your way for nothing.
- UX or 'user experience'
  - Guestbook: you could create a personalized guidebook with instructions on the property, done through

Hostfully or Airguide with fancy templates. Or you could do this on your own with tools like Canva or other free sites.
- Resources: Hostfully, Airguide, Touch Stay

Steak

The steak means better amenities, operations, etc. These are all tangible things which the guest can touch, feel, and experience intrinsically.

Increasing the number of amenities helps your place appear in more search results when a tourist is very specific and has applied one or more choice filters on one of the STR platforms.

Furniture
- Bigger beds
  - If you're expecting guests from the Netherlands or Nordic countries, where folks are taller, or from North America, where people are, ahem, wider, you'd do best to super-size your sleepers. You'll also stand out in France, where the average couple's bed is a double at 160cm wide and 190cm tall, and the typical single bed is 80cm wide. If you provide king size, at 180cm wide, or even better at 200x200cm, that'll get you more reservations and more stars.
  - Do what hotels do, and cheat. They often have two 1m-wide beds, and if they get a couple booking, they'll push them together and lay a 2m x 2m thin top mattress (about 6-8cm thick) over both beds. These are very comfortable and most guests can't tell the difference.
  - You'll want a waterproof fitted sheet over all mattresses, followed by another thick fitted sheet which hides any feel of plasticity.
- Extra sleepers
  - You can literally create couchettes from thin air. Without taking up any more floor space, you can accommodate more people. Check out single sleeper sofa chairs, which are surprisingly stylish while providing a good night's sleep. Fold-out couches have also greatly improved, not to mention the less-stylish 'BZed' which can work for cost-conscious consumers. Adding sleeping places is the best way to appear in more search results. Cost-conscious groups will dart to your listing. One caveat if you want to avoid the party crowd

is to keep your prices high, or not list all possible sleeping quarters but include "more beds upon request" in your listing without upping the total number displayed. This will allow you to speak with the prospective renters and gauge if they meet your expectations.
- Robotic furniture
  - The Jetsons imagined it, now you can own it. Push a button and your bed folds into the wall. Flip a switch, and it climbs into the ceiling. Hide a desk in a bookcase, or a dining table which slides into a counter when you're not using it. Great for getting the most out of small spaces. You can get these futuristic designs from Ori, Bumblebee Spaces in the US, or Madrid-based Beyome in Europe.

Luxury Amenities
- Wellness: According to Sotheby's, cold plunge pools, massage rooms and other wellness amenities are sought after in 2023. A fully enclosed sauna kit can be delivered in IKEA ready-to-build fashion, adding some bling to your basement.
- Outdoor: A jacuzzi costs a lot less than you may think, can be used year-round, and could be almost as successful in attracting guests as a pool. Fancy tents for napping or yoga or meditation could be an addition worth considering. We'll get into proper full-on dwellings in the Expand section.

Automations
  Messaging
- Most customer journeys are predictable upon booking-confirmation with deposit and administrative requirements, sharing address, directions, upsells like taxi transfer and things to do, check-in time and instructions, guides and manuals upon arrival, check-out reminder and procedure, invoice delivery and rating request. A template could be created for each of these steps, as well as anticipating exceptions like late check-in, cancellations or partial refunds. Each message could be managed through a sequence which can be setup in some property management systems, triggering the next one when the expected outcome happens after the previous message.
  Security/Access
- The way your customer accesses your property can either be the biggest infrastructure boon, or the biggest drain on your

profitability. A physical key for entry is absolutely the worst in every way. Read on to see why, and explore better alternatives.

A key can be copied, and open your property for theft, which your insurance company might not cover, because you gave a stranger the key in the first place. Squatters are a huge worry for owners of investment property and second homes in France. If there's no sign of break-in, the police will do nothing. It could take you months and a long, expensive legal battle to dislodge the usurpers.

A key can be lost, or broken. This is especially troublesome if it happens during the stay of your guest. You or your person overseeing the property must rush over there. Imagine it happens at midnight in sub-freezing weather. The locksmith's eyes light up like extra zeros when he hears how desperately and urgently his services are needed.

Keys need to be duplicated, for the cleaner, for the maintenance person, for the property manager, and at least two for the guests. This not only drives up costs, but multiplies the risk of theft or damage because you have no idea how the different service providers are handling the security of your key. Very likely, it's hanging in their shop out in the open with your address and possibly name on it.

Foremost of the key's drawbacks is that it must be handed over to the guest in-person. Who's going to do that? Your *conciergerie*? Sure, if you've made a conscious decision that's the way to go for you, and you're willing to pay 20-25% commissions.

One of your 'slashers' (freelancers) could hand over the keys, for a fee of €10-20 each check-in. Some lucky hosts have their cleaning person agree to do double-duty, both greeting and doing the *ménage* afterward. Neighbors and friends are not a sustainable solution, as they'll get very tired of the task quickly, if the rental becomes successful with lots of turnover.

You could do that yourself if you're nearby and available. That costs you nothing, but your time isn't free. If you're making the average French wage, you're paid €30/hour. When you do the check-in yourself, don't expect the guest to always show up at the appointed time. When they do, don't expect you can slip away before they ask you a barrage of questions about where everything is and how it works.

Sure, you're making a better impression with a personal greeting. However, you may be surprised to know that experiments in hospitality show little difference in ratings from guests welcomed in-person and those who were not. GuestReady France, which manages more than 1 000 properties in the country, only does self-check-in. They got higher ratings from guests who checked-in by themselves than they did for the previous in-person procedure. The only exception is when the traveller collects the keys from KeyNest, which is sometimes a bothersome guest experience, picking up from a local shop which isn't always open or where the personnel don't know the protocol.

There's a multitude of things you can do (detailed elsewhere in these pages) to satisfy guests from a distance, or anticipate their every question with information provided before arrival, and guides and instructions for how all the amenities work at their fingertips once inside.

A much better setup would be to automate property access and pilot the door locks from a distance. Several systems are available on the market, which are inexpensive, easy to install (most locks in France are on the same European standard) and maintain. Houses with a main single entry point are a piece of cake to install.

Apartments with dual (or more) entry go from tricky to impossible. If the street entrance is a simple code, and the door of the flat has a standard lock, you're golden. Codes can be shared from a distance, and owners will be informed if the building changes the code. Even double-entry, with a second interior door in the foyer of the building requiring a different code, is no problem.

The intercom system, where someone in the flat has to pick up the receiver and 'buzz' the visitor in, requires a McGyver-level workaround, which may violate the building's code of conduct (*reglement intérieur*). A device can be connected to the receiver in the flat which automatically buzzes the main entrance door open once the person selects your button on the wall from the street. Ask an electrician, who can probably work out a solution with one of the hardware companies listed below.

One final benefit of electronic entry is that it offers a sort of nuclear deterrent in the long-term rental business. If your tenant is late with rent and refuses to pay, you could deny them access. Consult with a lawyer before actually going through with blocking the tenant. The visible presence of such a system may be deterrent enough for the tenant to uphold the terms of the lease. If not, and they tamper with the system, or replace it, that would provide evidence and cause, supporting a case for eviction action.

Resources, fully automated access: TheKeys, Nuki, Somfy, Relais GSM, Igloohome, etc. Nuki's system works with Apple's Home app, connecting with other smarthome devices as well.

Semi-automated access: Pick up from nearby place of business, or from a neighbor. Key lockers exist for multiple units such as from KeyNest, At the Corner, Keycafé, ProximiKeys or Monkey Locky. You would need to get diverse owners on board if you don't own the whole building. Or you could look around if there are any free slots in nearby key cases. 'Click-and-collect' boxes could be deployed on a per-use basis, and some locations are partners with the key case companies.

Better than nothing: lockbox, hide-a-key. Note: some French cities are cracking down on lockboxes. In Lille, any found on public property (fence, lamppost, etc.) are cut and seized, and the owners fined.

Insurance
- STR: In most cases, having a separate policy specifically covering the vacation rental activity is overkill. Your regular home insurance policy should already cover the most common cases of damage and liability. Also, if the reservation is through Airbnb, they offer their Air Cover policy for up to $100 000 in damages.
- Deposits: One interesting area where STR service providers have cropped up is in managing the deposit (*caution*). This is a pain for both travelers and hosts. Guests are reluctant to give hosts or property managers these funds ahead of time for fear of not getting them back even when the stay happens flawlessly. Hosts want the security of knowing it's there if needed, but otherwise don't want to deal with the accounting headache and compliance issues. Check out Swikly.
- LTR: For long-term rentals, the market is quite developed and concerns not just property damage, but when tenants cannot or will not pay anymore. Organizations in this space include Cautioneo, Garantme, Luko and the quasi-governmental Visale program.

Other
- Pandor, from the Fipark group, rents a container which fits on an open parking slot, transforming it into a closed, lockable box. This would be ideal if you have an unattractive, unsecured parking spot in a location which is highly sought-after.

As you can see, it doesn't have to take much effort or expenditure to improve your property or the business you make with it. The next chapters go into optimizations from adding technology or people.

CHAPTER EIGHTEEN
Toolset tack-ons

If you wish to go it alone, and self-manage, there are tools which can enable you to do rentals better.

A whole industry of software, plug-ins, add-ons and other tech wonders have sprung up around this new sharing economy. And, no, we're not talking about the booking platforms. The consultancy AJL Atelier counts 420 of them. This is, of course, insane. Try not to get distracted by shiny buzzers and whistles, and concentrate on the ones which will make a real difference in your operation, no matter how you choose to rent your space.

Let's say you oversee a small building with four units. You could do STR, sure. But alternatively you could run it like a hotel. You could do serviced apartments (mid-term on Homelike). Or LTR. Or roommates (*colocation*). Or coliving. Or commercial leases. There are different and distinct tools for each of these. Some overlap, but it's extremely difficult to create a tool which is good for any two of these uses, much less satisfy everyone who's doing just one.

Many of these tools are multifunctional, so you need to make sure you're not paying twice for the same thing. You also need to verify that your chosen tools integrate well with other tools and the booking platforms.

At My Property Payday, we recommend that you set a goal for the maximum number of outside tools (2-3) and the maximum cost (5-10%) those tools are allowed to take away from your profits. As soon as you get above those figures, you might as well delegate everything to a concierge (STR) or property manager (LTR) who won't cost you much more, but should assume the software burden for you.

PMS for Accommodation

A property management system, or PMS, is a suite of tools, typically offered in SaaS format (online platform) which encompasses several useful components. Each of these can also exist separately, but our recommendation is to choose a bundle.

This software segment can be considered mature. Hundreds of PMSs exist, with very similar positioning. Venture capital investments in property management software tumbled in 2022, but rose nearly everywhere else in the applications space. Consolidation is trending, with Guesty acquiring Kigo, Eviivo buying Xotelia, Hometogo snapping up Smoobu in 2021, Situ absorbing Rentivo and Hospitable merging with SmartBnB.

You should be demanding that your PMS suits nearly all of your needs, and be aggressive in negotiating the pricing, even if you have very few properties. Once you make your choice, it can be painful to migrate to another system down the line. When you do, it can be nearly impossible to take your data with you.

Small co-hosts used to 3% OTA commissions will immediately have Airbnb apply a 15% commission rate once they start connecting to a channel manager or PMS, considered professional tools by the platform. This isn't such a big deal, as guests will have a smaller rate applied to them. But you should take this into account for your pricing strategy.

STR elements

Must-haves
   Channel Management
   The main pain points that channel managers solve are calendar synchronization and price injection across different platforms. Your dates and tariffs will change constantly. If you're using multiple platforms, you'll want to update once, and have availability and costs accurately reflected everywhere.

The rest of your content, like your description, amenities, photos and such will remain quite static. At the start, clicking publish once and having that content propagate correctly on different sites via the channel manager is a plus.

We know of no less than 50 French booking sites for STR accommodations. We're talking platforms which have French headquarters. These are in addition to the global sites which are very active in France, but come from elsewhere lIke AIrbnb (US), BookIng (NL) with 19 million French visitors monthly, Expedia/HomeAway/Vrbo (US), Holidu (DE), Plum Guide (UK) and Wimdu (DE).

Abritel, despite being acquired by HomeAway, remains more popular than the latter in France. The platform has deep roots in its native market. Don't assume because your channel manager feeds to

HomeAway that you'll have access to Abritel as well. Most tools don't connect to Abritel. As your property is in France, make sure your channel manager does.

Le Bon Coin is one of the Top 10 most visited websites in France, and ranks in the Top 5 or maybe even Top 3 of **all** platforms used by French people to book their stays... and practically no channel manager connects to them. They're a mostly free classifieds site, similar to Craigslist (which has no local take-up in France). Scams are present, but everybody still goes there for deals. There's low or no platform fees, depending if you transact with the host directly (always possible from the start), or ask Le Bon Coin to act as an intermediary (limited responsibility).

Gens de Confiance is a fast-rising classifieds purveyor which works on trust. You must be invited by three members before you can transact on the site, which is mostly used in app form. They have a sizeable vacation rentals category. *Clientèle* is high-end, folks who would never rent or reserve on Le Bon Coin. We don't know of a single PMS which connects to them.

Pricing varies wildly, from a percentage of your gross revenues (often 2-6%), to a cost per listing (€9-30/property/mo. is common) or a combination of the two. Rentals United wants to charge you €19/unit/mo. **and** 1% of your revenues.

Standalone tools: Bookiply, Channelmanager, Homerez, Hotelrunner, Rentals United, Sync Rentals, Bookingsync, SyncBnB

Messaging/Communications Management

According to iGMS, on average, a vacation rental manager sends 2 500 messages per month. You should expect to send 10 messages per booking. That's a lot of back-and-forth.

The majority of messages are for the same basic subjects, like which amenities do you have, will you accept a discount, check-in time and how to access the property. The majority of these inquiries can be handled by thorough descriptions and clear instructions. You'd be aided by a library of canned answers. You can develop these yourself, which would be best, as they're in your own voice. Many providers include such ready-made templates that you can draw from right within their interface, in several languages.

Standalone tools: Host Tools, Smartbnb, Wishbox, Your Porter App, Duve. Expect to pay at least €7/property/mo. for one of these inbox solutions.

Price Optimization

This acts similarly to Airbnb's Smart Pricing, but in a way that supposedly works. Only a dum-dum would use Airbnb's Smart Pricing, which drags your property kicking and screaming in a race to the bottom. In September 2023, Airbnb CEO Brian Chesky was quoted as saying "Airbnbs should cost less than hotels," and "we encourage hosts to lower their prices," promising to keep them in line during the 2024 Olympic Games. This company puts the interests of guests before those of hosts. Don't take advice from someone who benefits directly when you follow their advice. You'd do well to get a partner on your side.

Many PMS's claim to have dynamic pricing, but all they really have is an API connection to another tool. This means you have to pay for the PMS **and** for the other pricing tool. You can save money if the PMS has a pricing algorithm **native** to their application.

Standalone tools outside a PMS can sometimes perform better. The question is, does it outperform their cost enough to justify the expense? Some charge a pretty penny for access to your area, and even more for a connection plugging their recommendations directly into your listing. Beyond charges 1-2% of your gross bookings, for example.

There are three main problems with these tools: Who, What and Where...

- Who: again, the prices collected are for the most part from people who don't know what they're doing. According to Skift, only 15% of STRs are professionally managed, meaning 85% are run by individual hosts, the majority without revenue management credentials. There's little comparison to hotels which are more astute and in-tune with true like-for-like comparisons in the larger tourism accommodation market.
- What: the data on the OTA platforms only shows what's remaining, not what's been booked. When a listing disappears, the pricing tool counts that as a reservation. There could be any number of reasons the host unlisted which have nothing to do with booking, such as maintenance or occupying the property themself. There's also little idea to help distinguish which accommodations are truly 'comps' (similar m², amenities, quality, target population, etc.) and which are nothing like your place.
- Where: the numbers are nearly all from one platform, which is sizeable, but by no means representative of the entire market of rental lodging. Remember from The Sharing Opportunity chapter that the 'sharing economy' portion of the hospitality industry in 2019 was only 6%, and Airbnb represents a subset of that portion. Even if Airbnb's share has grown phenomenally since then, do you want to base your whole pricing strategy on what's happening in less than a quarter of the market?

These systems are all helpful, but less-so for properties in France. The pricing tool companies are all based in the US, which has more homogenous dwellings side-by-side, and doesn't take into account the 120-day rule, or other local regulations, giving a distorted view of earnings potential.

A word of caution- these pricing tools can cost as much as some PMS. They know that posting optimized rates can mean more to your revenue-generating capability than nearly everything else. It's too bad they so often fall short of what they promise.

Here at MyPropertyPayday, we believe all these tools have flawed methodology. Our view is covered at length in the 'Money: meters matter mostly' chapter.

Standalone tools/services: Resources like AirDNA, Airbtics, Pricelabs, RateGenie, Wheelhouse, Beyond Pricing, Room Price Genie, Rented.com, DPGO, Mashvisor and InsideAirbnb offer data on nightly rates posted on Airbnb. Expect to pay around €5/property/mo. for one of these, or 2% of your gross booking revenue to delegate the pricing and injection of said pricing on the OTAs.

Task/Staff Planning

This is perhaps the least-liked but most necessary part of your STR operation. You'll have to do cleaning and linen supply, check-ins/outs (physical or remote), plus re-stocking, repairs and maintenance. Given the different skill-sets and facilities required, this means dealing with at best 2-3 people/providers, and at worst a half-dozen that you'll have to juggle. Quality varies wildly and availability changes constantly.

It will happen that you have a check-out at noon and a check-in at 4 p.m. the same day. Will the *service de ménage* show up at all, much less on-time and finish mopping up before the new guests arrive? Will they have clean linens on site, and if not- will they be delivered on time to make the beds? When the cleaners tell you as they leave at 3 p.m. that, by the way, the toilet is backed up, will you know which plumber can provide emergency services? If there is no one to greet the plumber, how will they enter your property? If the guest informs you their plane is delayed, and the new expected arrival time is 11 p.m., well after your greeter has gone, who will do the check-in? If you are off-site, how will you know if and when any of these providers has come or gone?

Task and staff planning tools are designed for these situations. They help you manage the services to be performed and by whom. Nearly all come with a mobile app and checklists the providers can use on-site. The tricky part is getting them to do so, while using your chosen tool instead of their preferred one. Even if they don't, and you have to update the tool in their place, it can be useful for your management on the day, and your analysis after. Who shows up on time, and who is late? Does one do the same job in half the time as another? What are the average cleanliness ratings of each of the three cleaning companies you've used?

Some of the software providers just have an app. This means you'll need to find the personnel to perform the necessary duties. Others provide not only a tool, but the services to go with it. Not all of them are available in France, nor in all regions of the country.

Standalone tools/services: Care.com, Properly, Turno (formerly TurnoverBnB), HouseCall, Tidy, Operto, Resort Cleaning. Expect to pay €7-10/property/mo. for one of these.

Billing, Deposit & Payment processing

A billing or payment processing system is useful for you to accept direct bookings, avoiding the platform fees. It's also helpful for platforms where you're the merchant of record, such as on Expedia's network (Abritel, Vrbo, etc.).

For deposits, most platforms allow you to display your requirements, but offer no way for you to collect it beforehand, like Swikly does. Some hosts have this as a dissuasive measure, without any ambition to put a failsafe process in place. They count on recourse after the fact. If you want a more secure system, there are startups to help you for a transaction fee.

Standalone tools: Piloc, Swikly, Chekin, Stripe, Ximplifi, Siga, MerchantWarrior. Expect to pay €4/property/mo. for one of these, plus a percentage from 1-3% on each transaction.

Nice-to-have options

Direct booking site

We could have put this option in the must-have. It depends on your strategy. It is conceivable to bypass the OTAs like Vrbo and Airbnb entirely. Just put up your listings on your own site, and *voilà*, you're in business.

As most hosts are only doing this part-time, relying on the OTAs to draw inquiries, a direct booking site can be more trouble than it's worth for this population. You can spend a lot of money on building, hosting, maintaining, advertising, SEO and such, only to have a trickle of visitors many years later.

There are tool providers which specialize in STR, with templates, design themes and functionalities meant to wow cyber surfers, and convert them with effective calls-to-action. You could also choose your own CMS or content management system like WordPress, and simply add a provider's booking widget to that.

Fully 60% of hotel distribution is direct - showing the massive potential for STRs to get more direct bookings. But don't expect overnight (get it?) success. New websites with little content, which is static and never gets updated with new articles, can take years to generate traffic levels of a couple dozen visitors per month. SEO consultants are expensive, and they'll cost you way more than the 15-20% you'd give up to an OTA for bookings through their platform.

An approach with much greater returns and zero cost is to chat up your network, starting with local contacts. Let neighbors, nearby businesses, associations of fellow entrepreneurs, tourism boards, and even competitors (yes, them) that you exist and you're ready to serve their visitors from out-of-town or overflow guests. Point them (and friends/family) to your direct booking site to reserve. Or better yet, give them your phone number. This old-fashioned system is so seldom used, it wows modern guests, who convert at higher levels because they get to speak to an actual human.

Le Clos Saint Lubin, an operator of *haut-de-gamme* villas south of Fontainbleau did just that (and nothing else- meaning zero paid advertising), including inviting all these local constituents to their grand unveiling cocktail, and they've never lacked for bookings. Word-of-mouth works... if you work it.

Standalone tools: Boostly, Signal from Beyond, Direct Booking Tools, Aloware, Yada.ai; Enso Connect is a CRM to maintain contact with those who reserve direct and may be enticed to become repeat visitors. Expect to pay €3-7/property/mo. for one of these. For advanced functionality on a WordPress site and marketing assistance from a premium provider like Boostly, that will set you back €58/property/mo. plus a one time implementation fee, expected to be around €1 000.

Additional service sales

You could establish affiliate programs with nearby businesses like taxis, restaurants, food delivery companies, tour guides and activity purveyors. Many will agree to both a discount for your guests and a kickback for you. However, it can take literally years to build this out, make it work and put systems in place to collect your due.

New providers come with ready-made networks of suppliers ready to offer their services to your guests. This works better for properties in urban settings, or established tourist destinations, which both have many nearby businesses catering to travellers.

Often the systems of additional service tools plug into the ones you're already using. Or, they have offers you can easily cut and paste into your communication sequence templates with guests prior to arrival.

Standalone tools: UpSellGuru, Tourdesk. Expect to pay at least €7/property/mo. for one of these.

* * *

Guest experience

Post-reservation, there are many things which could make the stay a memorable one for your guests. You could provide them with an App which includes information about the area and activities, such as Yaago (20€/property/mo.) and BookOne do.

This is perhaps the most expensive area outside of the PMS or Channel Manager itself. Be wary that their offering doesn't overlap what you already have in your suite, like a universal inbox, templates for communication, guidebooks and such.

Standalone tools: Yaago, BookOne, Touch Stay, Your Welcome, Duve, Hostfully, Airguide. Prices vary wildly, but you could pay €10-20/property/mo. for one of these.

City tax and police registration

The company called 'Chekin' doesn't actually do check-ins, but rather collects the city tax on your behalf, and also handles the tourist's registration with the local police. The former is necessary for reservations through platforms other than Airbnb (which collects city tax on behalf of hosts). The latter is required when the traveler has a nationality outside of France. For this, they charge €4/mo./property.

Standalone tools: Chekin

Ratings/review treatment

Also called online 'reputation management' or ORM, these companies automate the collection of reviews. If you're just starting out, you may be surprised to learn that it's common to have less than half of your guests leave reviews. To grow that number even a little bit can require a lot of chasing down, and even incentivizing before they consent to provide a notation. Properties with few reviews attract few bookings, and those with poor reviews can stagnate with no bookings for weeks or months.

These tools can follow-up with positive reviewers, asking them to also note in other places which can be helpful to you, such as TripAdvisor, Google or Trustpilot.

One useful trick they support is when you think a guest might not have enjoyed their stay, you can pre-empt the platform's rating request with your own internal one. Often grumpy guests calm down once given a forum in which to vent. If that first place when tempers are still hot is your own survey, by the time the 2nd request from the platform arrives after check-out, they may feel they've already expressed themselves, or perhaps they're in a more serene state of mind. Your private poll collects the flack that nobody sees, and the public platform either gets nothing, or a more mitigated number of stars.

Another common method uses peer-pressure or social guilt. At your first opportunity upon check-out, when prompted by the platform to provide your host review, you can instantly give five stars, and send the proof of this to the guest, asking them to review also. Only the most cold-hearted of voyagers won't be influenced by this gesture. Some systems support and automate this.

It's a good practice to collect your own reviews. Airbnb, for instance, forbids hosts from posting the reviews from Airbnb guests anywhere but their platform. The review is content that Airbnb 'owns' and you can't use that to promote your place outside of the platform. If you do, you can get your account suspended.

Standalone tools: Revyoos, TrustYou. Expect to pay €1-2/property/mo. for one of these.

Accounting

Qlower claims to help reconciliation, tax preparation and such for both STR and LTR in France.

Standalone tools: Qlower

Considerations in your choice of PMS

This is a lot to sift through, we know. We did it, and still we feel a bit bewildered.

So, to better help you narrow down your list, here are some other points you may wish to take into consideration-

Locality: Your property is in France, which carries with it a plethora of specificities, not only in terms of language and currency, but taxes, regulations, utilities and such. Here are the providers either based in France, or with a long history of local operations: Avantio, Smily/BookingSync, Bookiply, Rentaleo, SuperHôte, and RentalReady.

Language support: Almost all PMS solutions already provide interfaces for owners, renters/users (and property managers) in English. Many claim dozens of other languages. However, some deploy clunky auto translation tools or AI which can easily annoy your prospective guests. Also, once the technology starts speaking their language, travelers might assume you do so as well. You need to manage expectations. It's not good to suddenly go silent when they ask for late check-out in Hungarian.

Access management: Previously, the 'Make it Better' chapter covered the advantages of keyless entry. Some PMS are integrated with certain hardware providers like Nuki or Igloohome. This allows you to quickly generate codes for new guests and staff, get notifications for entry and exit, and turn off access. If you already bought the hardware, see if the PMS works with your unit. If you didn't, see if they'll lease you a lock which works with their system.

Built for various property types: Guesty is one of the few tools which claims to be adapted to apparthotels, serviced apartments, camping, multi-unit buildings and such. If your property portfolio is heterogenous, or has very specific needs, then Guesty is worth a look. If not, then these varied capabilities won't benefit you.

Promotions/coupons: These can boost bookings, especially when used in 'drive-to-store' marketing campaigns. Though, there are ways to do the same things within the booking platforms, like volume discounts or slashing prices for a small empty window in the imminent calendar dates.

Manual reservations: This will almost never come up if you have a direct booking site. Even if you don't, workarounds are possible, like blocking the dates in your channel manager while accepting payment outside the system via Wise or Paypal or many other solutions.

Owner portal: This is of interest if you are a property management company (and want your owner-customers to transparently see what's happening). Or, if you're working with a *conciergerie* or agency, it's important that they give you, the owner, this visibility.

If you're the sole *propriétaire*, self-managing your own property, an owner portal is of no interest to you. If the property you're managing belongs to several people, say a family, or an SCI, an owner portal could help your fellow co-owners keep tabs.

Automation & AI: Regardless of all the fervor around chatGPT, it can take years to train a chatbot to handle about half of the general inquiries of an industry as vast as travel. It would take even longer for the chatbot to give adequate answers for the specificities of each property in a portfolio of dozens. We know because our main author worked for a chatbot company serving the travel sector. Suffice to say, take the claims of tool makers with a grain of salt. You can get limited benefit from this work-in-progress, but it's risky to count on the AI tech too much.

Outside of PMS', many of which have recently deployed this, and AskPorter, hundreds of free/cheap chatbots exist, but most require at least some programming knowledge to work properly, plus constant training and maintenance.

Price: At this stage, you're likely working with one or two properties. You don't need an enterprise-level solution, and don't want to pay extra for buzzers and whistles that bring limited value, and that you'll likely never use. If you have a high-value property, favor a PMS which prices per property per month, and target €15/unit/mo. or less. If your space isn't available year-round, make sure the PMS contract is month-to-month and monitor if it makes more sense to cancel after high season, then pick it up again a couple months before the next active period.

If you have a regular-value property, or one in an area of high seasonality, you can consider a PMS which charges a percentage of the booking revenue. This way, you won't be penalized for having no bookings in low-season. Make sure they don't include platform, cleaning or ancillary costs in their calculation and target no more than 2-5% of your net earnings.

Ratings: There are way too many review sites, and far too few verified ratings. The sites want to be the first stop for your evaluation, but we recommend you go there last. Otherwise, you'll see dozens of solutions which all appear nice, which is unhelpful at the start of a search. Instead, first create your shortlist of 2-3 possibles, and then see what actual users of those solutions have to say. You'll need to go beyond the number of stars, and actually read the text. Folks are candid about what works, what doesn't, and which tradeoffs they're willing to accept.

Resources: vacation rental software comparison sites G2, Get App, Capterra

LTR tools and elements
Traditional

Although rarely called a 'PMS' for LTR (more commonly rental management software or *logiciels de gestion locative*) these tools help you manage your spaces that are rented for more than 30 days at a time. They are far less sophisticated, because they don't need to be. Renters change much less often and handle services such as cleaning for themselves.

These tools are adapted to the specificities of the French market in terms of reporting obligations, tax preparation and contracting. They often come with a market place or ready-made partners like insurers, accountants and maintenance suppliers. Virtually none of them have an English-language interface.

Surprizingly, considering they do so much less than an STR PMS, they can cost up to **twice** as much. Pinql, for example, charges €29/mo.

You'll want yours to do ad management on platforms like ParuVendu and PAP, help with tenant screening, provide lease agreement templates, checklists pre- and post move-in, payment collection and reminders, and support legal procedures up to and including expulsion.

Resources: Appliceo, GererSeul, Homega, Insitio, LOCKimmo, Pandaloc, Pinql, Rentila, Ublo.immo

Coliving

Since this is a new category, there are not a lot of tools out there designed to address the specificities of operating a coliving establishment. You could try to use another LTR tool which was made for managing traditional tenant relationships. This workaround should function for your internal needs, like accounting, but is unlikely to have a tenant-facing app with an attractive interface and capabilities to manage the social aspects. You could create a group chat (through WhatsApp, Signal, Telegram, etc.) to organize movie night, home chef class, yoga instruction, as well as cleaning, repairs and such. Beware adding too many channels as that could make your operations challenging to manage, or simply have people miss messages because they're not checking or not using that app.

A poll from the Co-Liv Summit showed the top two things colivers are looking for in this type of living arrangement are digital tools and community. As the 'master of ceremonies' for your coliving facility, you should seek our tech which can enhance the resident and community experience.

Keep in mind as you scour the marketplace, that app companies will favor large operators with many more beds than you are probably managing at this time. Their enterprise target will be reflected in their toolset and integrations to things you don't have or need (like an ERP system), as well as their pricing (upwards of €500/mo.), which can be cost-prohibitive at lower numbers of tenants.

The apps are also squeezed when they try to go upmarket, because most coliving operators are also tech companies in their own right, creating in-house tools. These 'all-in-one' providers consider their proprietary apps to be a key differentiator, attracting colivers to their space instead of a competitor's coliving quarters.

Features you should be looking for in a tool which are specific to coliving include, for Residents: resident-led event creation, community groups, polling, in-app payments, community feed & messaging, digital concierge, incident reporting, local commerce, customizable marketplace, booking spaces and amenities; for Staff: virtual tours, tenant & services directory, building information, channel manager, listing portal to accept direct bookings, visitor management system, dashboard and reporting.

Resources: District Tech, Glynk & Cosine Labs, res:harmonics, Spaceflow, Sowebuild and TheHouseMonk Coliving SaaS applications consciouscoliving.com/coliving-apps-tech-guide/

Activity tools

Checkfront and Bookinglayer are the only tech service providers we found working on activities (and events to some degree). Both also claim to handle accommodations, but appear to be lacking the necessary elements of a full-fledged PMS for STR.

Their primary advantage is the ability to accept direct bookings. A channel manager to manage listings on other sites seems to be missing, which is a severe drawback.

Resources: Coworking apps, Security & Access Control Solutions

Others
Outside of hundreds of tools for accommodations, and two for activities it's tumbleweeds and crickets from the tech community. We know of no channel manager for parking, nor storage, nor events...

If you get into these businesses, expect to manage multiple parallel listings, calendars and communications channels simultaneously all by your lonesome. Or, you could simply settle on one platform per category, and run all your reservations through there. Either way, you'll need to juggle the calendars yourself and immediately block one when you get a reservation on another, or have to deal with double-bookings, cancellations and frustrated clients.

Some hosts are still using homemade solutions to manage their listings. One such configuration is through Apple's iCal or Google Agenda. You can have several calendars overlayed on one-another in the same view. This can get quite confusing with many properties and multiple channels, but is still workable for someone with one or two units. You could follow one of the online tutorials to set this up, and it could conceivably suffice, even across different uses for the same space.

If all this information leaves you even more confused than before, rest-assured you don't have to deal with any of it, if you don't want to. There's another way: you can make it someone else's problem. That's precisely what we'll cover in the next chapter.

CHAPTER NINETEEN
Outsource

If you've read this far, then you're likely very interested in the possibilities we've discussed. But you may be saying to yourself, "that seems like a hell of a lot of work!" You're absolutely right.

Those who choose to take on all the challenges solo must be true do-it-yourselfers. They must also be a Jack-of-all-trades, above average at a wide range of tasks from communications, to bookkeeping, to sales, marketing and data science. For the rest of us, we need help.

How much help depends on whether you want to remain in the pilot's seat, or relinquish the controls. If the property is your primary residence, you almost have no choice but to keep the captain's hat. Even when you do, there's a whole range of tasks you can delegate to others. No matter your strengths or weaknesses, or your preference for hands-on or hands-off management, your ideal balance is out there. This chapter aims to help you find it.

In addition to software, there are labor-saving humans ready to offer their services for your property business. This can go from a simple co-host arrangement from time to time, all the way to full-service property management taking the entire burden off your hands.

Level 1 - Helping Hands

<u>CESU freelancer payments</u>: There used to be widespread paying of service people *au black*, or under the table. Then, the government created the CESU program where the worker gets benefits and the payer gets 50% back off their taxes. It's not a true half-off, because the fisc tacks on about 80% social charges. Thus €16/hour turns into €14.40/hour when all's done. Take this into consideration when setting the rate with the cleaner.

So if you charge €48 for cleaning, which is the same amount your cleaner charges you, you can actually pocket an additional €4.80. These

little tips can add up over a year of renting. You may use this technique to either increase margin, or make your rental price more attractive. Your concierge (level 3) can manage the process on your behalf, and you still get the tax benefit.
- Resources: myCezâme, Brigad, Flash Service, o2, Saint Honoré Cleaning, Spic'n'span, Untempspourvous

Cleaners: Some hosts try to do this themselves, until they get lots of bookings or try to scale their operations. It's better left to professionals.

The pros should have flexible availability, preferably provide linens as well as a service to clean and turnover, replenish consumables, and maybe even supply extras like a welcome kit. Some go farther than that to become a veritable girl Friday reporting back to you with checklists, handling check-ins, even late ones, coordinating maintenance and installation when telecom service is changed or a faulty machine is swapped. Chances are you won't be so lucky, and you'll need to develop relationships with several to meet all your needs at all times.

Greeters: These folks can do physical check-ins, and check-outs if you want to maintain a personal touch. This person could also open the space for people parking cars, caravans, dropping off or picking up storage boxes. Some providers have made check-ins their primary business. These include Dolnn and Check & Visit, although the latter specializes more in LTR.
- Resources: Check-In Services greets guests and cleans flats in Paris only.

Photographers: Those with a keen eye not only have sophisticated equipment, they see what we don't. It can cost no more than €50 or €100 to go from simple to stunning.
- Meero

Stagers: A 'stager' or interior decorator will cast your property in the best light. They'll remove the clutter, eliminate items which are too personal, while adding touches of personality. They'll help the prospective guest project themselves into the space, which is the step just before reserving. Even if their role is not a permanent one, serving only to prepare for stylish pics, it'll be worth it.
- Resources: Flights of Fancy (English-speaking), Aveo

SEO specialist: A search engine optimization expert will help you determine what people are already looking for. To drive more direct bookings, they'll make sure your site uses those keywords and has that

content, then helps you convert them once they get there.
- Resources: Romain Giacalone of Welcomz

Copywriters: You're reading a book, instead of scrolling social media for tips and tricks. Perhaps this means that you value comprehensive, well-researched and time-tested content, exposing techniques that really work. An editorial-minded person has sifted through the junk and come up with pearls of wisdom for you. That's exactly what you'd get from a pro writer focused on the STR niche. Instead of the reader flipping over the can for a list of ingredients, they'll be treated to the flavors, the sensations, the wonderful experience that they'll have settling into your space.
- Resources: There are many, many folks out there who can help make your listing better. Alex Wong is but one of them who appears to have a good track record. So is Louise Brace. Try to get them to commit to a price per word, and target 15 to 30 eurocents.

Editors: Listing modifiers swap out the words and make updates to the pricing and calendar when you can't.

Communications agents: the greatest need is prior to arrival. Guests rarely reach out during the stay, or after the stay, unless there's a problem. If there is, you'll likely want to handle this yourself, or by one of your full-time employees.
Where do you find such people?
- Providers like… Albert to answer the phones or e-mails when you're away or sleeping. Arceah claims to do that plus provide accounting, training and advice for hosts. AngelHost has a 24/7 Reservation Desk speaking English and Spanish, but we're unsure about their aptitude in French.
- Some PMS vendors like RentalReady or Guesty can bundle guest communication services with their software. These services respond on your behalf at all hours and in several languages. From within the solution, you can have a view on these dialogues, and intervene in the conversation flow if needed. Expect to pay an even higher cost for these call center agents than for the technology. Prices start around €30/unit/mo. and can go as high as €75/unit/mo.

Accountants: Amarris is an accounting firm which either provides a DIY platform for rental income declarations, or full-service advice.
- Resources: Amarris, Qlower

***

Other helping hands

Handyman: Click askAndy to find a plumber, locksmith, etc. urgently.

Staff: Brigad provides on demand staff for hospitality (mainly hotels) for short and middle term jobs (mainly wait staff).

'Slashers': These are folks who have other jobs, but help out the hospitality industry from time to time. A surprising segment are recently retired folks. BornToHost conciergerie in Cannes uses this population extensively, and guests love them.
 - Resources: Teepee, Yoopies, Gofer, JeMePropose

Level 2 - Co-pilot

In a co-pilot scenario, you have someone who shares the burden of managing your property. They work about as much as you do, but most likely on different tasks. You can even port their share up to 80-90%, if you like.

Distribution of labor is commonly divided on lines of tasks that can only be completed on-site (by your co-pilot), and those which can be done remotely (by you):

On-site- cleaning, supplies, linens, check-in, in-stay visits (urgent repairs, keep noise down reminders, etc.) check-out, maintenance, renovations, install furnishings, replace appliances, and such.

Remote- listings, pricing, guest communications, finance, compliance (ID check, tourist tax collection, etc.), upsells/extras like taxi transfers and tours, handling reviews, promotions/marketing and so on.

Separating responsibilities this way is very effective whether or not you, the owner, are geographically located close to your property. Your rental business goes on as usual, whether you are on vacation, travelling for work, or simply out-of-town for the weekend. As you become comfortable with this arrangement, or as you acquire additional property, or the management of units far from where you live, you can extend this with more co-pilots in other areas.

Co-hosts: These are helpers and independent workers positioned specifically on the STR market. You can find them on dedicated sites like Cohostmarket or the Airbnb Community forum. Groups on Facebook in France dedicated to the *LCD* market (see Glossary at the end) are also worth mining. Co-hosts are also mixed in with 'slasher' sites (see level 1 above). Most of these sites have a way for you to search based on location, at least, and by discipline at best. You can also post an ad with

your requirements. For a complete list of platforms and resources to find people go the the Providers section at the end of the book.
- Resources: Cohostmarket, Airbnb Community, Toit Chez Moi, JeMePropose

<u>Online Property Management</u>: Some providers turn this model on its head. They'll propose to do everything remotely, while you, the owner, do everything on-site. These include companies like Evolve, and Pass the Keys. In addition to a 10% fee for listing management, rates and guest communications, Evolve charges 3% to accept payments via Stripe, and they charge $250 if you engage with them and subsequently change your mind.

Unfortunately, these "online property management" companies operate exclusively in the US and the UK, respectively. We don't know of any company with a similar model in France. However, if you dig with the companies you'll find listed in level 3, or in the Provider section at the end, you'll discover that they'll consider hybrid management instead of full conciergerie services. They don't just do that, but you may be able to work with them on a share of labor which works for both parties. This is especially true if your property is in an outlying area, and not in a city center, or in the heart of where tourists go.
- Resources: Evolve, Pass the Keys

Paying for the services of co-hosts will vary wildly depending on what they do, or where the property is located. The co-hosts will typically request a percentage, but we recommend you settle on a fixed price for a task completed. It'll make your accounting a lot easier. Also, their tasks remain the same whether or not they complete them for a 4-bedroom or a studio, in high season or low season, for a two-week or a two-day booking. They shouldn't share the benefit when you charge a higher amount. If you do, they're liable to turn down jobs when you charge the guest a lower amount.

When you add up all the expenses you have for your helping hands or co-pilots, and the cost of the tools used to run your rental business, and the total ends up costing more than 15% of your take-home revenues (before taxes), you should take a good hard look at your setup. Sure, you may have very efficient systems and people in place, but somebody needs to conduct that orchestra. Without you running things, telling everyone what to do, and following-up to make sure they do it, the whole operation crumbles.

There's an easier way, which costs about the same as all the above, once you factor in your labor. That way is discussed next.

* * *

Level 3 - Auto-pilot
At this level, you turn over all the controls to a professional property management company. Sure, you'll still need to do some minor things, like stow your personal items and vacate the premises before the guests arrive, if you're living there. But you won't need to do anything else.

Short-term STR
Julie Guérin, host of *La Conciergerie* podcast claims there are 3 000 STR property managers in France. Whatever the real number, there's one close to you, or at least a co-host, or someone who wants to become one.

According to an iPropertyManagement study on short-term rental property managers, there are 140 000 globally, 43 000 with more than 20 units worldwide, and 15 000 with more than 20 units under management in Europe.

Traditional STR property managers in France charge 20-25%. Professional property managers drive revenue premiums of 35% over individual owners, according to Beyond Pricing. This alone easily justifies their commissions of 20% on average.

If your concierge is worth their fees, you should expect that you'll make more money with them than without them. They shouldn't just save you labor, but be a motor for accelerating your rental revenue.

If your place is in a major city, like Paris, Bordeaux, Lyon, Nice or Marseille, there are many companies, called *'conciergeries'* to choose from. Because in those cities there is demand year-round, not just from tourists, but from business travelers, students, families visiting from out of town and such, these operations can be quite sophisticated with many employees and advanced resources.

What should you look for in a conciergerie?
You may have a preference for a type of property manager. Some lean towards a local specialized operator, like Tybnb in Brittany. Others favor a national leader, like Welkeys, with personnel across France. Still others might like the security of going with a strong global company, like GuestReady, present in eight countries.

All should cover the basics, to start with. Listings including pro photos distributed across multiple channels, calendar synchronization, communication, payments, incident resolution and reporting back to you, the owner. Here are some other areas to explore evaluating their capabilities:

PMS
The concierge should not charge you extra for the property

management system they use for their internal operations. That cost should be baked into their commission fee. The service station that does your car's checkup doesn't charge you extra for their engine diagnostic system. It should be the same for property management.

If you want to know more about PMS, read the 'Toolset tack-ons' chapter preceding this one. If there's one PMS that you particularly like, or features that are important to you, this could be a part of your selection criteria for which concierge you go with.

Pricing Algorithm

Here's an example of the difference an effective pricing algorithm can have on your bottom line. Concierge A charges 20% commissions and generates €2 000 gross booking revenues in a month without an algorithm. Concierge B charges you 25% and brings you €2 500 in a month by using an algorithm. Which one brings you more value? Concierge B puts €275 more in your pocket (€1 875 vs. €1 600 for Concierge A) that month. Concierge B has a greater capacity to consistently deliver value, and if they generate €275 more each month, at the end of the year that means €3 300 more for you. So, there's no contest.

You want a concierge which uses an effective pricing algorithm which updates prices often and dynamically. If they don't, keep looking. You don't need amateurs who are simply guessing. You need a sure thing.

By the way, some concierge services are so confident in their pricing algorithm, that they'll provide you a guarantee, whether or not your place is rented.

You want a concierge who goes beyond simply looking at what other hosts are charging in your area, doing an average, and setting your price at that level. Of those surrounding hosts, 80% are individuals self-managing one property. Almost none of them have a background in hospitality finance or revenue management. When it comes to pricing, they don't know anything.

If the concierge doesn't have their own proprietary system, that's OK. Something is better than nothing, even if it's through an API connection to an external tool. Many integrate with commonly available pricing systems, from Beyond Pricing, Pricelabs, AirDNA, Wheelhouse and others. Pricing systems are covered at length in the 'Toolset tack-ons' chapter preceding this one.

As with the PMS, dynamic pricing should be included the commission fee of the concierge. If they want to charge this as an option, that could be 3-5% on top of the 20-25% commission your concierge charges. You should insist they make it *prix fixe* instead of *à la carte*.

* * *

Native-level English-language greeters
If they're doing physical check-ins for you, make sure they have on-premises people who can speak both French and English at a very high level.

Dashboard
Your provider should give you access to an owner portal (detailed in the previous chapter) with current basic information about revenue, occupancy and such. It should also allow you to block the calendar for yourself. As the official 'host' in the government's eyes, you must provide a valid invoice for every one of your guests. You should also collect the tourist tax and pay on time. Your provider should enable you so that you or your accountant can do this easily.

Something extra

Platform: With similar services, a little plus can put one over the top. Maybe it's access to an attractive local platform like Abritel or Le Bon Coin, which isn't often offered, and not easy for you to manage yourself. Or maybe it's the ability to accept direct bookings instead of paying the platform fees. Ask what else your provider can do for you.

Possibilities: Business travelers on multi-month assignments. Visiting professors to nearby universities. Traveling nurses on longer stays. Expats just landing for several months while looking for a permanent home. A constant flow of new employees from out of the area being trained at the corporate headquarters just down the road. There are platforms, networks and connections to getting consistent bookings from these populations. Can your concierge help you in any of these areas? They'll need a 'carte G' demonstrating the legal right to property manage long-term, collect rent directly from tenants, and deal with leases, insurance and such. Do they have access or links established that don't exist elsewhere?

Most concierges only deal with short-term rentals to tourists. As you've read in this book, there are many, many more ways to make money with your property. Maybe you can find a concierge who's willing to take on one more, or all of these revenue-producing possibilities? If not, you might want to engage a second agency to deal just with parking, or events, etc.

Partners: A concierge could help your guests with airport transfers or discounts on taxi services. They might have a deal with a luggage service which can put their bags on consignment nearby before check-in or after check-out. If it's your primary residence and you have no place to stash your personal belongings, some concierges partner with companies who can store boxes for you temporarily, and bring them back upon your return. Will they offer these additional services to your guests, and share a cut with you?

Where do you find such concierges?

My Property Payday has compiled a list of more than 100 *conciergeries* / STR property managers operating across France and Europe. The 'Providers' section of this book includes a great many of them. Members can access the list, and non-members can submit a request for quotations.

You could also try on the search engines, which is a bit hit-or-miss because they are called by many different names (keywords) in both French and English. You'll have to weed through mostly real-estate agencies which only do buy&sell, or letting agents who only do unfurnished units long-term. If you do ask the internet, make sure to put the name of your postcode/town or region in the search bar.

How do you evaluate their services?

Ask them to provide you links to three of their properties. Are they well-noted? Do the reviews specifically commend them for their hospitality? Are the listings native-level English and enticing? Do the photographs appear professional and attractive?

Do the properties resemble yours? Are they houses or apartments? Studios or 1, 2, 3-bedrooms. The kind of dwelling says a lot about the population to whom the concierge caters. Studios and 1-bedrooms appeal more to young people, solo travelers, those on a quick getaway. This population wants quick response, info at their fingertips, and then to be left alone to enjoy their limited time in a new place. Places with 2-3 bedrooms are sought out by families, groups of friends, or couples traveling with other couples. They have many logistical complications they expect the host/concierge to help them with. Is the concierge culturally equipped to welcome the kinds of guests you expect to host in your property? Can they handle the complexities of a larger property.

Diversification

At publication, Sun Key Locations is the only multi-use property manager we at My Property Payday are aware of. This goes not just for France, but outside France as well.

Hopefully, more property managers will begin to equip themselves with the personnel, tools and processes to effectively cover several different uses and populations throughout the year.

* * *

Long-term LTR agents providing management "As-is" or "Classic"

If you already have the rental property, and it's furnished, you could choose a service provider to manage that property for you. This is called 'property management' or 'lettings management' (*gestion locative* in French).

You could have them run as a co-pilot, or on auto-pilot. Auto-pilot would be where you remain the landlord, with a direct contractual relationship with the tenant, but you delegate the management of that relationship to a 3rd party, the property management company. Co-pilot is where the property manager just does the finding, vetting and contracting (leases) and you, the owner, manage yourself after move-in. We'll get into subleases and arbitrage in the next section.

There are 6 500 LTR property managers in Europe with less than 20 properties in their portfolios according to industry consultant Simon Lehmann. There are also hundreds of bigger property management companies with several thousand properties each in their enormous portfolios. About a third of the 7.5 million private LTR properties in France are professionally managed. This service is typically done by real estate agencies.

In France, the average charge a traditional property management company will ask you for is between 5% and 9% (which is half what landlords are charged in the UK for the same service). Traditional LTR property managers charge 8-10% of revenue in the USA and minimum 10% in the UK.

The market is very fragmented, with many small players, and varying degrees of service quality. It's not easy to sustain as a going concern in the field, and they often need at least 150 properties under management to break-even. Since many of the tasks like maintenance, repair, and tenant relations take place in-person, there's a very local aspect to the business, requiring presence in order to react quickly, which is the number one thing you can do to retain high satisfaction from renters. In smaller towns or rural villages your choice of providers may be severely limited.

The top two concerns among French landlords are ensuring full payment of rent on time, and avoiding tenant property damage. The local expectation is that by going through a property manager, the owner can mitigate such concerns. Indeed, non-payment insurance is a common add-on provided by property managers, and included in their bundled fees. Officially, you're not supposed to ask the renter for a '*garant*' if you already subscribe to one of these policies, but many landlords do.

If you are purely interested in property management, there are many new companies which handle just that part. These startups in '*gestion locative'* include players like Flatlooker, Homepilot, Bernie, Gest'in, Kaliz, etc. These companies take over management, but do not make improvements or sublease, as is the case with the coliving startups we'll get to in the Expand section.

The proposition of *'gestion locative'* startups is that they can do a better job than the owner, because they have digital tools which make them more efficient operationally. They also possess social media know-how to manage reviews and customer satisfaction, especially among the younger segment of renters. Inevitably, they've built out their service offering with partnerships of benefit to landlords and/or tenants for insurance, moving, saving on utilities etc. Because their services are more digital, their costs are nearer the 4% lower-end.

You could also pick a traditional player to manage your property. Many of the well-known real estate brands offer property management in addition to buy/sell transactions on home purchases. These include global brands like Century21, ReMax, (held by the same US company, Reality), French brands like Foncia, Efficity, La Forêt, (all owned by the same French holding co., Emeria), or Guy Hoquet and CityA immo (owned by French holding Groupe Arche which also owns Bien'ici) local independent agencies catering exclusively to expats like Leggett, Miyako, Imodia, French Touch Properties, Vingt Paris or the Adrian Leeds Group, or *'mandataires'* loosely associated with Orpi, IAD, Safti et al.

The term *'mandataire'* refers to an independent agent with only a loose affiliation with an agency that doesn't really provide them with any services or support. This type of agent has grown from nonexistent a dozen years ago to capturing 24% marketshare, primarily because the agent can make more money in this loosely-controlled setup. They are a 1-person shop, and you're totally dependent on the knowledge, abilities and availability of that one person. While this is not ideal for a transaction taking 3-6 months, it can still work if the person is very good at their job, and not distracted by the handful of other homes they have to sell.

However, for management of dozens of properties leased over years, it's likely more than one person can handle. Also, if they keep only a handful of properties under management, they'll never get to the scale necessary to become profitable, and thus going out of business is an imminent threat you'd do better to avoid.

Inevitably, the management part of traditional agencies is often something they consider to be the ugly stepchild of their business. They make a lot of money from transactions, and usually barely break-even on the management side. Fully 60% of real estate agencies only do transactions- no property management. The monthly or annual rent represents peanuts compared to the amount of commissions on a purchase. The agency charges a percentage for both, and they can charge whatever commission they want for a transaction. However, for property management, they're limited by law how much they can bill, and the ceiling is very low.

Most landlords who have contracted with a traditional agency are disappointed in their service provider. Fully 61% of those who have delegated property management to a real estate agency are dissatisfied according to the CLCV. Rentals are obviously a loss-leader for these companies, who make all their money on buy/sell property transactions.

Still, some classic real estate companies are able to make the management part a growing concern. Inevitably, it's the specialist property managers who can make a profit, in large part because they are not distracted by transactions. Depending on geography, these can include companies like Valority.

The specialist property managers also tend to adopt a different attitude toward the business, because they are compelled to serve both tenant and landlord over a long period of time. They must build mutually beneficial relationships and maintain satisfaction for all stakeholders. The vast majority of residential real estate agents never complete two transactions with the same person in their lifetime. Since they'll never see either the buyer or the seller ever again, for some the temptation is too great to tell half-truths, cut corners or not always act in the best interests of their clients. If you go with a more traditional agency, we'd advise choosing a specialist property manager that does not conduct buy/sell transactions.

CHAPTER TWENTY
Partner

Short-term rental platforms see huge potential in providing add-ons and experiences to their main business of supplying accommodations.

In an ideal world, you would become an affiliate for their services, sending prospects their way in an automated fashion, where your compensation is equally automatic. It's tricky to track if you're actually paid what you agreed to. But partners know that if you have any doubts, you could cut them off at anytime. It's on them to be transparent, and provide reports back to you, showing the business they closed from your referrals.

Once you close these deals, they should be added seamlessly into the regular flow of communications you've setup with your guests. The e-mail templates you create to share confirmations and check-in instructions can have paragraphs about taxi transfer, or things to do, or restaurant recommendations, or even a calendar of activities planned at your property. The guidebook, or brochures inside your property can similarly have such information with unique identifiers so the partner knows the lead came from you.

Each one of these mentions should have its own link, or QR code. When the guest clicks on the link, two things happen. First, the source of the link should be known as coming from you, who is entitled to compensation if they book that other add-on. Second, the guest lands on the page of your partner, who must do the heavy lifting of convincing that person to buy, process payment and then deliver your kickback.

Workout or Wellbeing Instructors
   Definition: physical activity or health classes in your space, run by another person who does all the work
   Potential: up to 20% of €20/person/session
   Risk: low

Explanation: Almost all sport or esoteric pros are independents, without any usable space to their name. Sometimes the municipality offers their facilities, which aren't always adapted, nor inexpensive. You could partner with these purveyors, who might be happier *chez vous*. The same could go for their students.

Resources: Ownsport, Superprof, Personal Yoga, YogMee

Food Truck

Definition: invite a taco wagon, pizzaiolo putt-putt or other rolling restaurant to park on your private land to sell to guests and neighbors.

Potential: up to 10% of €20/person/event

Risk: low

Explanation: Food truck businesses are quite busy on the weekends or at high-season. They should appreciate an invitation mid-week, especially if you have neighbors nearby that might also order. Propose a profit-share. Be prepared to negotiate for them to come back often. They might expect a minimum of 40 people to 'privatize' but all you want is for them to come by and take the risk of the number of orders. If you are hosting an event or have a large party booking, this is the ideal time to call them in.

Resources: Eventigo

Guides

Definition: a person or platform to show tourists where to go, what it signifies, and delight them with interesting or funny stories along the way

Potential: up to €3 on every €10 tour

Risk: low

Explanation: A physical guide takes your guests on walks. When you send them a paying customer, they could relay a retrocommission your way.

An audioguide allows your guests to visit sites in your area at their own pace, whenever they want. Examples included for people staying at properties managed by Sun Key Locations:
- ✓ A Guide to the Gardens at the Palace of Versailles: Hidden Messages from the Sun King
- ✓ The Chairfather: Père Lachaise Part II

You could buy vouchers from Voicemap.me, and resell them to your guests at a slight markup. Or, for just a few euro, you could gift your guests a free tour, which should reflect well on your ratings.

Resources: Voicemap, GetYourGuide

Pet-sitters

Definition: Invite a dedicated caregiver for pets to use your space for their activity.
Potential: up to 50% of €10-€25/day/pet
Risk: high
Explanation: Listings go from €10-€25/day/pet. The lower-end are people who come to the owner's residence. The higher-end are more professionals with qualifications and installations on their premises which are designed to welcome fur babies.
You could offer a 50/50 split, which seems quite generous. After all, you're providing the space, which you've secured, bought the equipment and are paying the insurance and taking the risk if something goes awry.
Resources: Holidog; Yoopies; Amimalin; Animado; Caniminet; Animaute; Gardicanin; Emprunte Mon Toutou

MICE purveyors
Definition: Meetings, Incentives, Corporate Events run by others on your premises
Potential: up to 20% of €50/person
Risk: medium if alcohol is served
Explanation: You could always simply put your space up on the platforms for this usage. However, there are companies whose job it is to put on corporate events. They work with several companies. Partner with them to rent out your place on multiple occasions.
Resources: Momentys, As One, LDR, Shortcut Events, also surrounding businesses, your local chamber of commerce

Teachers of Education Classes
Definition: a classroom in your home, run by an instructor who does all the work
Potential: up to 20% of €15/person
Risk: low
Explanation: Independent educators and coaches are always looking for good venues to conduct in-person classes. This may not be big money, but if you find one with a regular following, it could be worth your while.
Resources: L'Ecole des Secrets

Storyteller (*conteur*)
Definition: Invite a teller of tales to your place to entertain with spoken words
Budget: up to 10% of €10/person
Risk: low
Explanation: The ancient tradition of storytelling is still alive and well in France. It's not just for children, although you'll find more aimed at this

public than any other. Quite popular in rural villages during summer, you could give your guests a special treat in the off-season, too.

Resources: l'Allégresse du pourpre

Aggregators

As mentioned in the 'Toolset tack-ons' chapter, there are a number of companies which have already struck a deal with hundreds of suppliers. You could easily tap into their network by adding their tech service to your operations. This involves little to no work on your part.

Don't expect to make as much money from this approach, as you're adding yet another middle-man. Also, these companies may have well-established relationships in the US, but few in France, and none where you operate.

Resources: UpSellGuru, Tourdesk

Expand

CHAPTER TWENTY-ONE
Additions

This book began by stating all the ways you could earn money from your space, without further investment, without taking on additional risk. This section, called 'Expand,' includes ideas for those who are ready and able to put down **extra** money, or at least extra time to make more profit from property.

By now, you're certainly looking at property from a space point-of-view, meaning you're not simply taking it at face value. A single-family home isn't just a year-round living place for for one family. The current usage is simply one among many ways that you could exploit the space. You have an eye toward the immense possibilities.

As a curator of investment property, you see not just what it is now, but what it could be. A couple with two children and another on the way is selling their 3-bedroom apartment to trade up for a 4th room for the newborn. If you buy the flat, you could similarly rent unfurnished to a family of four on a standard 3-year lease, but you don't have to.

You could do a shared rental (*colocation*) or HMO (houses in multiple occupation) for students during the school year. A coliving space could be created for young professionals. Business travelers and displaced workers could rent a room by the month. If the building allows it, a holiday let or short-term vacation rental could be hosted there. You could do a combination of the aforementioned at different moments of the year. Use what you've learned to transform the space into a project which meets your objectives through smart plays and diversification.

After reading and applying the techniques of the previous chapters, you should be reaching the full revenue potential of what your own property could bring, while respecting your preferences and lifestyle. If there's still room to improve, your best bet is to go back to the previous pages of this book, or seek outside guidance to bring it up a notch.

You're nearly always better off focusing on what you have, rather than hoping to get more from something new. Not only will your payoff be better (€0 invested vs. X% increase), you'll also improve your efficiency. When you eventually DO go forward by adding the next element to your Property Payday machine, you'll be better at it.

We'll now continue your education in the following chapters by showing how to leverage other people's money, blow out your existing space, acquire new property no matter your budget, and unveil the ways you could use that property to earn rental income. Many more options are available to you for secondary residences, such as coliving, impractical in a primary residence. If you have some spare euro in your *portefeuille*, we'll show you how you can spend it on property to grow your returns.

CHAPTER TWENTY-TWO
OPM: Other People's Money

The first strategies we'll look at, can be executed by anybody. Little to no money is required. The finite resource here is your time.

And your spleen.

You see, there is no free lunch. When you play with other people's money, or OPM, you're displacing their risk onto your shoulders. You're also working full-time or near to it, to get out from under their yoke as quickly as possible, and in any case, before the bill comes due.

WeWork found this out the hard way. They positioned themselves as a Proptech, or a lifestyle brand, when really all they were was a subleasing company. They convinced venture capital firms to give them funds. Then WeWork spent that money on discounted long-term leases, 10-years or more at commercial properties around the globe.

WeWork was making record-setting leaps in the UK, with the shared-space startup becoming the single largest non-government renter of office space in London, covering a total of 2.6 million square feet. At one point, WeWork occupied more Manhattan real estate than any other company.

Then, they sublet all that space at higher rates to several companies and individuals renting a seat for as little as $20 per day. In just a couple years, they were valued as a $47 billion company.

Even if the founders of WeWork hadn't wasted or pocketed a load of the VC money themselves, they still would've had a day of reckoning when commercial real estate demand weakened. That's exactly what happened when Covid-19 hit. Workers started doing *télétravail* overnight. Many of them still haven't come back to the office for the majority of the week, three years later.

WeWork's tenants fled, or used fewer seats, or broke their leases, or simply stopped paying. Meanwhile, the commercial landlords who own the spaces where WeWork operates, continue to collect rent. This came to a head in November 2023 when WeWork declared bankruptcy.

Keep their story in mind when looking at the following plays, which extoll you to carry a similar structure. Many videos and blogs and online classes and poor quality books are out there from self-proclaimed wizards touting these schemes. Be very wary.

We're not listing these plays because we advocate them. At My Property Payday, we don't think you should engage in **any** of them. But you should **know** about them. Purveyors of this sludge know they're peddling filth, and so they often *cache* their nature in ambiguous language. We're going to call them by name with intentionally simple language. In this way, we hope it's clear to you when you come across a peddler.

Risky business

The following plays are to be attempted only if you have a big appetite for risk-reward. It's best if you start with a bankroll of at least three to six months' rent and living expenses in cash to weather a storm. This amount of time is your minimum 'out' to exit an LTR lease legally in France.

French law prohibits renting on a sublease for a higher amount than the main lease. However, this is only in the case where both leases are of the same type. If both leases are long-term unfurnished, the sublease can't charge more.

In contrast, if the main one is a 'residential' lease (*bail d'habitation*), and the sublease is a 'commercial' lease (*bail commercial*), you **can** charge more. Ask your lawyer or accountant to draw up the paperwork in a way which protects you.

This is a loophole that coliving property management startups take advantage of. They will offer to sign a long-term unfurnished residential lease with the owner (often much longer than the 3-year minimum), then they'll outfit the place, and offer it to their clients on a room-by-room and month-to-month basis.

You could agree to this arrangement if you own a second property, and prefer the tranquility of hands-off passive income which is guaranteed. Or, you could propose this structure to other people who own the property that you're lacking to create rental income.

Arbitrage or Rent-to-Rent

This is where you find an owner who is willing to rent their property to you on a long-term basis. Then you rent that same property to another, or several others on shorter, higher-price leases, or lease-free on the sharing platforms.

Many coliving startups deploy this model, but they add a twist. They actually pay for renovations, supply the furnishings, and create the software which is used by tenants to plan usage, activities and pay for rent. Companies doing this include Habyt and June Homes. They get this initial money from venture capital companies.

This model means their capital outlay at the start is considerable, before any rental income starts flowing in. Keep this in mind for the play you're considering. Will you be able to rent it as-is? Or will you need to invest to make the place attractive to your intended renter? If so, where will the money come from? If you're thinking credit cards, or a bank loan, you may be rapidly going from knee-deep up to your neck.

We personally know several people who built a mini empire up to 20 subleased properties in this fashion… before declaring bankruptcy. It takes so little to turn this dream into a nightmare. A space which sits empty. A dwelling that you had a harder time renting, so accepted a price damn near your lease amount. A tenant who doesn't pay, but stays. A tourist who trashes the place at an unauthorized party. A law change prohibiting the use you planned to make of it. A setback in your personal life siphoning funds you had earmarked for lease payments.

In the 'States, there is life after bankruptcy, several very hard years later. In France, it's not really an option, nor one you should consider. Liability follows you, and can even trickle down into the next generation, unless your children refuse the entire inheritance.

JV

A joint-venture is where you have a business partner who's sharing the financial burden or out-and-out bankrolling your rental activity in exchange for a cut.

In these relationships, you typically have the money-man and the hustler. The one who supplies the money often does nothing else, except for oversee the work of the other partner. The hustler must do everything else, either themselves, or find the people who do the work.

Any good partnership would be 50-50, but we can clearly see here that it's not. The one supplying sweat equity is working a lot harder than the one bankrolling the project. It's extremely rare to see these kinds of arrangements lasting long, even to the term of the first investment. Either moneybags gets bored, or disappointed with progress and pulls out, or the hustler feels taken advantage of, or burns out, and abandons.

Flipping

This is where you find a diamond in the rough, and you find some way of purchasing it (usually going in with another party), with the intention of fixing it up and re-selling rapidly for a healthy profit. If the Preface and Taxation chapter didn't turn you off on this idea in France, we don't know what will.

To summarize, the upfront costs are so great (notary, agency, renovations) that it's almost impossible to hit break-even in ROI without holding for 2-3 years minimum, in a fast rising market. Look around in 2023, and you'll see that's not the market we're in.

Crowdfunding for your own project

If you haven't already made a name for yourself, you can forget this one. You're unlikely to reach the funding target.

Also, right off the bat, you'll have to give up 8% to the crowdfunding platform, and owe that same 8% back to your investors. It's a great way to start in a hole.

Resources: Seedrs, KissKissBankBank, Ulule, Crowdcube

All of the above ideas are long-term plays couched as 'get rich quick' schemes. Those who have very little can be attracted to them because they have no other assets to play with. Some have been lucky in these gambles. When they start to accumulate real capital themselves, something strange happens. They never go back to the same well.

They may be holding a microphone and extolling you to do what they did. They may tout these methods as fantastic. If they're such good deals, why aren't they doing them today? Why do they now put their own money in more conservative investments? Perhaps because they know just how lucky they were to get out of those early deals alive.

CHAPTER TWENTY-THREE
Blow out space; Extend calendar

Now that you know how to make money from your property on the sharing platforms, there are sure ways to create more of it:
1. Create more availability on your rental calendar by freeing up dates when you could go away.
2. Extend your calendar past six months in the future to accommodate additional dates for rental.
3. Rearrange your property, or clear it out to create more space.
4. Blow out or add more square meters onto your existing dwelling which can be rented by adapting it for different usage.
5. Construct new additional usable space on your existing grounds, separate from your main dwelling.
6. Leverage collective property owned by the extended family

More dates

Do you have a nearby place you could stay? If you do, and you don't mind going there more often, your property could become more productive.

In selecting your hideaway, it should meet certain criteria. The first is that the hideaway should cost less than half of your projected earnings. This is a good rule of thumb, but if you want to be more precise, figure net revenue by taking your ADR and subtracting platform fees, cleaning/ etc., and the taxes you pay on those earnings (around 15% for most people in France).

Then, factor in all of your expenses for the hideaway including transportation, lodging, half the meal cost (you'd have had to eat at home anyway) and sales tax. Net earnings should be well above net expenses to make it worth your while. Stay with family or friends for free, and the calculation is easily done. However, it may cause tension if you're there for 40 nights a year, so having several hideaways is a good idea.

Second, your hideaway should be near enough that you can get over to your main property quickly in an emergency. Your guest could lose their keys. A leak might start. If you have a maintenance person or property manager, then your hideaway could be anywhere. Neighbors aren't a sustainable solution.

Reconfigure
Definition: without building any new m², you could rearrange the layout, possibly creating another room.
Budget: between €1 500 and €2 500 per square meter, or about €1 000 if you're simply moving one plaster wall.
Risk: low
Explanation: A 20m² bedroom might have a layout which allows you to add a wall, creating two bedrooms at 10m² each. A single bed in a 15m² bedroom could be switched out for a queen/double or bunk beds, increasing your sleeping capacity by one and opening your place up for larger groups and families. Move your home office desk to the master bedroom, and your old office space becomes a new bedroom.
In France, you cannot rent out a room/space for accommodation which is less than 9m² or 2.2m high. An exception can be made for a space with a smaller footprint, but much higher ceiling, allowing for a minimum of 20m³ overall.
Resources: Moving a wall which is not load-bearing can be done by most homeowners themselves, which would save €100s.

More m²
We know people who have transformed their garage for a personal sports trainer. Others made their attic into a yoga studio. One flips their living room into a co-working space during the day. Others shift boxes and furniture out of offices to turn them into bedrooms.
On-site storage: Do you have a space in your dwelling where you could move more stuff?
Off-site storage: Is your garage filled with items you use rarely. If you don't have room on-site, you could move those to a smaller storage unit, or use the platforms to store with your neighbors. Then, rent it as a monthly parking spot for more than the storage costs.
Sell or donate items: It was sure nice of grandma to give you her antique dining table and 10 chairs, but when was the last time you used it? Big bulky furniture eats up m² which could be put to better use. You may be surprised how little value it has, and how fast that value is falling. Clear out space, move stuff from here to there and *voilà*, you have another room to rent.

***

Additions

Here are some ways you can get more out of your space, listed from the smallest to the biggest budget.

Studio (Music, Podcasts, Influencers)

Definition: Create a space, probably in your basement or garage, for a local band to practice, or a new media purveyor to record.

Budget: €0 to €5 000

Risk: moderate

Explanation: You could offer to host jam sessions musicians in your home rehearsal studio. This wouldn't be for entertainment purposes, but to help out a band which needs a place to practice.

Pro studios in Paris usually charge around €15-30/hour for a minimum of two hours at a time. These businesses equip the space at a minimum with soundproofing or deadening acoustic covers on the walls and ceiling, a drum set and cymbals, at least three amplifiers for guitar/keyboards, bass and vocals, and 1-2 microphones and cords. They may charge extra to rent a guitar, bass, keyboard or mixing table by the hour.

If you don't want to invest in all those musical electronics, you could offer to store the gear for the group in-between sessions. This might limit you to one potential renter, but if the group is serious and practices 3-4 times a week, it could make more sense than having several groups coming and going throughout the week. The band might be willing to pay €100 to €150/mo.

Podspace has made a professional-level video podcast studio in Paris and other locations in France. They claim to rent it out for €100 per hour. You could easily do the same, either competing with them, or becoming the only game in town if your space is in a completely different region.

Resources: Audiofanzine, Zikinf, Podspace

Kennels for pet-sitting

Definition: installing separate secure cages hosting animals, most likely dogs, on your premises (not at master's residence), during the day or overnight and walking them or giving them the opportunity to exercise outside

Budget: €200 - €2 000

Risk: high

Explanation: You can find many pet-sitters (*gardien d'animaux de compagnie*) offering their services for €10-€25 per day per companion and €20-€30 for overnight.

Resources: Holidog; Yoopies; Amimalin; Animado; Caniminet; Animaute; Gardicanin; Emprunte Mon Toutou

* * *

EV *borne électrique*
Definition: Providers will contract a profit share with you by installing an electric car charge station on your property.
Budget: €500 - €1 500
Risk: low
Explanation: A UK association of property investors says an electric car charging point is now the top value-adder to any home. Nearly a million people in France (and another million in the UK which might drive to France for holidays) currently own electric or hybrid vehicles. This number is rising exponentially. While the UK investor's claims seem exaggerated that a charging point could add up to £35 000 to a home's resale value, it should certainly pay for itself in a short time.
Is your home on a busy street with frequent passage from non-residents? Do drivers have the ability to park in front, within 10m of your land? Are there few chargepoints in your area? Then this could be an inexpensive and lucrative add-on to your property business.
You'd also have a ready answer for guests who ask to juice-up. Rather than freely opening your digital spigot, which can potentially add €20-€30 per day to your expenses, you offer them a solution which actually makes you money. Plug Inn, for one, suggests you charge €4.50/hour.
For owners of multi-unit buildings, Bump offers more powerful chargers in greater quantity, installed at their expense, also sharing revenues.
Resources: WattPark; izi by EDF which uses hardware made by Wallbox; Bump; Fastned; Plug Inn by Renault

Shed/Barn/storage build
Definition: a moveable structure, separate from the main building, but on the same land.
Budget: €600 - €7 000 (for a hangar €7 000 - €14 000 up to 600m³)
Risk: high
Explanation: Any new construction of a shed, veranda or garage greater than 5m² is subject to a *taxe d'aménagement*. The cost is quite prohibitive, especially for an investment. The state has created a simulator to help determine estimated taxes prior to building or buying.
The tax is €1 004/m² in the Paris region, and €886/m² outside. This means if you build a new shed in your backyard in Essonne, if it's 4m² there's no tax, but if it's 6m² the *fisc* will charge you €6 024. The entirety of the tax bill is due at once at the time of construction.
The tax can be avoided by setting multiple 5m² structures next to one another, or making your shed less than 1m80 tall inside. Tiny houses, trailers and other such dwellings on wheels appear to escape the onerous tax. Also, those which were built without authorization at least

six to 10 years ago.

Resources: Leroy Merlin, Castorama, Bricorama, ManoMano

Jacuzzi/Spa

Definition: outdoor above-ground heated lounging water pod with jets for two to seven bathers

Budget: €700-€9 000

Risk: moderate

Explanation: The advantages of adding a water spot are covered in the swimming pool idea further on. However, that assumes you have the land required and the resources to pay for it. A jacuzzi or spa is an inexpensive alternative which takes up less space. It also costs less to maintain.

On some platforms, having this amenity in your listing allows your property to appear in the search results of travelers looking for a 'pool.' You'll be visible to a wider swath of potential paying guests.

Resources: Atelier Nordic

Sauna/Hammam

Definition: indoor or outdoor hot box

Budget: €2 000-€9 000

Risk: high

Explanation: Even if guests use it sparingly or never, the fact that your place has a sauna raises it into the echelons of wellbeing and high-end. You might get chosen over nearby places that don't have one, and you could certainly charge more.

Also, if a guest's main motivation is mindfulness, that isn't achieved overnight. Longer stays could be in your future, should you surround your spaces with such amenities.

Resources: Auroom

Tree house

Definition: a wooden structure, separate from the main building, up in a sturdy tree

Budget: €3 000 to €20 000

Risk: high

Explanation: The French call these a *'cabane perché dans l'arbre.'* They're not as prevalent as in the US, nor as elaborate. So, if you have one, it can be a rare treat for your guests. Consider it an amenity to attract folks to your grounds overall, rather than a destination.

In order for it to meet the requirements of overnight guests, it'll have to be rainproof, equipped with electricity or mobile juice and at least nearby facilities for *pipi/caca*. If you're renting outside the summer, it'll need to be enclosed with a safe heating source, and in-home style bedding.

You'll have to secure the area at a minimum to avoid falls and liability. There are no insurers we know of offering policies specifically for this, so check what your homeowner's insurance covers.

Swimming Pool

Definition: splish, splash in your own personal water hole

Budget: €15 000 to €50 000 for a sunken version, plus €500/year maintenance

Risk: moderate

Explanation: France has 4 000 municipal swimming pools and other public aquatic parks. But many cities are closing them because of energy costs, and water restrictions. This makes private swimming holes even more sought after.

The *fisc* is convinced adding a swimming pool will increase the rental value of your property between 5% and 10%. They'll apply two taxes to your new construction, a *taxe d'aménagement* (if greater than 10m²) and the classic *taxe foncière* will be increased for the entire property. Thankfully, if you declare on time (within 90 days) you'll be exempt from paying the *foncière* for the first two years.

Luckily, a pool actually increases the resale value of a house more than the government's take, +19% on average, according to Meilleurs Agents. It's more of a '*patrimonial*' play down the road, rather than a means to increase rental income today.

Which doesn't mean that you won't make more money. It's just unlikely that your ROI will be better than break-even solely from renting. Hosting swimmers will bring you nominal new funds. The biggest boost you're likely to see is when you rent your entire property, including the swimming pool.

Reservations for your whole place should see increased demand vs the pool-less competition. Also, you should be able to charge a premium per square meter versus the surrounding options.

There's even a new provider who will rent a pool by the month. All they need is a flat space of 15m² (6m long by 2.5m wide), and access for the truck. The pools are tricked out shipping containers, which have stylish wooden siding.

The cost is €1 600 per month, or less if you rent for several months. Delivery is included within the Tarn-et-Garonne department (just north of Toulouse). Onsite, they fill it for you, verify that the filters are working properly and check the chlorine levels. At the end of the rental, they haul it away.

If your rental is in a region which frequently hovers above 30°C during the summer, or experiences regular heatwaves (it seems everyplace in

France has them), a pool could be the amenity *sine quoi non* in order to get reservations. Ask yourself if you think you could get €400 per week more, or €60 per day more than you would normally, and would your occupancy rate approach 100%? If so, maybe pool rental could be right for your property.

Resources: Trident Piscine Mobile

Tiny house / Yurt / etc.

Definition: a moveable structure (or one that meets France's definition of '*demontable*'), separate from the main building, usually in a yard or vacant lot of land

Budget: €20 000-€100 000

Risk: moderate to high

Explanation: A true 'cottage' industry has been stirred up. Many variations exist, from moveable units on a trailer frame, shipping containers, and standalone kits on a foundation. According to one tiny homes report, the market is expected to grow $3.7 billion by 2026.

One owner in Oakland lives solely on the STR income he makes from renting tiny houses parked on his urban property. North Hollywood's Alexandria Park is an entire village of tiny homes. Samara tiny house manufacturer started by an Airbnb co-founder, raised $41 million.

In France, Easybox transforms shipping containers from 5m² to 30m² into all sorts of configurations, including live-ins that can be delivered to your premises from the back of a flatbed semi truck. Mykub sells stunning units up to 50m² for €100 000. MCF Tiny Houses go for €40K-€100K. Vagabond Haven retails tiny houses in Denmark, Finland, Italy, France, Spain and Portugal.

Parcel has a unique model where they will tow their company's tiny house onto your property, manage the comings and goings, then split the commission with you. This arrangement should be low or no-cost to owners, but they don't serve everybody, just farmers. You must have a plot of land designated for agriculture where they can park their tiny house.

One US builder of pre-fabs up to 40m² called Rent the Backyard posts dramatic videos of dropping down their creation via crane over the main house onto the lawn behind. They will do a profit-share with you to help subsidise the $100 000+ cost. They haven't yet delivered to Europe, and we're not sure their designs would meet the specs here. In the US, a tiny home build costs around $300 per square foot versus a traditional build which costs around $150 per square foot.

If your tiny house is on wheels (most likely on a trailer frame), it must have its own license plate in France. Like most accessories which are towed, it can't weigh more than 3.5 tons, be more than 4.3m high nor

2.5m wide. It can't be parked on a terrain for more than three months straight without a declaration of *travaux*, or works to the municipality.

Setting a tiny house without wheels bigger than 20m² on your French property, even for your own use, requires approval (or at least a lack of prohibition on the PLU or '*plan local d'urbanisme*') from the city's planning commission (*mairie*). One trick is to have the footprint of the structure not go over 20m², while astutely configuring mezzanines or rooftops to add useable space that won't cause administrative headaches.

Greenkub's wooden structures are designed to do just the trick while blending seamlessly into the surrounding natural environment. They can be delivered with or without kitchens, showers and toilets. Before deciding on which configuration, ask yourself how much you (and your guests) will be willing to depend on the main house.

The call of the wild will inevitably be followed by nature's call. The WC of choice in a tiny house is the dry toilet. Guest habits will need altering, and the pile-up will need frequent disposal outside the structure. Manufacturers claim you can compost the creations, preferably far from all houses, big and tiny.

Resources: Parcel; Tiny House collective; Easybox; Greenkub; Maestro Chalet; Rent the Backyard; Tinyzood; Samara; MCF Tiny House

Build up, Push out, Dig down

Definition: add m² in any direction you can to your existing properties through construction

Budget: between €1 500 and €2 500 per square meter, more if you are raising the roof, excavating the basement or reinforcing the foundation to add a new floor.

Risk: moderate (if touching the roof or foundation) to low (if not affecting the existing structure, like a lateral addition).

By constructing more square meters, at worst, you're creating new space for your own enjoyment. If your property is worth more per m² than the works cost per m², you're already ahead of the game at completion. In order to realise your gains, you'd have to exploit the new space in the sharing economy, or sell. If neither are in the cards at the moment, this becomes a long-term play.

Build up

When you raise the roof you are remodeling to re-arrange the layout, creating new space upstairs which can be monetised.

Push out the walls

You could add a wing

Dig down

Depending on the project, it may require approval from the city's planning commission (*mairie*) and plans drawn up by a qualified architect which respects the PLU or *'plan local d'urbanisme'*. In terms of time, figure one month for the plans and submission, two to three months for possible modifications and approval, followed by three to nine months for the build and completion. You could be generating extra revenue as early as six months from the time the light bulb goes off in your head.

ADU or in-law unit.
Definition: a fixed standalone structure, separate from the main building
Budget: €30 000 to €100 000
Risk: moderate
Explanation: An in-law suite is a great option to create possibilities for income. They're nowadays referred to as "Accessory Dwelling Units" or ADUs for short.

This is very similar to the tiny house concept, but here we're talking permanent construction. It will be either a completely separate building, or may share a wall with the main property. In either case, it has its own entrance and facilities (kitchen, shower, toilet). It can depend on the main home for utilities and waste removal, or have its own meter.

All such long-lasting construction will require a building permit, and qualifications. It will also be subject to the *taxe d'aménagement*.

An ADU could be rented either short-term or long-term. You could also rent out your main home for more money, and quickly move into the ADU during your guests' stay. For maximum revenue, move into your ADU full-time, and rent out your main home as often as possible.

Converting shared property
Family vacation home - convince relatives to pitch in and share profits by renting when it's not in use. Show them this book (and tell them to buy their own copy ;-) to assure them you know what you're doing. Entice them with simulations of rental income and their share of the take.

Inheritance
If a loved one has left you a place, you could exploit its earning potential.

If you're lucky enough that your relative is still around, there are tax advantages if they transmit the property they planned to will to you **before** they pass. Inheritance taxes in France are very high, and can be considerably avoided by anticipating the moment of transmission. The earlier they give, the greater the tax advantage.

The French government incentivises moving assets from the passive to the active economy. Since 80% of the *patrimoine* or assets owned by people in France consists of real estate, the *gouvernement* encourages people to put that to work. Apartments which remain empty are taxed higher than those which are rented out on long-term leases. Owners have a financial incentive to rent if only to avoid paying more to the state. The government's plan is working, because vacant lodgings dropped from around 3.3% of all residential property in 2013 to 1.1% in 2022. Still, there are 3 million unused properties.

The administration also allows the decoupling of the intrinsic value of the physical property (*foncier*) and the ephemeral value of the usage (*usufruit*) of that property. Your relative can pass on one or both of these elements to you. When they keep the 'usage,' you both save on inheritance taxes. The one who has the *usufruit* is entitled to reap the rental income, but you can work out a deal with family, perhaps splitting the gains.

Your relative might save additional taxes by joining with you (and maybe your siblings) in the creation of an SCI. When one shareholder passes, their parts go to the others without an inheritance payout event.

To explore these scenarios, a physical meeting of all concerned parties, held at the offices of the family notary, is necessary.

CHAPTER TWENTY-FOUR
Acquisitions offsite

According to bespoke BTL provider Beanstock, 70% of adults in France would like to invest in rental property, but only 10% have actually done it. If this is one of your desires, what's stopping you?

For some, an aversion to risk has held them back from investing in property. All investments pose some degree of risk. The question here is how much risk are you willing to accept? The information here aims to help you measure and mitigate risk, and weigh that versus the potential gain to see if it makes sense for your particular situation.

For others, it's a question of time. You imagine having to deal with tenant or guest issues, maintenance emergencies, turnover of renters and all the hours spent advertising finding and vetting new ones. Certainly, if you're going to do it yourself, you'll need to have a bit of free time. It would also be greatly helpful if you actually enjoyed this kind of work, and relations with clients. If this is not you, or you don't have the time, there are people and organisations who can do the work for you. Some have been mentioned earlier, such as in the Outsource chapter in the Optimize section. Others will be introduced here.

"How?" is the main question of people who are ready, but don't know where to start. This 'Acquisitions' section aims to offer a primer of how to go about acquiring revenue-producing space. You'll also be turned on to providers who can answer your questions and accompany you.

For most of us, it's a question of means. This book began with figures detailing the enormous amount of debt property owners are carrying versus their income. So, the main aim of these pages has been to get the most out of what you already have.

There's another point of view, which purports that debt is a great way to build wealth. By leveraging home loans, putting 20% down, you actually get 100% of the exclusive use of something which is worth 5x more than your initial investment.

***

STR resources

Look at supply and demand in your geographic area of focus. AirDNA's rentalizer has a tool which helps many investors identify where a property might produce good rental returns. It works better in their home market of the US, where properties are fairly homogenous in the same area. Take it with a grain of salt in France.

For example, we know of a building in Neuilly-sur-Seine with two comps. Both apartments had the same surface area. Both were sold within a month of one another in 2022. They were on different floors in the same small structure, a five-story building with less than 40 total units. One was sold at **twice** the price/m² as the other.

Nightly rates: AirDNA, Key Data, All the Rooms

LTR resources

If you're settled on exploring a purchase for long-term rental options, here are a list of resources and providers which can help.

Demand for rentals: LocService has a very useful tool (called a *tensiomètre locatif*) indicating if supply (*offres*) or demand (*tension locatif*) has the upper-hand in the city where you're searching. Note, many smaller towns or property types don't have enough data to establish an accurate measure.

Just before back-to-school 2022, LocService announced the college towns which had the greatest disparity of rooms available versus how many students wanted them. La Rochelle topped the list with 11 inquiries per offer (*demandes par offre*), quickly followed by Paris (9.5), Lyon (8.2), Rennes (6.9) and Metz (5.9). According to Altarea, in Lyon the ratio is 7:1. The Crous operates 83 run-down student residences in Paris which are always 100% full. Conversely, student demand in Lille, Bordeaux and Nantes has practically disappeared.

According to Masteos, these college towns offered the greatest gross yield potential in July 2022: Mulhouse (12.64%), Saint-Étienne (11.07%), Perpignan (8.91%), Troyes (8.86%) and Le Mans (8.27%).

Rent prices: Maps (gouv) *carte des loyers* ; Paris (mairie) *encadrement*; IDF (région) *encadrement* because the entire Paris region is in zone tendu;

Sales data - Historical transaction amounts and some property details, like number of square meters: PatrIm (government data) ; Etalab (notary publics) ; both are lagging indicators, meaning data is from six months ago or older. Meilleurs Agents mixes several data sources (including these) pretty reliably.

Maybe you've applied the principles in the previous chapters and have accumulated enough extra income to add to your property portfolio.

Whatever you've done, you've done it right, so give yourself a pat on the back.

Now, don't forget what got you here in the first place: working it. Apply that same attitude, that identical work ethic, that winning hands-on approach which helped you build your wealth.

Remain an active investor, not a passive observer. Even if you delegate the day-to-day operations to a service provider, you should maintain frequent and controlled oversight. They work for you, and should meet your demands. You have a right to high expectations.

They may be a professional in the real estate industry, but you're no longer a novice, and you've proven your capabilities in this arena. You are on equal ground.

There really are opportunities for every budget. One of the following could make sense for you.

CHAPTER TWENTY-FIVE
Small budget

In this chapter, we'll highlight some profitable plays that don't break the bank.

Crowdfunding
Definition: Thousands of individuals like yourself pitching small amounts into a project previously only accessible to banks and institutions. This differs from the subject covered in the OPM chapter, as you're investing in someone else's project.
Budget: from as little as €10
Risk: high
Evaluation: Crowdfunding in France raised €2 billion, in 2022. Two-thirds of all projects were in real estate, according to Mazars and the FPF (*Financement Participatif France*). The average rate of return of a Crowdfunding project in 2022 was 9.4% according to Mazars and the FPF. On average the investor gets back their money in 21 months. They can be bought inside a PEA-PME which, when invested for at least five years, the funds including interest can be pulled out tax free.

The promise of these startups is to invest as little as €10 in property and get up to 15% per year return from shared rent with other investors. Arrived Homes and Lofty in the US have a somewhat similar model of raising money from crowds to purchase fractional shares in rental units.

They package these deals in such vehicles as crowdfunding, and SCPI that may be through a life insurance policy or some other mechanism. Usually a builder (*promoteur immobilier*) or renovator (*marchand de biens*) will have a project for which they're raising funds. It could be a new apartment building, or block of buildings or a complex.

It's more reassuring to go through one of these startup sites because they should have done most of the due diligence for you, such as "Has this promoter bailed on investors in the past?" Sadly, that's happened a lot, and serial fraudsters have just closed down a previous company and started a new one to take the money and run. Banks were sometimes burned by these unscrupulous promoters in the past, so now they demand strict insurance coverage, and only give their best APR to honest executives with a solid track record.

The platforms hosting the fundraise should also have checked the feasibility of the project, whether the finished product should sell or rent for as much as the promoter says, as quickly as they predict. Hello Crowdfunding indicates 13.5% of projects are not delivered on time. If the project doesn't meet their guidelines, the fundraising marketplaces say they won't allow it on their site.

Though this is playing at the equivalent of the penny-ante table, it's still very high risk, high reward. The AMF, monetary regulator in France, put out a specific buyer beware warning to investors in the crowdfunding sector. Venture here with only as much of your bankroll as you're willing to never see again. Make sure that the amount you choose will still allow you to maintain your lifestyle as before.

A safer bet in a similar product might be to buy SCPI stock (*Société Civile de Placement Immobilier*) which is the French equivalent of a REIT (Real Estate Investment Trust). See information on these later in this chapter.

Rather than own a stone in a rockhouse, you could own a share in a promising Proptech company. GuestReady has completed three successful rounds on the Seedrs crowdfunding platform. Smartrenting raised on Crowdcube in December 2023.

Resources: Bricks, Wiseed, Homunity, Linxea, Primaliance, France SCPI, Iroku, Upstone, Louve Invest, Baltis, and Club Funding (which raised €125 million in 2022)

Land

Definition: a vacant plot, zoned for habitation or agriculture or to remain natural with occasional temporary lodging

Budget: €10 000 to €90 000

Risk: low

Evaluation: Every plot of land in France has a cadastral number. You can look it up on the Geoportail government site. Contact the local *mairie*, give them the *numéro de cadastre*, and request an ownership name. Get in touch with the owner and let the haggling begin.

The average price paid in France for empty land on which you can build lodging was €91/m² in 2020 up 3.7% from 2019. The average plot size was 924m² (for €84 100). Construction cost on bare terrain averaged €1 527/m² for an individual house.

In France, it's very popular to buy land, and then contract with an independent architect to build a single-family home. In fact, this 'from scratch' method called 'CCMI' (*Contrat de Construction de Maison Individuelle*) is much more prevalent than buying from a builder. Kaufman & Broad (KB), Nexity, and other builders are active in what's called 'VEFA' (*Vente en l'Etat Futur d'Achèvement*) making tens of cookie-cutter homes in a new development (*lotissement*). In 2012, 90 600, or 60% of new habitations delivered were 1-off CCMI builds. In 2020, VEFA builder KB delivered a piddling grand total of 358 individual houses in chock-a-block 'villages,' and they were the #7 real estate builder in 2021.

If you think Green Acres is the place to be, Eloi can put you in touch with agriculture pros looking to sell their farms. This requires a bigger budget and a higher tolerance for risk.

You can invest in a forest for as little as €1 000. The cost of one hectare is €4 630 an increase of 4.2% year on year in November 2023. It's more of a patrimonial play because revenues from the exploitation are only about 1% annually. However, the last 10 years the land value has increased by 40%.

Resources: Geoportail

Parking

Definition: Renting a garage with a lockable door, or any other offstreet driveway or spot behind a gate. Sometimes called a 'box' in France, this refers to an enclosed space with a lock on the door near to dwellings, able to house at least one standard-size automobile or several rooms' worth of belongings. Rented on an hourly, daily, weekly or monthly basis.

Budget: €10 000 to €35 000

Risk: low

Platform fees: 10% to 15%

Evaluation: While far from sexy, investing in parking can produce fantastic returns. The average price paid by renters of a parking garage in Paris is €169/mo. and the very top-end go for as high as €500/mo. Yields from 5-8% gross are routinely superior to long-term apartment rentals, in many cities double that of flats, which typically produce 3-4% gross (LTR unfurnished). Strasbourg, Saint-Étienne, Nîmes and Montreuil offer the highest potential yields outside Paris.

Tailwinds from the market are increasing demand. There are fewer and fewer car street parking places in Paris, down 16% to only 141 000 places (in 2017). That's one for every 14 residents in the city limits, and one for every four of the 617 000 cars with Paris plates.

According to YesPark, the city of Paris will cut their street parking in half to only 70 000 spaces in the next five years. That's right, half of all street parking places in Paris will disappear by 2026. It's no wonder in

Spring 2021, there was a 60% increase in requests for underground parking on SeLoger.

It's no wonder such a scarce commodity tends to hold its value. More than 30% of driving time in Paris is spent looking for a parking space. After finding one, Cocoparks claims each driver spends an average of €600 per year on parking fees, not to mention fines.

The mayor of Paris, Anne Hidalgo, is anti-car, and only wishes to exacerbate the tension. During the pandemic, the mayor allowed restaurants to take over parking spaces in front of their bistro, so patrons could better respect the health protocols. Restauranteurs built elaborate terraces to block the street for the exclusive use of their customers. It's been three years, and the structures are still there, blocking thousands of spots, unavailable to drivers. There's talk of making them permanent, which would further reduce the available street parking for residents.

Paris is just one example of a city creating economics which benefit holders of parking spaces. These conditions exist to some degree in all the medium to large cities in France.

Hotels, shopping centers, conventions and institutional facility managers with sizeable but underused lots are also using platforms like OnePark, YesPark and ZenPark to boost their revenues.

Public parking spots are supposed to be 2.5 meters wide by 5 meters long. Hardly any of the spaces are so drawn. So, French car owners have just gotten used to guiding their cars into these minuscule spaces, and extracting their bodies from them. It's amazing what they put up with. And some are very happy to pay for the privilege. In some *quartiers*, renting a parking box is the only sure way of having some place to put their car.

If you're lucky enough to find one with electricity, it could be a goldmine. The average price paid by renters of an electrified parking garage in Paris is €195/mo. or 15% more than one without electricity. With more and more electric cars on the road, demand to power up in-home or in-garage is growing phenomenally and won't abate anytime soon. A standard 16 ampere or 20A plug is sufficient to fully charge a Tesla model S overnight. You may also consider adding a charging station (figure €1 300 installed, minus a possible €300 subsidy) so your renter gets their battery to 100% in just a couple hours.

A box with a plug could be of interest to many besides car owners. Armies of electric scooters, bicycles, *trottinettes* and other individual mobility contraptions are scattered about cities. They've all got to be charged somewhere, and stored from time to time.

Bands want to practice without disturbing the neighbors. Artisans need to store equipment in-between repair jobs. Folks living in cramped quarters nearby could want *une pièce en plus* for their household items and furniture, especially if they're undergoing renovations for several months while continuing to live there.

One Paris investor claims to double their income by renting to four motorcyclists at €50 a pop, where one car would usually net €100/mo. Up until September 2022, street parking for two-wheelers was free and sidewalk *stationnement* was tolerated in Paris. No more.

While electric scooters can still park for free (not likely to last), 94% of two-wheeled motorized vehicles in France use internal combustion engines. Each day, 100 000 of these circulate in Paris, and every one of them now needs to pay for parking. Paris claims 43 000 paid street parking places for motorcycles, but this could be a stretch as some spots are counted twice, usable by both 4-wheelers and 2-wheelers.

Enforcement from camera-equipped vehicles plus automated ticketing from independent providers like Streeteo makes it easy for the mayor of Paris to collect fines on a massive scale. Impounding roundups are frequent and costly. A whole population of *motards* who never had to pay before are now forced to. They'd be attracted to a safe and dry box for around €2/day.

Yespark claims a 70% increase in demand from motorcyclists since 2021. Saemes, Indigo and Vinci also run paid underground parking lots with some scooter slots, but not nearly enough. The 12p5 platform shows 5 000 monthly spots for motorcyclists in Paris from €35-€65/mo. All street spaces and subterranean parking lots combined will still not be able to hold all the motos and scooters that come to the capital.

A parking space equipped with videosurveillance can also net you more. An automatic garage door opener could be a plus, if feasible. Most boxes have ceilings too low for a door machine and a car, or doors unadapted, or simply no power to lift. Folks in France don't seem to mind opening their garages manually, and they'd definitely prefer a tight security lock to the convenience of automation.

When you choose to exit, local real estate agencies are very happy to take on the sale of your parking property for a reasonable fee (5-10% commissions). It's easy money for them: little to no inspections, few on-site showings, a captive audience of prospects with cars living in the neighborhood and a steady demand from investors outside the area. There are even agencies, like ParkAgence who specialise in selling these properties.

Resources: WePark, MonsieurParking, 12p5

Mobile home

Definition: an independent unit on a lot owned and managed by a separate company

Budget: new €30 000 to €70 000; used €20 000

Risk: high

Evaluation: In 2020, about 22 million Americans, or 6.7% of the population, lived in mobile homes. The largest mobile park landlord is Sam Zell's Equity LifeStyle Properties (ELS), which owns 170 250 units across the country and the asset is the main part of his $5.3 billion fortune.

So yeah, there are some folks that have made some money with this play. The economic environment of France may not lend itself quite as well to producing income. Let's look at the pros and cons.

Advantages- no *taxe foncière* nor *taxe d'habitation*; Max rental revenue for a week in high season from €700 to €1 200.

Disadvantages- Extremely seasonal; If it's in a managed park, you won't own the land and must pay ground rent of €3 000 to €5 000 per year; Fragile construction (exposed pipes commonly bursting in winter, for example); design falls quickly out of fashion; Small, inactive resale market for an asset guaranteed to lose value over time; Tons of competition, not only from prevalent *mobil homes*, but from more desirable and unique dwellings like yurts, '*roulottes*,' tiny homes also catering to budget travelers.

If you're sure you can make your money back, or perhaps turn a small profit within a decade, and enjoy for yourself from time to time, go for it. For most others, this will not be a money-making investment.

Resources: article- "How much can you make"

Fractional Ownership

Definition: this is when you secure a portion of the time usage of a property (timeshare), up to actually legally owning a portion of the property.

Budget: €50 000 to €300 000

Risk: high

Evaluation: This is an $8 billion industry with an unsavory reputation. More than 10 million US households have bought in, and 85% of them regret their decision.

Almost all vehicles of this type are designed for the personal pleasure of owners. They're not designed to produce income, and to do so would require the consent of your fellow owners. If you have that consent, and the building authorises such use (STR, for example) then these properties very well could be generating income.

The tremendous advantage is that you could get access to an exceptional product at a fraction of the cost.

The disadvantages of timeshares are numerous, as John Oliver pointed out in his 25-minute video segment. As an investment product, yield will likely be lower. Expenses are higher, with no way to control them, as the buyer has no choice but to have the property managed by the same company who sold you into the plan… for life. That company often unilaterally raises its fees, and the owner have no say.

As with all collective ownership or 'timeshare' schemes, there's no easy way out. Like multi-level marketing, or a pyramid scheme, you've got to recruit someone new before you can get off the roller-coaster yourself. There just aren't extensive resale markets for such products. Real estate agents either don't want to (they'll make chump change) or don't know how to (complexity) sell such products. You could go back to the agent who initially sold you the property, if they're still in that business. If you bought from a developer which doesn't property manage, chances are they're long gone. There are timeshare exit companies around, but they can gouge clients even worse than the initial seller.

Still, there are several new companies getting into the game of fractional property, and their model could be better, notably because you actually **own** a percentage of the property (usually in an SCI). According to Prello, people who own their second home outright only stay in their property an average of 40 days per year anyway. Why not only pay for what you use? When you're not there, the property manager is generating revenues without you having to lift a finger.

These startups are mostly focusing on the high-end luxury market, which is less susceptible to downturns. Properties are typically standalone, with greater appeal, and a higher per-night rate.

Services are packaged by the startups, which claim specialization catering to the hoi polloi. The right property could marry both lucrative nightly rates plus high occupancy. If you live within a short travel-time away, you could enjoy for yourself at the last-minute when there are gaps in the calendar.

Buyers beware there's a backlash against these kinds of arrangements. The revolt is led by powerful home owners' associations (HOAs), neighborhood groups and municipalities. Since the occupiers are technically owners, there might not be much these groups can do to prevent usage by fractional title-holders. However, they could restrict rentals, or disturb your guests.

Also, these are new companies in a new market that's extremely volatile. Pacaso cut staff by 30% in 2022.

Resources: Pacaso; Altacasa; Mansio; Sonhaus; Prello; Adrian Leeds Group

Proptech *parts*

Definition: own stock in French tech companies operating in the property sector.

Budget: €1 000 or more

Risk: moderate

Evaluation: Some of the more established Proptech companies in France are currently private, but accepting micro investments from individuals who are not business angels.

Resources: Masteos, IAD, GuestReady, Smartrenting

SCPI

Definition: this is the French version of what's called a Real Estate Investment Trust or REIT in the US and elsewhere

Budget: €10 000 or more

Risk: high

Evaluation: Many real estate companies are looking for capital, and have opened their equity to individuals. US company Wander operates a portfolio of luxury properties around the world that they run as short-term vacation rentals, and their entry ticket is $10 000.

REITs around the world almost universally lost money in 2022. Indexes were down -24% in the US and Hong Kong, and -20% in Australia. S&P Global Intelligence compared 133 REITs in North America and saw they collectively lost -58% of their value in 2022.

Strangely, the French version, SCPI, did quite well in the same period. In 2022, these investment vehicles raised more money than ever before in France. The average rate of return of an SCPI in 2022 was 4.53%. They haven't done as well in 2023, so expect rife volatility.

Resources: Wander

Whatever you choose, start somewhere.

CHAPTER TWENTY-SIX
Financing

Unless you have at least €100 000 cash, you're going to be looking at a loan to finance your investment purchase. Banks in France won't offer a home loan for less than €100 000 anyway.

Maybe you're an all-cash buyer, like 29% of purchasers in the US and 40% of purchasers in France. You may be tempted to skip this chapter, but then you'd be missing out on the advantages of bank loans and generous rental property tax deductions in France. You'd also lose the '*effet de levier*,' or lever effect afforded by putting up a small amount of your own cash for something that's worth 4x to 5x your initial outlay, producing commensurate rental income.

This section intends to serve as a primer for your property loan exploration.

If you're not a French resident, you're in luck, because there's no restriction on foreign ownership of property in France. This is not the case in Canada, which recently enacted a ban on foreign ownership from non-residents through 2025. Italy has something similar in place for non-EU residents.

Non-residents might be asked to pay a slightly higher APR (3-4 decimal points), or put up a bit higher cash amount for the down payment (5% more). This is a small price to pay versus the benefit they receive, as explained in the following paragraphs.

If you're from the UK, where many properties are sold on the disadvantageous leasehold basis, you're in luck again. Almost all properties in France (apartments included) are sold on a freehold basis, meaning you're acquiring both the walls <u>and</u> the land/ground. You don't have to pay a separate 'ground rent' as it's packaged in the entire lot which belongs to you at completion.

Leasehold in France is called '*Bail Réel Solidaire*' or *BRS*. All programs are run through an entity called an '*organisme de foncier solidaire*' or *OFS*. It's only accessible for low-income households wishing to purchase social housing (*HLM*). Costing up to 40% less at purchase, the resale market is capped. While in the UK, a freehold with less than 100 years left on the lease is considered a dangerous investment, in France the leases only **begin** with a maximum of 99 years and go down from there. The new BRS program has gotten off to a very slow start, as only 300 units were delivered in 2022.

Your winning streak continues as you look at the interest rates (*taux*) available to borrowers in France, which are at least half the APR (*TAEG*) you could expect in the UK or the US. In June 2022, the average APR for a 15-year loan in the United States was 4.48%. At the same time in France, for an identical 15-year fixed term, the average was 1.3%... more than three times <u>less</u>.

Later in 2022, the US hit a peak of 7.2% APR. This means in the space of only 8 months, the US went from a historic low of 3% to a 20-year high. This level of volatility doesn't happen in France.

French rates are half those found in Portugal. They are habitually one point less than in Germany or Italy.

These low French rates are accessible, no matter the usage of the property in question. This is welcome news for Britons, who are used to paying a much higher rate for investment real estate (5-7% APR is common), than for their principal residence. Brits also pay more APR if it's a second home, or if they're buying through a limited company. These distinctions aren't taken into account by French banks, which offer the same rate, no matter who's living there, and regardless if the buyer is a company.

In 2021, the average rate held for outstanding loans was 1.53%. That's for **all** loans on the books, not just the homeowners who refinanced recently.

Almost all French loans are fixed-rate. Just like in the US, 99% of mortgages in France are offered with fixed interest. Compare that to the uncertainty of variable rates, which are dominant in other European markets like Spain: 52%, Sweden: 50%; the UK: 42%, Italy: 19%, the Netherlands: 13%, Germany: 10% and Denmark: 9%. The fixed period in France continues for the **life** of the mortgage, unlike the UK, where any fixed period at the beginning (2-10 years maximum) is followed by variable rates the rest of the way.

French borrowers pay the bulk of their interest in the early years of the loan. Mortgage Interest represents approximately 40% of the monthly repayment in Y1-Y2, 30% of monthly in Y3-Y4, 25% of monthly in Y5 and so on.

* * *

Loan capacity

Before you go shopping, it's important to know how much you have to spend ('*capacité de prêt immobilier*' aka '*taux d'endettement*' aka '*estimation d'emprunt*'). This involves knowing the way that banks think, and the criteria they use to judge a borrower's profile.

The first thing you need to know is that a French bank will focus more on **you** than on the property. Since this concerns an investment, their reasoning may be *étrange* to you.

In the UK, banks evaluate BTL purchases more on the quality of the project, rather than the salaried position of the borrower. Once the borrower, who's already owned a home previously, passes the hurdle of showing £25 000 annual gross income that doesn't come from rentals, they'll turn their full attention to the project.

UK banks want to know they're investing in a good deal. If they consider that it is, and the landlord appears to know what they're doing, the bank is likely to give the green light. Yes for 40% debt-to-income ratio. Yes for entrepreneurs. Yes for buying through a company. Yes for an interest-only loan. Yes for seniors who wish to continue reimbursement when they're 100 years old. A French bank would say no to all these things.

The *taux d'usure* and 35% max

In France, there's not one but two ceilings you'll confront when asking for a loan. The first, the '*taux d'usure*' doesn't exist anywhere else but France. It dictates the maximum total interest rate a bank can offer. It artificially squeezes out certain populations. In Q4 of 2022 alone, 1/5 of loan denials were due to this.

It's a moving target, changed monthly, with different levels for each type of loan and length. In November 2023, the usage rate was set at 5.91% for a 20-year or more home loan.

The second is the '*capacité d'emprunt*.' No more than 35% of your income can be used up in a bank loan. To get an idea of how much a bank would loan to you, start with one of the free simulators online. The website calculator won't provide a definite response, but it will give you a good first draft ballpark. Reliable ones should be found at Service Public (government), Beanstock (agent & service provider), Les Furets (aggregator), or Pretto (broker). Or, you could search '*simulateur ou calculatrice de capacité de prêt immobilier*.'

To give you an idea, a couple earning the minimum wage (SMIC) which has saved up the required down payment should be able to qualify to borrow €150 000 over a 25-year period. The mortgage payments would be normally equivalent to their monthly rent. However, they'll have to be satisfied living in a smaller dwelling they own, rather than a bigger one they rent.

An online simulator will also allow you to play around with the figures:
- ♦ "What is the lowest down payment we can give and still qualify?"
- ♦ "Can we borrow 10 000 from Mother?"
- ♦ "If we waited 3 months when my trial period ends, would that work?"
- ♦ "How about we assume the flat we're going to sell is worth 20 000 more than the estimation?"

If you explored a bunch of different scenarios with a bank, you'd have to change your story several times, lessening the bank's confidence in you. A skittish banker is not likely to grant you a loan. So, use the online simulators first to see which scenario would most benefit your situation. Then, take your story to the banker, and stick to it.

Term

In most cases, 20 years is the maximum loan period you're likely to get for an investment property from a French bank. If you go in for a shorter term, you could get a more favorable APR, as 15-year is lower than 20-year, 10 is lower than a 15-year, etc.

The 30-year loan periods you can get in the US are unheard of in France. In 2022, it became illegal for banks to loan for longer than 25 years. New builds are an exception, but banks are still limited to 27 years for those.

You may get a bank to go all the way to 25 years for a loan on a main residence, but don't expect that term length for an investment property. The longest you're likely to be offered is a term of 20 years for a mortgage on a rental.

This book is about rental income, so we won't go into detail about a main residence mortgage. However, knowing a bit about how banks think on this subject can be helpful to your process.

The way banks evaluate dossiers for an investment versus a main residence differ in one key area. An investment assumes you'll continue to pay for lodging elsewhere. So, the bank will add your house payment (loan) and/or rent (lease) to your debts. This will increase your debt ratio versus your income, and in doing so, reduce the amount that you can borrow. If your obligations are already at 35% or more of your net income, the amount you can borrow is **zero**.

However, if the loan is to purchase your main residence, it is assumed your other lodging payments will disappear. Your other home loan monthly payment becomes €0 after you sell that property. Your monthly rental payment becomes €0 after you break your lease. That dramatically frees up the amount of new debt you can take on. The bank will be very happy to fill you up with debt in the form of a home loan up to the limit of 35% of your net income.

The bank may be suspicious if the target property, meant to be your new main residence, is far from your current home and place of employment. You could say that your job allows you to work remotely, or that you plan to commute (many people do this M-F, even working internationally, then coming home for the weekend).

The bank may wonder why your family of three plan to leave your 3-bedroom dwelling for a 1-bedroom property. You could say you're downsizing, or junior is going away to university.

Of course, you needn't proceed in this deception if your loan capacity for an investment is equal to or greater than the amount needed to finance the purchase.

If you're wondering about the legality of this approach, it's true that in the UK the post-loan switcheroo would be considered fraud. Not so in France. Once a borrower takes possession of their property, they can use it for any legal and authorized purpose. That includes choosing to rent instead of occupy your new acquisition. French laws allow you to change your mind at some point in the future after your transaction clears. Mortgage contract terms may ask you to reveal a change of usage to the bank, but the French laws do not oblige you to comply.

Down payment or Deposit

For a standard profile buying an investment property, you can bet the bank will ask you to front 20-25% of your own money toward the purchase price. The bank will not finance associated charges such as the Notary fees, or the real estate agent's commissions, unless the mandate is '*honoraires charges vendeur*'

The bank may offer to finance renovations, which will go into the overall *enveloppe* or loan amount.

Non-residents

You may be the King of Siam, but that won't help you get a mortgage from a lender in France. French banks have a strong preference for financing fiscal residents in France. This has to do with two main reasons: risk and reward.

On the risk side, you must remember that the French bank won't assume any. Look ahead in this chapter for the section about loan insurance. That's just for starters.

The UK and US are more attractive than France for multiple property owners, older investors, licensed professionals (doctors, lawyers, etc.), entrepreneurs and company directors. This is because financial institutions in France are both constrained in the ways they can evaluate a property purchase, and banks also tend to see these profiles as too risky. If the guy who vouches for the income of the borrower… is the borrower himself (as the head of the business) the bank won't trust that endorsement at all.

If a significant portion of a borrower's income is variable, i.e. comes from commissions or a bonus, the bank in France will not count **any amount** of this revenue if it comes from a job they've held less than three years. French banks will only consider the fixed salary, and ignore the rest, regardless if it represents 50% of the total compensation and is consistently earned.

In France, those who wish to invest in multiple properties can hit a wall quite quickly. This wasn't the case in the past, as half of rentals in the land are owned by landlords with two or more other properties. They'd be hard-pressed to add to their portfolios today. The marketshare of these *multipropriétaires* will surely diminish in the future.

New strict regulations prevent lending which pushes the applicant over the 35% debt threshold. If that income is from a foreign source, or made by someone from one of the professions listed above, the bank is less likely to trust it, and may not count it in their calculations.

People over 60 are doubly discriminated against. They may have €1 million in their account, but if their income/pension is €2 000/mo. net, with no debt, they'll be capped at a €700 per month mortgage (€700 is 35% of €2 000), regardless if the property can easily fetch rent of €1 000/mo. In addition, the term offered will be much shorter, as the banks are extremely reluctant to have mortgage clients in their 70s, and they definitely want to avoid **any** period of repayments from 75-year-old clients, who are uninsurable.

The bank does have slight manoeuvrability, as one fifth of the loans they award can be "exceptions" which invite further scrutiny from the oversight authority. However, French banks are lending for BTLs in less than 5% of these exceptions. So, no matter your profile, your chances of getting an exception granted for your investment are slim and none.

Banks in France regard collateral as a last resort. They're not in the business of repossessing, nor selling assets (even if they've appreciated greatly) like houses. They have a particular aversion to auctions, where the outcome is incertain.

These are considered extreme cases that take them away from their core business, and light years away from their comfort zones. **You** are their customer, and they want no other. Certainly, they have no interest in deploying the effort or expense of reselling your house. However, if the owner stops paying the mortgage, the bank is more likely to exercise their right to force the owner to sell. As all transactions go through the notaire, the notary will collect for the bank before the owner sees one eurocent.

On the reward side, if you don't live in France, and don't direct deposit your salary or pension into the bank where your loan is held (a requirement in 99% of funding cases), they'll say, "*à quoi servez-vous?*" meaning "what good are you?" The bank can't sell you any other of their 100s of overpriced services like insurance, car loans, consumer lines of credit and such. Nor can they sting you with the average €215/year that people in France pay for basic banking like a checking account and debit card (commonly offered for free in the UK and US).

If your income goes up, the French bank won't benefit in any way. If you have children, the French bank can't draw them into their lair, where they'll pay dividends for 20 years. You, the borrower, will probably soon forget they exist, which doesn't bode well for the French bank developing a relationship with you. If they can't treat you like a '*vache à lait*' or 'cash-cow' they'd much prefer you find another farm.

Some non-residents would be better off by waiting, if it is their intention to move to France or retire there in the future. Once their '*carte de séjour*' or residence permit is four years old, the banks treat them just like the locals.

Other non-residents who can't wait, might try to get a loan from their home country. Although it almost certainly will be more expensive than a loan from a French bank, at least it lets them get in the game. Having a seat, any seat, at the table of rental property investing in France is well worth the trouble.

Brokers

Your best first point of call could be with a mortgage broker (*courtier en prêt bancaire*). You may be looking at the historically low rates, and saying, "Why the hell do I need a broker? It's not worth the broker fee to have them negotiate from 1.1% down to 0.9%!" It's true a broker will typically charge you around €1 500 (making an additional half a point compensation from the bank behind your back). It's also true that -0.2% over 10 years of a €130 000 loan would only save €1 440.

However, for certain profiles, especially non-residents and newcomers, a broker can be the difference between getting in the game, and staying on the sidelines. For others, no matter their status, the terms and conditions of the offer can have a much greater impact on its attractiveness than the APR. That's the real reason to pay for a broker, if they're good.

Pretto is one startup broker in France offering lower fees. Others like Blue Sky cater more to non-residents . Still others like French Private Finance hold out a white gloved hand to the very wealthy.

Brokers will be able to negotiate with the type of commercial banks known as a '*sociétaires*' which includes such brands as Le Crédit Lyonnais,

Société Général, La Banque Postale, BNP Paribas and HSBC.

HSBC is leaving the French market, and will be called the CCF in 2024, which was its name before HSBC acquired them two decades ago. It's unclear how this will affect their mortgage business. One thing is for sure, if you're a client of HSBC in another country, the CCF won't give a damn.

One thing to keep in mind is that brokers in France DON'T work with '*mutualiste*' banks, who are similar to credit unions in the US in that they are 'owned' by their clients (*actionnaires*).

It's no wonder that in France only 40% of loan agreements were negotiated by brokers, versus 80% in other markets, like the UK.

The fact that credit unions don't work with brokers means that for at least half of the market, you're going to need to go to the banks one by one. *Mutualiste* banks include the Crédit Mutuel, Banque Populaire, Crédit Agricole, CIC, and the Caisse d'Epargne. An added layer of complexity is that these banks are decentralized. The Crédit Mutuel of Caen might tell you '*Non*' but your same dossier could get a '*Oui*' for financing from the Crédit Mutuel of Toulouse. So, don't write off a bank brand completely if one of the branches turns you down.

One tremendous advantage of the *mutualiste* banks is that they can make decisions quickly at the branch level. The director of a Société Général branch in Lyon or Marseille has to check with the headquarters (*siège*) in La Défense for every single home loan application, no matter how basic, and wait weeks for a response. In contrast, the CIC branch manager in *Perpète les oies* (Podunk town) can agree right away, and her word is as good as gold.

Another advantage is that the terms and conditions offered by the *mutualiste* banks are often more attractive than the *sociétaire* banks. You may wish to take the best deal through a broker, and see if you can get better by going directly to a *mutualiste*.

Insurance for mortgages

Around 1.5% APR for a mortgage in 2022 is not the totality of what folks pay, though. The French system has a separate rate for loan insurance (*assurance prêt immobilier* or *garantie emprunteur*). This insures that if you die, become incapacitated or can't work, that the remaining balance of the loan will be paid off. Investment loans don't require the 'can't work' coverage, so their insurance is a bit lower, albeit still exorbitant.

The loan insurance rate varies wildly based on the profile of the borrower(s). If you're in your 20s and in good health, you might pay only 0.005% to 0.30% more. If at least one of you is over 50 years old and has diabetes, you might pay up to 2% more. That's right, the insurance could end up costing **more** than the loan!

The health checks are also incredibly invasive. It starts simple enough, with a form (*questionnaire de santé* or *déclaration d'état de santé = DES*) posing 14 yes or no questions. You're allowed to omit any incident 10 years old or older, including cancer for which you're now in remission, and all operations like a caesarian, getting your appendix out or tonsil removal. If you answer yes to any of them, you're in for further inspection.

If your questionnaire turns up something they'd like to know more about, they'll ask you to drop your drawers for the lab coats. Even if you check 'no' for every single one, you'll almost certainly be asked to endure these exams if you wish to borrow more than €400 000, or if you are (or you'll become) over 60 years of age during the loan term. The bank's insurer may require a complete physical, blood and urine samples, a mammogram and other comprehensive examinations, performed by their own physicians. These are not your family doctors, or GPs with your health in mind. They're there to find weaknesses, or more likely, a pretext to charge higher interest.

US homeowners are used to paying for this coverage as well (without the body prodding). However, in the 'States, once the owner has at least 20% equity in the property, they can forego loan insurance, which protects the bank. Most US folks replace it with a policy in which the beneficiary is themselves, not the bank.

Not so in France, where homeowners need to keep paying this insurance even if they have 99% equity in the property, and the risk to the bank is infinitesimal. To the last *centime* of their mortgage, 20+ years later, the borrower will have to carry this insurance.

Loan insurance isn't actually a legal obligation. It's just that there isn't a single bank in the land which will let you borrow without it. There have been not one, not two, but **three pieces of legislation** (*loi Murcef, loi Lagarde, loi Hamon*) passed in an attempt to release the banks' stranglehold on the consumer. In 2022, fully 88% of mortgage insurance policies were still held by the same institution (or its subsidiaries) which issued the loan.

Another specific text enacted in June 2022 limited the banks' ability to subject borrowers to the health questionnaire: not for cancer survivors in remission for 5+ years; not for hepatitis C sufferers; not for diabetics.

While the laws have helped, you'll still need to go into battle mode to successfully exercise your rights and win the negotiation. An enormous part of your profitability depends on your efforts in this regard, or those of the representatives you choose to send into the fray.

While it's damn near impossible to do away with the *assurance emprunteur* altogether, there are three things you can do to reduce the insurance burden.

First, ask the bank to defer (*délégation d'assurance*) the insurance by giving a proxy to a 3rd-party provider, which is your right under the loi Lagarde (at the time of the initial loan offer). If you go through a mortgage broker (*courtier d'assurances*), they can negotiate this clause from the bank for you upfront. French banks make a lot of margin by selling you their own bloated in-house policy (*assurance groupe*) packaged with the loan. They're not inclined to acquiesce to your request to shop around, unless you draw them into a corner, or you hit them with the Hamon hammer (right to change law).

You corner them by asking for the preliminary offer rate first, without mentioning that you want delegation. Once they've given you the percentage rate in writing, then make your request. At that point, they can either say '*oui*' or '*non*' but they can't reneg on their offer. If you ask for delegation right off the bat, your APR offer will likely be higher.

If they turn you down, but you still like their rate, you can proceed, knowing you have the ability to leave in the future anyway. Since 2014, the loi Hamon has given consumers the right to get out of abusive contracts, like forced packaged insurance with loans. Even if your contract expressly says you can't, you can take your business to one of the many low-cost alternatives, like April. These upstarts are typically 60-80% less expensive, for comparable coverage.

The banks play an unfair game of convoluting their policies, which makes an exact like-for-like switch tricky. They have the right to refuse, within reason, if the competitive coverage is lower. "*Désolé*, our policy covers up to €205 000 if you're struck by lightning, and theirs only goes up to €200 000. *Refusé.*" Even if you have to upgrade to the next-level with the upstart, they'll still save you at least four or five figures.

You may have to wait a year to bail, until the 1st anniversary date of your loan signature. There's only a 1-month window each year on the date you signed up. Legislators recently freed this up to 'at any moment' but only for new loans from September 2022.

Second, if you're buying as a couple (mandatory if you're married under the *communauté* regime), you can play with the partitions (*repartition* or *quotité*). Let's imagine *monsieur* is a 55-year-old smoker, and *madame* is 44 and fit as a fiddle. He's riskier, so his rate is 1.2%, and hers is 0.8%. On a straight 50/50 split, that's an average of 1%, meaning on a €500 000 loan, they'll spend €5 000 on loan insurance for the first year (and possibly every year, depending on their conditions).

What if, instead, we ported 80% of the insurance risk on *madame* and only 20% on *monsieur*? That would bring their average rate down to 0.88%, and their cost to €4 400 the first year (and possibly subsequently). Already, they've saved €600 in Y1 and could stand to save up to €12 000 on a 20-year loan.

The insurer may push back if Mr. earns 60% of the household income, and Mrs. brings home 40% of the bacon. Usually, they give you quite a bit of leeway, so push for the best ratio which they're willing to accept.

Thirdly, and lastly, ask that they make it digressive (*digressif*). Instead of paying the same amount every year, as the amount of remaining capital (*capital restant dû*) decreases, the APR will apply to the reduced amount. The insurance portion might cost you €200/mo. in year one, and only €50/mo. in year nine.

Thankfully, there have been recent efforts to do away with health exams, and even questionnaires altogether, in the loan application process. Crédit Mutuel announced they would stop asking for existing clients. Crédit Agricole is thinking about it.

Alternatives

If you're still a bit short of your goal, there are some supplementary solutions you may be eligible for, or you may wish to consider. We outline them below.

PTZ

The *prêt à taux zéro* is a complementary mortgage to your main mortgage. The rate isn't really 0% as the name would imply, but closer to 1%.

It's awarded to certain acquirers, like first-time buyers, lower-income profiles and now those who commit to more sustainable housing. The new '*éco' prêt à taux zéro* program was extended to the end of 2023, loaning up to €50 000 toward the purchase of a dwelling which requires significant refurbishment works.

These offers became less interesting as the market rate approached the PTZ rate. In 2023, with the market rate racing toward 4% and perhaps higher, the PTZ is generating increased attention. If you have this option available to you it would be worthwhile to look into it.

Partial funders

There are a few actors out there who will 'go in' on the project with you. It's not a joint venture (JV), per se, but it works a bit like that. They'll front up to 20% of the purchase price, with a maximum limit of €100 000 (so, no properties above €500 000). Also, they don't ask for monthly payments, so there's no hit against your loan capacity. They don't ask you to pay them back until you sell, or a certain number of years have gone by.

There's a catch, of course. The compensation they expect approaches loan shark levels. They'll front 10% of the purchase price, for example, but they'll 'own' 15.5% of the resale value. If your future sale is a wash (same price as you paid) they'll still have made 55% on their investment.

In a rising resell market, you as the owner should make more than enough on the 80-95% you 'own' on the property to cover the partial funder. However, in a flat or down market, you may be giving up more than you want to. Their offer is likely to be more attractive to those who are a bit short of their dream, or who wish to gamble on a property above their price range. These part-financier/part-owner companies include Les Nouveaux Propriétaires, Eliosor and Virgil.

Home Equity financiers

For the lucky few, there's a small chance you could unlock some of the value of your property, and turn that property value into cash for further investment. In the UK and the US, and many other places, there are very common and well-known financial products which allow homeowners to do this, such as a 2nd mortgage, a home equity loan, etc. A HELOC or home-equity line of credit can be had in the US for 85% of the home's value, regardless of how much of the home you actually own.

While some of these offers do exist in France, they are so restrictive, or unattractive economically, that an extremely limited population could or would sign up for one. The only product resembling a 2nd mortgage in France would be a bridge loan (*prêt relais*). It's used exclusively when a proprietor buys a new primary residence and takes possession before their old property completes sale. It's intended to be used for a very short period, from weeks to months, and almost never for more than a year. And you wouldn't want it to be either, as the interest rates offered are not competitive.

To get a home equity loan, you would most certainly need to own your collateral property 100% outright. Even then, the bank would be reticent to loan you more than 50% of the value (verified by a 3rd party) of that home.

If you already own another property outright, there are limited ways to release some of that equity in order to fund a real estate investment. Players making offers in this vein include Les Nouveaux Proprietaires, Partners Finances, Solidus and StayHome.

The offers aren't straightforward home equity loans like the ones you may be familiar with in the US or the UK. They can resemble shared ownership schemes, or outright takeovers like a reverse mortgage (*viager*). Keep in mind that your goal here is to receive a big lump sum now which can be used as a down payment or refurbishment budget for a separate acquisition. You're **not** interested in getting a monthly or yearly annuity, because that's not going to help you complete a real estate purchase which you then use for rental income.

These are very new and complex business models which may not be right for everyone, even those with a keen grasp of financials. It's best to be accompanied by a legal advisor when evaluating.

Rent-to-own (RTO) or Leaseback

For those who covet a bigger, better property closer to where they want to be, but don't quite have the profile to get the corresponding bank loan, a number of startups offer a pathway to proprietorship. They are called 'Rent-to-own' or *'location avec option d'achat'* or *'leasing immobilier'* companies, which appeal mainly to first-time buyers.

You identify the target property, and if the RTO is OK, they buy it (you chip in 2%) and then rent/lease it back to you. The rental period is typically three years, and the monthly amount includes a savings portion which will go toward the purchase. The rent is much lower than a mortgage, allowing you to save for a down payment. The RTO watches your nest egg grow and advises when your profile will attract a bank to take over. The sale price is negotiated in advance, which should protect against upswings, but not downturns.

Hestia and Sezame are two French companies in this new area. Hestia doesn't actually own the houses it purportedly buys, but instead 'manages' it for other deep-pocketed institutional investors.

US company Flow is the most high-profile startup in the space, raising $350M backing Adam Neumann, the same founder who almost tanked WeWork. Ribbon ran such a scheme into the ground before being scooped up by EasyKnock, who has an equally spurious model. Big-money playah Loftium runs the riskiest venture of all in the US, named 'host-to-own,' where STR guests are expected to finance the nest egg necessary to make the house yours in a matter of 3 years.

Investors need not apply for these schemes in France because, as far as we can tell from what little information leaks from these secretive startups, the properties cannot be sub-leased during the 3-year rental period. Even so, such a scenario isn't likely to be cashflow positive, given the structure. The startups won't have the funds necessary to keep so many properties on their books past 36 months, and their backers won't stick around past that. They need relatively quick 3-year exits to finance new buyers.

On the other hand, investors need predictable models. So changing the game to something more capital-intensive and certainly less profitable after the 3Y mark is unappealing to investors. If sub-leasing becomes OK, this could be a way for a budding investor to get started, with minimal skin in the game.

* * *

iBuyers

A number of startups now do all-cash offers on homes. They espouse the advantages of transacting quicker (1 mo. less from *promesse* to *acte*) and avoiding the middlemen (agents) and expenses associated with marketing and selling real estate.

They are called 'iBuyers' as they use sophisticated algorithms to quickly determine the value of your property. Startups in this space operating in France include Casavo, Dili, Homeloop, Properstar, Vendez-votre-maison and Zefir.

These companies do not offer an attractive solution for most investors. They can buy your current home, but won't help you get a new one, nor an investment property. The offer they make is inevitably lowball and take-it-or-leave-it. If you're in a hurry to recover the money from your illiquid asset to place elsewhere to take advantage of a good deal expiring soon, an iBuyer might come in handy. Otherwise, pass.

Speculators and gamblers

Fans of Robert Kyosaki et al will ask, "is that all there is in France? No crazy financial products? No sanctioned pyramid schemes?" I'm afraid we'll have to answer in the affirmative.

In the USA, it's obvious we've learned nothing from the 2008 subprime fiasco. Again today, speculators and gamblers in the 'States are being allowed to borrow far beyond their means. Using "debt service coverage ratio" business loans, even self-employed people with little income, or worse, "Non-Owner, No Income" NONI profiles can amass a scary number of properties.

They all think the new eldorado is in building a vacation rental empire from OPM. If you don't, they'll tell you you're missing out. If you settle on one or two properties, they'll call you a '*petit joueur*' or loser. Don't listen to them.

Although property owners in France would all like a bit more flexibility from the system, folks here are pretty thankful for the safeguards. There was a bigger decline in house prices in the US, minus 20%, in both 2008 and 1990.

It's not as if the financial markets have penalized France in terms of capital gains from home sales. From 2008 to 2013, during the global financial crisis, and a period when mortgage interest rates were climbing, home sale prices rose 50% in the Paris region. Since 1996, French residential real estate sale prices rose 238% for houses and 214% for apartments, according to INSEE.

Residential values have increased here as much or more than practically anyplace else. When they drop, it's usually much less and slower than elsewhere. In the last 50 years, the USA has suffered 12 recessions. France faced only four.

We've got it pretty good, comparatively, those of us who've invested in French property. Nobody wants to kill the golden goose.

Finance for real estate in France is a vast subject. The preceding paragraphs are by no means exhaustive, but they could help you get to a standard loan proposal (*offre de prêt*) which is suitable, if not entirely optimised.

Those with superior economic acumen see the finance portion as the key to higher yields and building out their portfolio. If this is not your skill-set, or you have no ambition to become a mogul, you should do just fine with a traditional approach.

Experienced investors (*investisseurs aguerris*) go well-beyond the basics, with complex high-risk financial products, and heavily leveraged structures pushing the limits of their debt ceiling. These tricks of the trade include interest-only loans (*prêt crédit in fine*), BRRR (with the emphasis on the last 'R' for Refinance aka *faire racheter votre crédit immobilier*), bridge loans (*prêt relais*), home equity lines of credit (*prêt hypothécaire* ou *prêt sur valeur immobilier*), joint ventures and peer-to-peer deals. Many of these don't even exist in France, but some do, usually in a format less-attractive for investors. If you have the stomach for such adventures, do an internet search for these terms, or find further reading in some of the books listed in the bibliography.

CHAPTER TWENTY-SEVEN
Big budget

If you're lucky enough to afford buying property, now may be a good time to do so in France. In March 2023, the fifty most populous towns in France all saw their sale property values decrease.

Sure, interest rates have shot up during that time, but they're still lower in France than in most other places, as shown in the preceding Financing chapter. And if you're a fortunate all-cash buyer, interest rates don't concern you. When foreigners buy in Paris, nine out of 10 times they pay cash, meaning only 10% require a loan from a French bank according to estate agency Fredelion.

Big-budget Acquisitions

Since we're talking about high-ticket items, let's first set a couple ground rules for the discussion. We've already broached the subject of finance, so you know you'll probably need a banker on your team, and maybe a mortgage broker, too.

You'll also have to deal with an agent in 70% of cases (only 30% of transactions in France are FSBO or 'for sale by owner'). In 2021 in Paris, there were twice as many real estate agencies as bakeries.

Sellers in France pay 5.5% on average for the services of an estate agent (*agent immobilier*). Don't fool yourself, thinking you, the buyer, don't pay this fee as well. In most cases, the owner has priced at the market rate, and then added his estate agent fees on top. The final price is either shown as '*FAI*' for '*frais d'agence incluses*' (fees included) or '*hors honoraires*' (agent fees expressed separately). In the latter case, the agency's fees are spelled out (*mandat de vente aux charges acquéreur*).

Just like Purplebricks slashed agent prices in the UK, many startups have come on the scene in France with similar flat-fee or low-fee representation. Here, they're called néo-agences, and they go by names like Proprioo, Liberkeys, Hosman and such. They're not of much benefit to the buyer, but when one of these companies has the property's mandate, you know the seller stands to keep more of the proceeds from the sale. That might make them more amenable to price negotiations, as they could still be ahead of the game versus owners selling through a traditional agency.

When the buyer engages a house hunter (*chasseur immobilier*) which is extremely rare, the agency fees (*frais d'agence*) can easily double. Agents rarely share commissions in France, and are reluctant to lower their fees. Everybody in France expects the buyer to pay and pay. You may be a master negotiator, and regularly do better than others who play the game, but you should know these are the norms you'll have to fight against.

It's uncommon to employ the services of a sourcing company to find investment property. This field is quite developed in the UK, but less so in France. Still, there's no shortage in advisors claiming to have found the best areas in which to buy for maximum return. Many agents talk about 'off-market' properties, but outside of luxury homes, these are practically inexistent. Although there is no common MLS, nearly all properties appear on Le Bon Coin, Seloger.com ou Pap.fr. Aggregator apps like Where You Love and Folhomee gather all listings from these sites in one place.

There are organizations like Agora Store, Kadran and WinUp, which specialize in auctions (*enchères*) and distressed property. To participate, you'll need to do all of your due-diligence beforehand, and give a check (*chèque de consignation*) for 5-20% of the estimated property value at the start of the barking. If you do decide to bid before the gavel drops, know that you'll almost certainly need to be an all-cash buyer. Banks will sometimes propose a loan on an auction purchase, but know that if the bank doesn't follow-through with the funds, you'll still be liable to buy. There is no 'cooling-off' period (*délai de rétractation*) either with auctions; you're committed from 'go.' The entirety of the purchase amount will be due within 30-60 days.

The Notary public (*notaire*), your so-called friend and 'legal representative' in the purchase process, will likely cost you more than the other two, the banker and the agent. Property buyers in France are used to paying exorbitant 8%+ taxes to the notary public (*frais de notaire*). These fees are non-negotiable, as almost all of them go to the state. The notary only gets about 1.5%, leaving the rest of the 6.5% as fixed taxes. You might get lucky and have your notary knock off up to a half-point off his fee, but don't count on any better reduction than that.

The equivalent to notary fees in the UK are called 'stamp duty land tax' or SDLT. While it's much more complex to calculate SDLT, with price bands, and exceptions for non-residents and BTL, the end result is that it's much lower for most price points in the UK versus France.

Same thing in the US, where it costs less in taxes to purchase property. The US gets you on the annual property tax, which is almost universally more in the 'States than in French municipalities.

The agency and notary fees in France make buy-to-sell or home 'flipping' unprofitable. In France it doesn't make sense fiscally to flip homes. Owners must wait until the property increases at least 14% in value before it starts to break even. To become appealing for resale could take many, many years.

You'll also need an insurer on your side. It's preferable that your banker is not also your insurer. The reasons were amply covered in the financing chapter.

Finally, you'll need an accountant to come off the bench in the 4th quarter, not to score the winner, but to take points off the other team, the *fisc*! France has signed treaties with many countries to avoid double taxation. In almost all cases, income from France is taxed in France, and income from elsewhere is taxed in that other country. Only the very wealthy who pass a certain threshold are taxed on their global rental profits and property value, when declared to the local authorities.

There's one other thing to be said about taxes, and that concerns filing. Declaring taxes in France can be quite complicated, especially for property investors. In order to get the most out of your money, or simply to avoid errors, fines and penalties, you must employ the services of an accountant, adding to your expenses.

What, Where and How

Let's first look at 'What' to buy, 'Where' to find it, and then 'How' to use it.

What

The most popular big-ticket investments are going to be apartments or houses. When shopping for these, inevitably one of the first questions is "Should I buy new (*neuf*) or existing (*ancien*)?"

Our recommendation might surprise you.

New Build versus Existing

If you're buying for yourself, it's a matter of preference. You could be happy in either *neuf* or *ancien*. But this book is **not** about buying for personal comfort or pleasure. This book is about **income** and **profitability**. In France, in almost **all** cases, existing (*ancien*) properties will give you more of both.

Let's look at the issues with new builds which diminish performance-

***

Quality: you'd expect a new home to be better in terms of materials and quality, but sadly in France this is not always the case. It's a low-margin business where builders routinely only make about 2% profits. The temptation to cut corners is overwhelming. In a brand new complex East of Paris built by Nexity in 2021, after an average storm, massive quantities of rainwater ran into the apartments through the light fixtures and electrical outlets.

Even doing a slap-happy job, they rarely deliver on time, so you must be extremely vigilant on managing your treasury, so you don't give them too much too soon without rental income to offset your outlay. Today, fully 26% of those who reserve a new build end up backing out of the deal according to the FPI.

Size: New homes (including apartments and houses) are now 9m² smaller than they were 20 years ago. That's the equivalent of losing a bedroom. New houses have lost even more, being built 17m² smaller.

It's a form of retail camouflage known as "shrinkflation," ostensibly to combat rampant inflation. Builders give you less property, and still raise the price of their product considerably, to barely tolerable levels.

Value: You'd expect a new unit to be worth more, because they certainly cost more. The price of a newly built house in France rose 37% from 2018 to 2022. Today new French homes cost at least 20% more than the neighboring average at purchase. In 2021, the average paid for a new build nationally was €4 603/m². But as soon as the day after sale, the value of the new build falls dramatically to the surrounding level. The national average paid for all residential property, new and existing, was €2 330/m² in 2021.

It's not as bad as driving a new car off the lot (-30%) but close. The buyer doesn't recoup the original price paid until at least 5 years hence (in a market rising 4% annually). You can forget about flipping a new home in France for big capital gains.

"OK," you say, "that's understood for resale. But what about for income from rentals on new builds?" Unfortunately, it's the same or worse. Renters are often not willing to pay more to live in a new build.

For further evidence, look at the guidance for monthly rent by the city of Paris. Even the *mairie* says you can charge **more** per month per square meter for an apartment built **before** 1946 than you can for a flat built between 1946 and 1990. Rents go up slightly for builds after 1990, but not enough to offset the profitability hit from the high purchase price. Flats from before 1946 will inevitably offer a better yield on rents.

***

Financing: There are some financial advantages to buying on plan, or *VEFA* (*vente en état futur d'achèvement*), like lower VAT (*TVA*), lower notary fees (*frais de notaire*) and, of course, no agent fees (it's also possible to buy an existing home without an agent, and 30% do). But if you sell within 5 years the government will clawback these taxes, washing out any advantage. Buying new in France only makes sense for resale value if you buy and hold, for at least 10 years.

Popularity: Today, new build *VEFA* transactions number five figures annually, compared to more than 1 million transactions in the pre-owned sector. New home sales were only 147 112 units in 2021 (houses and apartments combined), and continued down 20% in Q1 2022 to only 30 000 units sold (FPI). If these were such a good deal, there would be more purchases of new builds, right?

In 2022 only 96 000 new homes were sold, a 31% drop year over year and the worst in 16 years (FPI). For the three months ending February 2023, there was a -27% drop in construction permits awarded, and a -38% decrease in new construction for houses, according to the FFB.

Only 6 000 houses in developments (*lotissements*) were sold in the whole country in 2022. That's about the same number as the metro area of Austin, Texas alone built that year. Maison Phénix, the former construction leader in France, went belly-up. Hexaom, the new number one, went bankrupt (*redressement judiciaire*), but will likely remain in business.

New builds have also fallen out of favor *outre-Atlantique*. In November, 2023, prices for new homes had fallen -18%, versus a 4% increase for existing builds year-over-year.

Sadly, there's simply not enough good new construction in France to meet the needs of a growing population. France has sizeable immigration and the highest birth rate in Western Europe. Demand for housing far outstrips supply. When it comes to new build, the locals say *"non, merci."* Not that shoddy construction. Not at that price. Instead, folks are getting by in older buildings with more people sharing a smaller amount of space.

The researchers at the Thomas More Institute predict by 2030 France will need 850 000 new homes built to meet demand. New constructed units must grow to 400 000 per year from a piddling 100 000 today to close the gap. They'll never make it.

Population growth, including immigration, divorces and the number of people who never marry by choice and choose to live alone, all contribute to growing demand. Everybody has agreed for decades that more construction is needed, yet the problem exacerbates. In 1994, the SDRIF identified that the Parisian region alone lacked 300 000 lodgings.

This deficit wasn't rectified, and might never be.

What is more likely to happen is people accepting to live in smaller spaces. Collective habitation is on the rise, including intergenerational with relatives or strangers sharing, even in spaces once considered to be private quarters. More and more people will accept to share out of necessity. In December, 2023, fully half of Americans 19-29 lived with their parents.

We predict people will feel richer for sharing, monetarily surely, but also interpersonally. This could bring about a tighter connectedness our elders harken back to.

France isn't alone in 'manufacturing' this housing crisis. California, with 39 million inhabitants, only built 118 000 homes in 2022. The UK built 380 000 new homes in 1969, then 200 000 in 1990 and a record low 136 000 in 2012. All the while the British population was growing, continuing to outpace building. Same story in Sweden for the last decade, where new builds numbered 20 000 to 60 000 annually, and the population grew 75 000 to 150 000 each year. Spain needs an additional 1 million properties on the rental market, but they do not build enough new homes. So prices on the rental market increase. In Spain, it's now 64% more expensive to rent a room (flatsharing) than it was five years ago.

Society's ills, and the inaccessibility of property price tags makes a perfect storm for landlords the world over, ensuring strong demand from renters for decades to come. It's the least we can do to offer decent accommodations at a reasonable rate.

DPE and **AER**

Going forward, because of the new regulations on DPE (*diagnostique de performance énergetique*) or energy efficiency, builders should normally improve their upcoming products. This will be great for society over the very long-term, good for owner-occupants over the middle term, but not at all interesting for investors who buy new over the short- to mid-term.

The current DPE must be supplied by sellers prior to purchase, and gives the property a letter rating: A, B, C, D, E, F or G. The new owner assumes this rating, unless they refurbish the property, and get a new, better rating established by a certified *diagnostiquer*. If the G-rated property (4.8 million units) has a renter in-situ, from 2023 the landlord is forbidden from ever raising the rent while that poor rating persists. That restriction will climb to F-rated properties in the future, and on-and-on.

From 2025, G-rated properties (6% of all dwellings) may not be rented at all. Owners can move in to live there themselves, but they can't have a tenant. From 2028, F-rated properties (18%) may not be rented. As of

July 2022, 5.2 million of the 30 million principal residences were classified as F or G. This lowest of the low DPE-rated properties represents no less than 45% of the assets in the Paris region alone. Residences in ski stations have a DPE of F or G about 50% of the time.

From 2034, E-rated properties (24%) may not be rented. Restrictions have yet to be announced for D-rated or above. This means that in five years, one quarter of all existing residences will be forbidden from being rented; **in 10 years, half of homes will be banned from renting**.

Some exceptions exist, like if the required renovations cost more than 50% of the value of the property; or if the exterior can't be insulated because the building is considered an historical monument. The biggest exception, unknown by most, is that the new law (*Loi Climat et Résilience*) and restrictions only apply to LTR. They don't yet apply to STR, or if you want to inhabit yourself.

A winning formula is to make a lowball offer on an existing unit that doesn't meet current or upcoming DPE requirements, and thus is unrentable. Of course, you should first check if the property lends itself to reasonably priced renovations which will make a significant impact on the energy consumption. Les Echos published an article indicating five types of renovations to avoid, considered too expensive and inefficient. The startup Ameliore Mon DPE can advise you whether or not it's worth it, and if yes, handle the renovations.

In September 2022, after the first wave of restrictions went into effect, there was a 10% drop in the number of apartments for rent, according to Bien'ici. This is in stark contrast to what usually happens at back-to-school time. This is one of the consequences of the new DPE requirements. Owners of energy hogs are either quitting the rental business, or selling up. Only 32% of those with a property classed F or G plan to renovate according to FNAIM. Instead, 1 in 4 plan to sell.

In February 2023, SeLoger remarked a -40% drop in rental listings for the properties with the highest energy consumption, and -25% less for all other listings. The tension locative for prospective renters is getting tighter. This is because the owners of energy inefficient properties have chosen *en masse* to sell. Fully 37% of all for sale listings on SeLoger in January 2023 were for *passoires thérmiques*.

Already according to the notaries, properties rated 'F' or 'G' sell for -2% to -25% less than those rated 'D,' which is considered the middle-ground. Bien'ici says between January and September 2021, the number of properties rated 'F' or 'G' put up for sale shot up 74% in Rennes and 70% in Nantes. In Paris, the number of these *passoires thermiques* put up for sale has exploded to 72%.

Most buyers shy away from such bad DPE scores. The worse the rating, the fewer requests are made to see the property. This represents a tremendous opportunity if you're a handy person, or you know how to work the *artisan* contractors effectively.

Renovate this type of property to bring it up to energy specs, thus increasing its value and making it rent worthy. A slew of new contractors and tech companies have started up to tackle the massive renovation challenge. In 2022, by far the segment raising the most VC money in Proptech (€350 million) was in improving the energy efficiency of buildings.

Many of these improvements are highly subsidized, especially for those with low incomes. Government help applies just as well to secondary residences.

A fantastic bonus of home improvement is that the inverse is also true at the higher-end of the rating spectrum. In December 2021, notaries found that homes classed A and B sold for +10%, and those rated C brought +5% in value.

You'll want to get reliable estimates on how much it would cost to bring the dwelling up to spec, and get the renovation contractors to commit to meeting the new minimum rating. Heero estimates that it takes an average of €450 per square meter to renovate and go from one letter to another, or possibly two higher on the DPE chart. If it's too costly to get to a 'D' rating, but 'E' is achievable, that may be a sufficient target to shoot for. Bought today, that still gives you a decade of rental income before future renovations, move-in, or sell-off.

One note of caution to keep in mind, the DPE methodology is quite new and demand is massive. In 2022, 1.9 million DPE inspections were completed by 10 000 diagnosticians, paid between €60 and €150 each. Earning so little, there's a great risk their investigations may not be so thorough, or the temptation to take a bribe would be great.

Most of the checkers (*diagnostiqueurs*) are not as rigorous as they should be. The magazine *60 millions de consommateurs* (similar to Consumer Reports) tested five of them in four different cities, and published their findings in the June 2022 issue. The results varied widely, with a **two-letter gap** found regularly between best and worst ratings for the **same** property. None of the companies was consistently accurate, although they all have a legal obligation to be so. You're better off being accompanied by an expert or reading the documents yourself carefully, and comparing to plans, titles and receipts. If you want a rough estimate, Hellowatt has a basic online simulator.

There also appears to be a loophole in the DPE regulations which seems to maintain the greenlight for STRs. The legislation specifically restricts dwellings which don't meet the norms from LTR, but curiously omits to mention STR. The minister in charge said this would be rectified in 2023, but nothing changed. Many STRs have no insulation or heating, as they're only used in the summertime (think of tents, yurts, cabins, treehouses, etc.). It could be a long time before this exception is closed with legislation *qui tient la route*.

Since the Spring of 2023, the AER (*audit énergétique réglementaire*) goes farther than a DPE and is necessary to sell a detached house or a building.

Denormandie

This is a fairly new scheme of tax reduction which applies to *ancien* or existing builds which require a lot of works. The renovations must cost at least 25% of the total operation. For example, on a home with a €150 000 purchase price, an additional €50 000 in refurbishments must be spent.

Those works must improve the energy efficiency of the dwelling by at least 20%, as measured in kWh/m²/yr. This transformation would only move the property one letter grade higher on the DPE, which should be achievable in many cases.

The refurbished property must be allocated to the rental market for the same six to 12-year length of time and under the same terms as the Pinel program. The tax breaks are identical.

However, it's less likely this scheme would be managed by a promoter, since we're talking existing builds that might be a standalone property, and not part of a collective building. If you do the subsequent property management yourself, or even delegate to an agency, the expenses will likely be less, and certainly more in your control than on a Pinel program.

The Denormandie plan has geographical designations in place. You're required to select a project in a specific zone to reap the tax benefits. So far, 222 towns have been designated "*Cœur de ville*," making them eligible for this scheme.

Property Investment

More and more people in France are choosing residential property as their preferred investment vehicle. The proportion of residential property sold to investors doubled in the last eight years. Investors today make up 30% of home buyers in France. Compare that with 28% in the US of all single-family home sales in February of 2022, according to housing data firm CoreLogic. In 2021, 24% of US single-family home sales were to investors according to Pew Stateline.

You could acquire a new property, separate from your residence, which is selected specifically for its ability to produce revenue. Since property types vary widely, it may be confusing to settle on what makes a good investment. So, let's look at the investors who came before us, and see what they bought.

Although the whole of France is split evenly 50/50 between apartments and houses, the vast majority of investors, 92%, have invested in apartments. More specifically, 60% of rentals are either studios (36% according to LocService.fr) or 1-bedroom flats. This could be a question of cost, as the average purchase price of an investment is €170 000, which makes it more accessible budget-wise.

However, there are investors who own multiple units. They conceivably had the means to buy houses, but instead chose to purchase several apartments instead. There must be a reason for this choice. Perhaps they wish to appeal to a wider number of potential buyers on the resale market. Or maybe they're going by smaller is better. You can almost always charge more per m^2 for a tinier unit.

Whatever the reason they've chosen flats, 93% of investors are satisfied with their investment. You, too, might be content to follow the crowd. There are no bonus points for originality in property investment.

Those who wish to use more creativity in their approach could produce a higher upside, or suffer a downside. For example, only 25% of renters begin their search looking for a studio, but they end up with one in the 36% of cases stated above, likely for budget reasons. Alternately, 20% of renters would choose a house if they could, but only 5% of the rental stock are houses. By going in a different direction as the other investors, you could have success providing to an underserved market.

Office transformation

One play which can be used to circumvent the strict regulation of short-term residential rentals in major cities, consists of buying a space that already has the commercial license. Converting an office into a vacation rental, or a multi-unit hotel or coliving space can be lucrative. There's less of an administrative headache, and quicker turnaround time than pursuing a change of usage which may never be granted. Edgar Suites grew their holdings to 52 apartments through this method alone.

These units are often on the ground floor, street-level, which most French people hate for their primary residence, but travelers aren't bothered about. Real estate agency Rez-de-chaussée specializes in selling these properties, and often has inventory with the commercial license.

Whether you go with new or existing, choose the target property which matches the spot your needle sits on the risk/reward speedometer.

Successions

Surprisingly, the fisc could be your friend for uncovering one type of buying opportunity. Their site impots.gouv.fr offers a new service showing which properties were recently acquired through succession and are currently not occupied (*successions vacantes*). While you won't see the contact info for the new owner(s), you should be able to see their names and the address of the property in question.

Hotel
Definition: multi-room building rented out a room at a time for short stays
Budget: €1M+
Risk: high
Evaluation: According to BPI, on average, you won't recoup your investment in a hotel before at least 10 years have passed. There are a number of hoteliers who are tired of waiting and have been looking to sell up for some time. Perhaps you know something they don't, or have digital skills and communications savvy that they lack. If you think you could do better, and have the funds, read on.

There are several advantages to having multiple rental units. Operations-wise, you can activate economies of scale to purchasing supplies, services such as cleaning, etc.

The flip-side of the coin are all the costly installations and round-the-clock personnel which you must employ.

If you thought the short-term platforms were screwing you by taking 15% commissions, you ain't seen nuthin' yet. Online booking tools, aka 'OBTs,' (and their travel management company parents, aka 'TMCs') like Expedia, Booking.com or Priceline charge hotels upwards of 25% commissions for reservations through their sites.

Resources: BPI article on regulations

Where

In the chapter 'Money: Meters Matter Mostly' we said real estate rental prices were in lockstep with sale prices, which is true in the long-term. However, in the short-term you can find divergences which can be exploited to your benefit.

When/where the rent:sale ratio is high (elevated monthly rental value vs. lower sale price) you can increase your gross margin. That is, until everybody else finds out, buys massively in an area, and drives up sale prices. This is what happened over the last decade in Bordeaux, where the price/m² rose 74% from 2010 to 2020, but rents only rose 3.6% from 2014 to 2019. Those who bought in early are still experiencing great yields, while those who buy today must content themselves with 2-3% net in most cases.

Home sale prices in Bordeaux dropped -5% in 2022, which is a dramatic fall versus the rest of the country, which rose 5.6% overall in 2022. However, prices would need to fall a lot more, and rents rise considerably, for Bordeaux to produce decent yields today.

Montpellier (6.72%), Lyon (6.31%) and Marseille (5.13%) were the cities with the highest average rent increases over the last decade. This will certainly not continue in these areas, which are all now subject to rent control.

The annual *Baromètre de la rentabilité locative* by the magazine *Mieux vivre votre argent* and their partners lists the net yield after tax of new rental investments in sizeable cities throughout the country. Their calculations assume all rental income is generated from LTR furnished (thus LMNP) and nothing else. The highest yield, at 4.34% was for Saint-Etienne, followed by Nancy at 3.38%. In the 2-percents were 14 cities: Rouen, Orléans, Lille, Nice, Paris, Dijon, Toulon, Grenoble, Marseille, Lyon, Caen, Montpellier, Strasbourg and Toulouse, in that order. All others were lower.

Paris owes its top 10 status to the incredibly low property tax currently being applied. In 2023 the Mayor increased property tax by 50%, likely knocking the capital down on the profitability list.

If you're not in one of these urban areas, you may be surprised you can still do STR. In 2022, the biggest leaps in coverage for Airbnb came from the Sarthe the Yonne counties, where hosts increased the most. Sometimes doing something different than the rest can pay off.

Income vs. Patrimonial

Local real estate taxes and charges from one building to the next can be night and day. You'll want both to be as low as possible for an income play. If you're counting more on property value increasing over a long period, these expenses mean less.

One sure rule is that the closer you get to the city center, the smaller dwellings become. The average size of an apartment in Paris is 59m² and 2.7 *pièces* (1.7 bedrooms). In the *petite couronne* of counties which border Paris, dwellings are 70m² on average, and contain 3.2 *pièces* (2.2 bedrooms).

A growing trend is for tourists to select accommodations near, but not in, the city they plan to visit. Many visitors to the capital in Summer 2022 judged Paris vacation lodgings too expensive, and decided to reserve in the periphery instead.

From Versailles, for example, the train whisks visitors to Paris in 15-20 minutes. Rentals are much more spacious, calm, and less expensive. Plus, most tourists will want to see the Palace and gardens during their trip anyway.

* * *

How

How best to exploit your new investment property? We'll look at many ways here.

Buy-to-let or BTL
Definition: purchasing property to run all flavors of STR and LTR, although BTL is traditionally associated with LTR
Budget: €100 000 to €1 million plus
Risk: moderate

Buying a residential property in order to let or rent it out on a long-term basis is the most popular real-estate investment in the country for individuals. Private citizens own 97% of such properties in France, and institutions have the other 3%. This is radically different from the UK, where about half of all rented properties are managed by corporations, and the US, where this is quickly becoming the case.

You could then select a tenant and manage the property yourself. Upwards of 2 out of 3 of landlords in France solo-manage their properties.

This 'buy-to-let' project would involve a study of the budget and terms a bank would likely offer in their lend agreement, extensive research on the location and type of dwelling, analysing likely scenarios of rental income factoring occupancy rates, subtracting expenses of upkeep and taxes, and taking into account your time, which is also money.

Or, you could delegate the heavy lifting to another company, which could do all the legwork for you from A-to-Z.

There's a whole new crop of service providers specialising in real estate investment opportunities for individuals and couples. These startups in *'investissement locatif'* (essentially BTL and LTR) include players like Beanstock, Masteos, Brick, Immocitiz, MyExpat, Bevouac, Investissement Locatif and Brickmeup. In 2022, this was a Top 3 Proptech segment raising €225 million in VC money. In the US there are BTL companies like Roofstock, Mynd, Awning and Doorvest, among others.

Their tool which should be of greatest interest to the owner is their algorithm, more accurately estimating the revenue-producing capability of a property and its valuation over time, while minimising the periods of vacancy. They scour the entire country for these *'pepites'* or 'good deals' for every size of budget.

To help you evaluate what a good deal looks like, let's first look at what an average deal looks like. The average annual gross return for LTR in France is 6%. Take the average rent of €16/m²/mo. and multiply that by 12 months to get €192, then divide by the average purchase price of €3

178/m². There can be a big difference between gross and net from one provider to another so make sure they show you their method of calculation.

Uncovering **which** specific product to invest in almost justifies their fees by itself. Sourcing companies in the UK charge upwards of 2% of the purchase price, or a flat fee between £3 500 - £5 000 just for the property search. Doing the legwork yourself assumes you have the knowledge, and you have a proven evaluation methodology, and you have the time, and you know where to look (neighborhoods, property types), and you can uncover and eliminate the pitfalls and you're comfortable negotiating personally.

Yield simulations they show are very attractive, and no doubt many of their clients actually realise performances at those high levels. However, you won't hear them guarantee returns. One of their contemporary startups, Youse, offered such guarantees and they went out of business because of it.

One enticing claim from these companies is that you needn't wait until you both own your primary residence **and** have built up a secondary nest egg from the supplemental income of your high-paying job. They say it's not necessary to be a homeowner first. Indeed, this is a worldwide trend, where young renters decide their first property purchase will be a second home, or an investment property. Packaged investment companies say you can start investing with a monthly paycheck of as little as €2 000. That's close to the average individual gross annual salary of €2 130.

This is likely due to a number of factors, some of which are possibly unique to France. For one, there are an incredible amount of very tiny dwellings on the market. A small number of square meters equals a lower price, sometimes even under €100 000, which the vast majority of the population could afford.

In Paris, upwards of 20% of all units are 20m² or under. The average size flat in other big French cities like Lyon, Marseille and Lille are a bit bigger, but still less than you'd expect elsewhere in Europe. In most other countries (besides Japan), the legal size limit is much higher, but in France, units as small as 9m², without either a shower or toilet, can be rented legally. Such *chambres de bonne* in Paris usually have a shared toilet on the floor (*palier*) or some steps up or down from the small studio. Even units which didn't have the required square meters on the floor, could still be rented if they met the minimum cubic meter threshold of 20m³, meaning high ceilings where a bed could be placed above the kitchen (we're not kidding).

We should add a disclaimer that every investment has its own set of risks. Before taking on a loan or buying additional property, get professional advice. Definitely avoid the get-rich-quick amateurs glorifying themselves as Tiktok influencers spitting out incendiary videos on BTL in the UK. These are nasty sue-happy characters using predatory practices to get you to sign up to their uncertified training courses.

The selection of the property is especially important if you expect your investment to pay for itself. The overwhelming majority of landlords in France, 84%, lose money each year (until they sell), or so they claim.

The majority of residential owners in France are also using traditional rental schemes for their property investments which are not fully optimized. They are simply offering their entire empty property on a standard long-term 3-year lease. Let's call this play 'LTR unfurnished whole.'

How does this compare with the other options? We've drawn up table 10 to illustrate the differences. In the Potential Revenue chapter, you saw an example of the money-making capabilities of a **primary residence** in Toulon. That example covered not just accommodation, but also storage, parking, activities and events. That *maison bleue* simulation respected the regulations in place, and used market rates for that particular city.

The following example (figure 10) takes a different approach. First of all, this is for a **secondary residence**. Now that we're in the Expand section, we can imagine that you own another property, separate from where you live, and you wish to earn rental income from this investment.

Secondly, this example only looks at accommodation income. Each line supposes a different income stream, which is the sole method deployed throughout the entire year. We are not mixing plays, and each space is used in the same manner year-round. STR examples have chosen an average nightly rate, which is the median between what is expected at high season and at low season.

Third, the scenario imagines that there are absolutely no local restrictions in the area. National laws still apply, such as lease type, minimum room size to remain a decent dwelling, etc. However, there's no rent control. We don't need to ask the municipality's permission to do this or that. We can do STR or co-living 365 days a year if we want. This example gives us the freedom to examine what the market would bear.

Yes, there are places in France that are like this! But rather than look at their specificities, we've chosen a general model, more likely to inform what might be the best move in your situation. To accomplish this, we've chosen national averages for all residential property across the land. The key data point from which we draw the other figures is €16/m²/mo. That is the average amount paid by tenants on an unfurnished 3-year lease across apartments and houses in all corners of the *hexagone*.

We've used this average for the 2-bedroom apartment, which, at 45m² is about the average size for a dwelling in the land. Smaller properties earn more than €16/m²/mo. and larger ones earn less.

The table details gross income generated nine distinct property types and for eight different BTL accommodation plays.
(figure 10):

Revenue potential by accomodation use for different size residential spaces
all figures gross   National averages   My Property Payday formulas

Usage	Occupancy	Space								
		Room	Studio	1-BR apt.	2-BR apt.	3-BR apt.	3-BR house	4-BR apt.	4-BR house	5-BR house
est. number of people:		1	1	2	3	4	5	6	7	8
number of units:			1	1	1	2	3	3	4	4	5
m2 total:		12	22	32	45	65	80	95	105	125
		€/YR	€/YR	€/YR	€/YR	€/YR	€/YR	€/YR	€/YR	€/YR
LTR unfurnished whole	90%	€3,370	€4,372	€6,083	€7,776	€11,232	€13,824	€16,416	€18,144	€21,600
LTR furnished classic	85%	€3,660	€4,748	€6,606	€8,446	€12,199	€15,014	€17,830	€19,706	€23,460
LTR furnished mobility whole	65%	€4,198	€5,447	€7,578	€9,688	€13,993	€17,222	€20,452	€22,604	€26,910
LTR unfurnished roommates	85%	n/a	n/a	n/a	€9,180	€13,260	€16,320	€19,380	€21,420	€25,500
LTR furnished roommates	80%	n/a	n/a	n/a	€9,936	€14,352	€17,664	€20,976	€23,184	€27,600
LTR furnished co-living	75%	n/a	n/a	n/a	n/a	€16,146	€19,872	€23,598	€26,082	€31,050
STR whole space	55%	€6,003	€7,789	€10,836	€13,853	€20,010	€24,628	€29,246	€32,324	€38,481
STR divided	45%	n/a	n/a	n/a	€17,002	€24,558	€30,225	€35,893	€39,671	€47,227

As you can see, despite having the highest expected occupancy rate, 90%, the 'LTR unfurnished whole' play produces the lowest revenue for all property types. It's also the least attractive fiscally, unless you're an owner of multiple properties.

Slightly more, around 9%, is made in the 'LTR furnished classic' setup. The 15% extra monthly rent (a modest figure which could be higher) is offset a bit by a lower expected occupancy. Not everybody wants to rent furnished, although many do. Even if it was a wash on the gross, renting furnished will make it up on the net by benefitting from the LMNP scheme.

'LTR furnished mobility whole' shows you can make even more bank on a *bail mobilité*. This should be especially attractive to renters of smaller spaces. We almost put 'n/a' on the larger property sizes for this usage. The renter already has to meet certain criteria. What are the chances they're also well-off with a gigantic desire for space? How many families with four kids are there who are visiting professors, expats, or folks undergoing months-long renovations in their main home?

Even though it only makes sense in certain circumstances, it's well worth trying to make it work for your situation. The table shows on average 'LTR furnished mobility whole' produces 29% more than the first line 'LTR unfurnished whole.' Plus, you can still take advantage of LMNP.

Usage lines 3, 4 and 5 are comparable in terms of revenue production. 'LTR unfurnished roommates' and 'LTR furnished roommates' are both known as a '*colocation*' in France, and all tenants are on the same lease. The same 15%+ extra monthly rent applies when you deck out the place with furnishings. The difference here is that, because you're renting out to several people, you can charge more per room, and thus more overall. That's the reward. The risk is you'll have more turnover, a possible increase in wear-and-tear and a more precarious population which might have trouble paying rent on time.

'LTR furnished coliving' produces even more income than all the above, and a whopping 46% more than the first line 'LTR unfurnished whole.' It could be even better, as we've chosen conservative figures. Many co-living property managers claim full occupancy, or at least 10-20 points higher than the 75% selected in this scenario. Each owner has the freedom to charge whatever rates, offer whatever additional services and events they want under a coliving arrangement.

We're very bullish on this play. As it's new, you can expect more volatility than with the other methods. If you go for the high-end, and make your space unique, with a concentrated focus on the community within, you could have a winner on your hands. Your renters could develop a strong affinity with the place, promoting it to their inner circles. If you go viral with these groups, they'll take good care of the place, and finding new tenants will be a breeze.

In 2022, coliving startups raised €140 million in VC money. Coliving startups operating in France include: Colivys, Colonies, Finestate, Friendlyhome, Homies, Koliving, La Casa Coliving, Lamaiz, Roof, Sharies, The Babel Community and Vitanovae. Batiarmor.fr is selling new build LMNP investment vehicles in Rennes branded as '*Nous Coliving*.'

'STR whole space' exploits the standard short-term play. In this ideal world, with no constraints, STR can reach its full potential, producing 89% more revenue than the first line 'LTR unfurnished whole.' This is almost double, and some STR practitioners claim to make three times what they would in a traditional lease. This may be, but unlikely if they do it year-round and have to contend with low season.

'STR divided' means running your property like a hotel. It's technically feasible, which is why we list it here. It may make sense in certain configurations, like a quasi-hostel at a ski resort, and could be legally possible, as long as it's not for all intents and purposes a hotel, with a front desk, services provided onsite and such. Tourists who want that kind of experience might prefer a hotel, since we're charging an average of around €60/night for a 12m² private room, plus shared bathroom, kitchen and living space.

Of course, if the 5-bedroom space was a hotel, you could probably charge more for it, and you would definitely have a better occupancy rate than 45%. Most hotels are 70-80% full, averaged throughout the seasons. This should give you some indication of how lucrative hotels can be, despite their regulatory constraints.

Furnishings

Take into account whether you will be renting furnished (*meublé*) or unfurnished (*vide* or *non-meublé*). While there are more costs to fit-out a dwelling (figure €100 to €200 per m²), most landlords who do so can charge 15-30% more than for an unfurnished unit.

Fiscally, in France furnished makes a lot more sense than to rent it empty. Any accountant (*comptable*) will tell you the same. To take full advantage of all the tax breaks that are available to you, consult with an expert. Meanwhile, here's a brief overview.

(figure 11):

General/Regulatory Aspect	Furnished	Unfurnished
Subject to rent control (*encadrement des loyers*)	Yes, but less-so: tolerance above max plus possibility to add amenities or bundle for higher rent	completely
Rent charged	15-30% more on average	regular price
Lease term minimum	· 1-30days for STR without lease. · 1-10mo for mobility lease or student let · 1yr for classic lease.	· 3yr for classic lease, which is the only one legally available under direct owner-renter agreement
Notice period (except for tenants over 65 years' old, who are protected)	· Tenant: 1 mo. at any moment; · Landlord: 1-3 mo. at end of term for any reason in most cases	· Tenant: 3 mo. at any moment (1 mo. in certain cities/circumstances) · Landlord: 6 mo.+ at end of term only in certain circumstances
Mixed usage allowed (ex. Student let 9 mo., then STR 3 mo.)	Yes	No
Roommate situation (*colocation*) or HMO	Yes	Yes
Coliving	Yes	No
Voids, time to find new tenant	1-2 weeks	1-3 months
Main residence of tenant (*résidence principale déclarée*)	Depends, can be if they stay more than 8 months, otherwise, no	Yes, obligatory

If you rent unfurnished, you'll still need to provide a minimum of furnishings, (see Regulation chapter). However, you won't be able to deduct the cost of these amenities.

When you speak to your accountant, you'll most certainly discuss which 'régime' or status would be the right one for you to select in relation to the French tax code. For most folks, *LMNP* or *Loueur Meublé Non-Professionnel* (most of your income is generated outside of your real estate holdings) will be better suited than *LMP* or *Loueur Meublé*

Professionnel (renting is your main job).

LMNP offers tremendous usage advantages, some of which are listed above. These give the property owner flexibility, options and a higher upside from potential revenue increases. The story gets even better when looking at the outlays involved in renting.

Far greater advantages await owners on the expense and tax side, as shown in the following chart.

(figure 12):

Fiscal treatment	Furnished (LMNP régime réel)	Unfurnished
Amortisation Property (deduct loss of property value from 'use')	Yes, across 25-40 years	No
Amortisation Renovation & major Maintenance	Yes, across 10-15 years	No
Amortisation Furnishings	Yes, for 5 years	No
Amortisation (any subsequent of above if cost €600+)	Yes (costly appliances are better to amortize than deduct outright)	No
Amortisation or Deduction of Notary & Agency fees (*frais de notaire* and *frais d'agence*)	Yes, across 25-40 years (same as property)	No
Deduct Mortgage Interest payments & bank charges	Yes	Yes
Deduct costs of utilities, internet & telephone	Yes	No
Deduct expenses for building fees (copropriété) or service charges	Yes	Yes
Deduct Insurance	Yes	Yes
Deduct Taxes (property and other related, like CFE)	Yes	No
Deduct Property Mgt (Letting Agency) fees and advertising to tenants	Yes	Yes
Deduct travel expenses to visit property, do showings	Yes	No
Deduct Accountant services for tax declarations	Yes	Yes
Rollover (carry-forward) deductions	Yes	No
Cap on deductions	No	Yes

As you see, there are a lot of things you can deduct, and all of them are available to you under LMNP with the real expenses tax regime.

If in any year, your deduction total is greater than your rental income, you are allowed to carry forward (*défalquer*) the unused amount and apply against next year's profits. You can do this up to 10 years for most elements.

Under the right conditions, with the LMNP régime réel, it is possible to pay absolutely no taxes on rental income for a decade. This is because the profits are offset by the 'losses' both real and imagined.

Let's just illustrate one of the magic loopholes: amortisation, which for us is the biggie. It's a strange and wonderful thing once you get your head around this contradiction - you are allowed to depreciate the full purchase amount of something (the property) as if its value is decreasing.

However, in almost all areas of France, for all property types, over time the resale value is actually increasing.

From 2016 to 2020 the national average value increase for residential property was 3.65% per year. That means if you bought a property worth €300 000 in 2016, that same property was likely worth €346 257 in 2020, so about €46 000 more.

Counter-intuitively, in the lovely green eyes of the fisc, during the same period the asset has depreciated from €300 000 to some lower amount. For houses and entire buildings in France, the value of the structure can be depreciated, but not the land because the land never gets "used up." The *fisc* arbitrarily chooses some percentage between 10-20% as the 'land value' portion. Let's pick 15% in this case. So €300 000 - 15% = €255 000, which is considered to be the value of the property at the time of purchase.

All €255 000 can be written off, but normally spread evenly across a 25 to 40-year period. That's right, even though the other expenses must be applied within 10 years, or the excess deductions are lost forever, for the property depreciation, the deduction party continues.

Let's choose 25 years. This could allow us to depreciate €10 200 per year during the 25-year period.

Amortisation alone cannot create a deficit, or increase the amount of a deficit. Only real expenses can create a deficit, which you can rollover (*reporter*) in subsequent declarations, up to 10 years' hence.

Setting up your LMNP activity isn't very straightforward, so it's best to have someone else do that for you. The all-in-one '*clef-en-main*' startups like Masteos et co. mentioned earlier in this chapter can help you, if you buy through them. Or, if you buy solo, have an accountant do the legwork. You'll likely need an accountant (around €300/year, also deductible) to correctly declare your taxes anyway, at least the first year, which is the most complex. The real expenses regime carries with it an onerous reporting requirement which is better left to the pros.

Here are the steps in the administrative process. First, go to the site of the *Greffe du Tribunal de Commerce*, and fill out the form P0i (*formulaire P0i*) also known as the Cerfa n° 11921*06.

The form has three purposes:
1. Declare you'll be running your activity as a *Loueur Meublé Non-Professionnel* (LMNP)
2. Get a SIRET number (all commercial activities need such a number, even if it's not a veritable business)
3. Choose standard deduction or real expense reductions (*micro BIC* or *réel*)

* * *

At first glance, the *micro-BIC* standard deduction of 50% sounds pretty good. However, it doesn't account for all the write-offs listed previously, which can take you well past deductions equalling 100% of your rental income, which can be carried forward for years to come.

A VAT (*TVA*) regime should be chosen, but this only applies if you are providing additional services. These encompass hotel-like extras such as breakfast, cleaning, tour guides and such, which are all classified at the 20% VAT rate. You'll want to think twice before offering any additional services, especially if they are bundled with your rental. See chapters on Regulation and Taxation.

You can avoid getting caught in tricky fiscal situations by correctly filling out the form, and being careful what you offer to those who stay in your property. Therefore, we recommend you don't offer these services, and hence '*franchise en base*' is the correct choice on the *TVA* field.

Within five months of submitting the form above, you should also register with the *Centre de Gestion Agréé* (CGA), which allows you to write off the cost of membership (required).

Before the next year's tax declaration period (April-May) you'll need to setup a professional account (distinct from your personal account) on the Impôts.gouv.fr website (equivalent of IRS or HMRC). After two years of activity, you'll be subject to the CFE (*Cotisation Foncière des Entreprises*) which is a small tax on the size of the property with a commercial activity.

In terms of timing, you'll want to do your LMNP paperwork and declare your activity at the moment of purchase. That way, you can already begin deducting your notary and agency fees on the transaction. Also, the LMNP activity must begin **before** you purchase furnishings, if you wish to deduct the expense of the furniture from your income. Declaration is what counts, not necessarily producing a furnished lease before the place is decked out. What tenant would sign that?

Speaking of acquiring items to fit-out your investment, there are companies who will help you do that. The 'Make it Better' chapter 17 details individual amenities of interest. Here, we're talking about furnishing entire flats for BTL from scratch.

Easy Mobilier is one such company offering packages with varying styles and budgets from studios (around €2 000) and properties with multiple rooms. They'll also deliver, construct on site and stage the furnishings, or you could do that yourself and save a bit of money. VIBESinBNB is another interior decorator catering to STRs, using the high-end Temahome catalog of French-built *mobilier*.

You needn't skimp on the quality, unless your budget is really tight, because the more you spend, the longer it'll last, and the more you'll be able to deduct. With amortisation, it's possible over time to get back a greater amount than your outlay. This effect is accentuated with pricier brands.

Of course, you shouldn't go overboard. Think of the population who will be staying there. Will they appreciate the added comfort and style? Or will they not care? You can err ever so slightly on the side of surprising your renters in a good way, and having a bit sturdier stuff to withstand wear and tear, especially if there are children or pets.

Finer amenities could enable you to charge slightly more. Better yet, they could attract the kind of renter who's more reliable, or willing to commit to a longer stay.

The cherry on the LMNP cake is that when you go to resell the property many years in the future, the fisc won't take any of the previous depreciations and amortisations into account. It'll be as if they never happened.

In the example of the €300 000 property purchase introduced earlier in this chapter, imagining the owner sold in 2020 for €346 000, the capital gain will be factored starting with the €46 000 appreciation since the purchase price. Even the €46 000 can have deductions applied to it, so the base amount can become much lower before applying the CGT rate.

One thing to watch out for is if your LMNP activity generates more than €23 000 in rental income in any one year, or that your rental income is greater than 50% of your income from other sources (married couples can add up both incomes). If that happens, then you'll automatically slip into the LMP tax regime.

LMP can be much less attractive, and onerous, for most people. Those with high incomes (salaries or dividends), or at an advanced age, where succession planning is top of mind, may prefer LMP. Here's how the two compare.

(figure 13):

Fiscal treatment	LMNP (non-pro) *régime réel*	LMP (pro) *régime réel*
CGT (capital gains tax) 'exoneration'	Yes, partial after being held 6 to 22 years, & total after held for 30 years	Yes, only if LMP last 5Y earning less than €90 000 last 2Y
Rental income subject to social charges (from 20,15% to 43,2%)	No	Yes
URSSAF signup required	No	Yes
Amortisation	Yes	Yes
Deduct expenses	Yes	Yes
Period to carry-forward losses	10 years	6 years
Losses applied against total income of household (including salaries, etc.)	No	Yes
Subject to 'wealth tax' or IFI (*impôt sur la fortune immobilière*)	Yes	No

***

It is possible to mix the two. This may make sense for those with many properties, or holdings which generate a significant income. Portfolio landlords could keep a couple furnished properties in LMNP which earn less than €23 000/yr, and run the rest as unfurnished LMP. This way, they get the best of both worlds fiscally, spread the risk and add a bit of flexibility in their portfolio.

An accountant with even greater qualifications (*expert-comptable*) and price tag is required to deal with the intricacies of LMP.

For Junior's studies

Meilleurs Agents completed an analysis of college towns in France, comparing the costs of renting versus buying for your son's or daughter's lodging while pursuing a degree (5-year master's). In 78% of the cases, they concluded it's better to buy than to rent.

Bogey/Delta

In the 'Money' chapter five in the Evaluate section earlier in this book, you saw the difference between the value of a purchase versus a long-term rental in terms of the cost by amount of time used. The amount that you, the buyer, stands to pay per month, versus how much your renter pays per month is often referred to as a 'bogey' or 'delta.'

As an investor, when looking at whether a property represents a good investment or not, you should be looking at that bogey.

CHAPTER TWENTY-EIGHT
Packaged investments

Why do all the heavy lifting, when there are companies who do it all for you, wrapping up opportunities in a neat little bow? Well, you can't judge a book by its cover. That pretty packaging may hide a dud of an investment.

Défiscalisation schemes

The most popular of these 'reduced tax' offers come under the name of 'Pinel' (and formerly Duflot, Scellier, Robien, Borloo, Besson et al). They're going away soon because the State isn't happy it spent €2 billion on the Pinel program for only 30 000 lodgings built.

Entire books have been written about these tax writeoff or *défiscalisation* investment vehicles. They're extremely complex to the degree that you almost need to be an expert in French real estate, accounting, legal and finance to make heads or tails of it, much less make money on a deal. The ones who **always** make money are the promoters, who pocket sky high commissions from the sale to investors, then recoup the exclusive management fees for decades to come, where they continue to stick it to those same investors.

If you're a tax resident in France, and you have the stomach for it, read on. Otherwise, feel free to skip to the next section.

From a pure yield point of view, suffice to say if you're happy with an absolute maximum of 1-2% **gross** annual returns on your money, there are many other ways to accomplish that which don't lock you in for such a long time, and don't require a lot of heavy lifting on your part or the hiring of an army of experts.

The tax advantage works like this in 2023, if you rent the qualifying property out for six, nine or 12 years, then you'll get a tax credit based on the first €300 000 of property value. For a six-year rental, the tax is reduced by 10.5% (or €31 500 maximum total or €5 250 maximum per year); for nine years -15% (or €45 000 max. total or €5 000 max/YR); and for 12 years -17.5% (or €52 500 max. total or €4 375 max/YR). In 2024, those percentages are going down to -9%, -12% and -14% respectively. After several years of these deals, the opportunities which remain are tantamount to social housing.

These schemes don't make sense for most of us, so we won't go into much more detail about them. Here are some bullet points if you would like to investigate further:

- Fiscal residence must be France: if you don't work for a French company, or split your time between countries like a digital nomad not spending more than 180 days/year in France, these investments won't help you. Similarly, if you get transferred out of France, or want to retire out of France, you've just lost the main reason you bought into this investment in the first place.
- Lower/Middle classes need not apply: this is a vehicle for high rollers or couples who earn a ton of money in France, and thus would be subject to the 40% or greater tax bracket. You'd have to accurately project your situation staying that way for a decade. If you have any loss of income, periods of unemployment or a maternity leave or two, you'll have less taxes to write off. Less taxes means less benefit.
- New Construction only: the previous chapter has a detailed section on 'New Build versus Existing' detailing many of the disadvantages. Here are some others:
  - Risk at purchase: delivery dates are habitually late. Sometimes, the finished product never arrives. French law has no provision allowing you to cancel the purchase because the unit you bought was not delivered on time. Delivery could be delayed indefinitely, with no requirement of proof on progress of building by the promoter. Meanwhile, the money you've given so far is tied up, and the funds you've promised the builder remain due in the future. Your only protection is having clear 'out' clauses with dates and amounts in your contract.
  - Cutting corners: more than half of builders don't respect the law, so says the *DGCCRF*, the national fraud commission. Offenses include abusive clauses, claiming they have insurance which doesn't exist, or taking money before contract signature or too much too soon during build, that is, if they ever start building. One promoter who delivered 20 houses in Les Mureaux in 2018 has subsequently had those homes judged unfit for habitation. They must be destroyed.

- Buy and hold: for a minimum of 6 years (and no tax benefit after 12 years) is what you'd have to do on these *défiscalisation* tax schemes. Surprisingly, many past investors in these schemes were flabbergasted to discover they couldn't sell the apartment for what they bought it for a decade or more before. That's because the promoters initially sold it for 30-50% more than the price of existing properties in the surrounding area. A 20% premium should be the absolute maximum versus the cost of ancien next door.
- Lose benefit if empty after 1 year: if you don't find a renter right away, you will lose all tax benefits associated with the scheme. The renter needs to have moved in within a year of your purchase or the delivery date (whichever's older). Investors with this knife at their throats accepted anybody with a pulse at discounted rent just to keep the tax break.
- Monthly rent limits: even if your flat isn't in a city with rent control, the scheme restricts how much you can charge, for the entire life of the investment.
- Run-down Urban areas only: the *gouvernement* rightly wants to incentivise new building where there's not enough quality housing to meet demand, especially from lower-income families. It's in the middle of this squalor that they want to raise shiny new units. Since real estate valuations are dictated first and foremost by location, location, location, you'll have to accept that the surroundings won't help you initially. It takes a lot of imagination in some areas that gentrification will happen
- Restrictions on usage: long-term leases of 1-3 years only. Even the tame mobility lease is prohibited, and don't even think about STR or mixed use to make more money or hedge your bets.
- Restrictions on who you can rent to: there are minimum and, if you can believe it, also maximum income thresholds your renters must meet. If they don't, you can lose your tax break. If they do on move-in, then make more or less than the thresholds later on, you can lose your tax break **and** be stuck with a tenant you can't easily change.
- Fantasyland simulations: industry insiders say the only ones who make money on these deals are the sellers, not the buyers. The investors are enticed by simulations which rarely reflect the reality they encounter. These estimations are rarely binding, so there's little recourse if a plan goes awry. *Pinel Arnaque* (scam) is but one blog post detailing the horror stories post-purchase.
- Other bills at the Exit: the building managers are notorious for

hiking the charges for upkeep. You bought brand new, so there shouldn't be hardly any maintenance, nor major repairs to speak of, right? Wrong. They're famous for coming up with new mandatory expenses, probably ones they anticipated way back when they cut corners in the construction phase. Every owner has to pay and pay. If they don't like it, go ahead and sell at a loss. Owners are lucky if they find a buyer who wants to assume such high monthly service fees.

Buyer beware for any investor looking into the Pinel tax writeoff scheme which ends in December 2024 (with reduced tax breaks in 2023). There's a great summary on the *Avenue des Investisseurs* blog which includes a free downloadable Excel sheet for comparing Pinel with LMNP. Spoiler alert - LMNP wins in a landslide.

A company in Bordeaux calling it's plan the 'Method Devila' (which the entrepreneur named after himself) build new townhouses and claims the same benefit the Pinel people do. Contrary to a packaged deal from a promoter, you own the property outright and do what you want with it upon delivery.

Consultim Groupe has many real estate investment programs, mostly Pinel and other serviced buildings. One interesting concept they called 'mobility' is managed to support different usages and populations throughout the year, like students, business travelers and tourists. While this is the right idea on the revenue side, dig into the fine print to ensure you're not paying exorbitantly on the expense side.

Consultim and Terrésens offer *residences de tourisme* ski residence management packaged investments.

Censi-Bouvard

The *dispositif Censi-Bouvard* also concerns new builds and is very similar to the Pinel *défiscalisation* tax schemes detailed elsewhere in these pages. You can skip this section, as by the time you read it, that ship has sailed. You must have activated before December 31, 2022.

The vast majority of people who exercise these tax reduction schemes either bought initially from a vendor in a packaged manner, or currently have a management company overseeing their investment. Property usage intentions range from tourism, to student housing, to senior communities to assisted living (*EHPAD*).

Censi-Bouvard is a segment of LMNP, but without all the advantages. Unlike other LMNP, the Censi-Bouvard investments cannot use amortisation. They are offered a -11% tax break instead (maximum €33K), which is typically less attractive. The tax break only applies to fiscal residents in France who commit to the plan (and all associated costs) for nine years.

Other Packaged Investments

There are 4 other categories we haven't addressed yet, and they, too, have their history of scandals and disgruntled buyers who regretted their investments.

Resorts (*résidence de tourisme*) or tourist complexes.

These are sold by such companies as Pierre et Vacances. It's a similar pitch to the timeshares, but you own the property. People may think it's neat to make money on their ski resort apartment when they're not there, and also *profite* themselves for a couple weeks a year.

They'll look after it for you, and you can have no other manager. The upkeep and fees cost a lot more than most folks plan for. The business is extremely seasonal, so you can expect to make nothing for months at a time... and all the while, the manager's cash register keeps ringing with your payments for overseeing an empty apartment.

Student Housing (*résidence étudiante*)

College housing property manager Roof says in France there are only 350 000 student housing places for the 2.8 million youths enrolled in university. The interior minister says a further 300 000 students are projected. That supports the theory that more beds are needed to meet student demand.

However, it does not automatically follow that packages from builders and managers of student housing make good investments. There are many ways yields could go south, the most common of which are overpaying for the property in the first place, and getting locked into high expenses from an operator you cannot divorce.

Count on an average cost of €70 000 for an outright purchase of a small dwelling in a huge building.

These are sold by such companies as Cafpi, Greystar, KaufmanBroad, Nexity, and Vinci.

Corporate Housing or Apartments (*Résidence d'affaires* or *Appart'Hôtel*)

These are sold by such companies as Vianova. You can expect the same deal as with the resort packages described above. The only difference is that they are less affected by seasons.

One curious thing to look out for is these run contrary to STRs. Appart hotels for business travelers are full during the week (when rates are low) and empty on the weekends (when rates are higher). The managers of these places often put them up for rent at firesale prices on the weekend, just to get some income. This is not what you want your investment partner doing with your money.

Assisted-Living Facilities (EHPAD for *établissement d'hébergement pour personnes âgées dépendantes*) **or Retirement Communities**

These are sold by such companies as Direct Immogéré, either within or without the *Censi-Bouvard* scheme. While the population is aging, and there should be greater demand for retirement homes, none of these businesses seems to know how to run a profitable business. In 2022, fully 85% of EHPADs ran a deficit. That year, the biggest player in the sector, Orpea, declared bankruptcy.

CHAPTER TWENTY-NINE
Style points

"There are no points for style…"

This book has aimed to be an overview, and offer a big-picture view. We don't pretend that it's complete.

The lines we've decided to stop at, forming the four perimeter walls of our 'book building,' are ones of aesthetics, of personality/voice, of engagement, and of 'extras.' Call them 'Style points' if you will.

Zillow studies paint colors, for example. Its latest analysis said that a white kitchen, long *de rigueur*, could now hurt a house's home price to the tune of $612, whereas a charcoal-gray kitchen allegedly increases the cost by an average of $2 512.

It's not as if these aspects are unimportant, but they are certainly less important than the fundamentals. They are the 'sizzle' and this book is the 'steak.'

Most influencers, podcasters, instagrammers and gurus of our era focus on practically nothing else but style. If you follow them too closely, you may start to ask yourself if you're not doing enough to promote your property and yourself on social media. I would instead ask **them** what they'll do once the style they've chosen falls out of fashion?

We know of a real estate agency in Paris which spends €25 000 per month on ads with Google and Facebook to generate leads… which produce €50 000 per month in revenues… before paying overhead, staff and taxes. In your opinion, does that business model make the agency rich, or the GAFAMs of the world rich?

Aesthetics- Do you get bored easily? "This year mauve is in, so you'll want to re-decorate your space!" or "He painted his studio like a comic book to attract guests." Are you one to ride the trends, or stay neutral for wider appeal? Would a guest absolutely need to have a selfie with one of your key attributes? Would you want them to?

Personality/Voice- do you want to pretend to be BFF with your guests or simply cordial? Some hosts try to differentiate themselves by adopting a certain tone, whether mother hen, local tourist tip resource, gay-friendly, or catering to outdoorsy types. LL Bean catalogs did this successfully in the '90s, adding backstories to their clothing line and the models who wore them. It got them good notoriety for awhile, until they became a trope for mockery on such shows as Seinfeld. Still, while the wave lasted, they probably made more money than their contemporaries with similar commodities. Can your way of communicating create a niche, resulting in extra cash?

Engagement- Apart from the platforms, how will people find out about your rental? Will you post on your own social timeline, FB groups, and the walls of the multiverse? Will you ask past guests to participate in pandering to future guests? If they do so, will you offer them something in return? Influencers routinely offer to post in exchange for a free stay, and in so doing flit about the world as digital nomads on another's dime. Should you take the bait?

Extras- including breakfast, gift baskets, vending machines, experiences, and such.

Focusing on these areas could set you apart, and that differentiation could lead to greater visibility, extra bookings and better ratings. Or, they could simply be a fruitless distraction, and time suck, chasing after the approval of a fickle public. Only you can decide if they make sense for you.

CHAPTER THIRTY
Nothing to lose

"Bob Dylan said it best…"

There's a population we haven't yet addressed in this book: those without property. If that's you, hopefully reading these pages you've come to believe in the power of property . If you aspire to use that power for your own situation, don't be left out. This last chapter is for you, because, "when you ain't got nothin', you got Nothin' to lose."

Using your rented Space

Sub-leasing
   With your landlord's permission, you could re-rent the space that you live in for accommodations, on a short-term or long-term basis. Greystar, a leader in student housing blocks, struck a deal with Airbnb to allow renters to do a revenue-share for their room on the STR platform. Platforms like Leavy, Troctachambre, Studylease and Smartrenting help long-term tenants make money while they're away.
   French law prohibits subleasing for a greater amount than the regular rent, however, there are ways around that. For example, if your monthly *loyer* is €1 000, you could get €1 000 for two weeks. You could earn €2 000 for four weeks which overlap May and June. You could charge €2 000 for one week, where your take is €1 000 and the rest goes to the landlord, cleaning, platform fees, food/supplies you've left for the guests and other charges.
   Also, the laws are different for long-term and short-term. If your sublease period lasts fewer than 30 days, you could conceivably charge what you like. See the arbitrage section earlier in this book for more ideas to make subleasing worth your while.
- Resources: Studylease, Leavy, Troctachambre

Storage at your rental

CoStockage claims you don't need your landlord's permission to store items at the place you rent. Still, it's a good idea to let them know.

Check out previous chapters for leads on storing items at your rental. Platforms to place your ad are shown at the end of the book.

Services for neighbors & travelers

Pousse is a startup doing plant sitting and watering charging €50 for 1 session for up to 20 plants.

Pet sitting

This is an activity well-detailed previously. A list of platforms to propose your services as a fur-baby sitter is found at the end of this book.

Package reception or Parcel-sitter

Two startups called Welco and Pickme put you on the map to receive packages for your neighbors when *les voisins* are away. Each provider offers about €1 per parcel to the guardians of cardboard treasure. The money could add up if you live in a densely-populated urban area with many apartments, but few nearby collection boxes (*boîtes à colis*) and no *tabac* shops which have already setup a Relais Colis dropoff/pickup point.

Pickme, Welco

Luggage storage

If your rented apartment is in an urban area, preferably no higher than the first floor, or with an elevator, you could sign up with platforms like Luggit or Lockers. They'll send travelers your way who want to lose the weight of suitcases while they explore.

Part-time side hustle

Consulting

You could advise or consult others on doing some of the activities spelled out in this book. The caveat here is that you don't want to venture too far into regulated territory. You'd need a real estate license (*carte professionnelle*) to represent for ongoing lease management, or transact property like a real estate agent (*agent immobilier*) whether for purchases or collecting money on behalf of others as in rental management. Financial advisors (*conseiller patrimoine*) on real estate holdings also require credentials. Pretending to be one of these professionals, or acting too much like them can run you into stiff fines or possibly jail time.

Fees could be charged on an hourly basis (€100/hour), a day rate (€500/day) or project/mission completion (€1 000 for accompanying/translating during the various steps of a renovation).

Co-host

This is where you 'help out' another, typically the host, with their STR business. You could be customer-facing, or operational. It's for both of you to work it out. It usually works best if you're dealing with the owner directly. Too many middle-men can muck up the works, or eat into one of the three party's profits.

Some have run the co-host model quite successfully, way beyond the imagined capabilities of one person. A member of Airbnb's program called 'Luckey' after the property manager they acquired, grew to more than 100 units managed in this fashion. With the shutdown of that failed experiment at Airbnb, he's now setup as 'Sociéte Hosting Services' a full-service *conciergerie* in Lyon.

One big disadvantage of this setup is the money-handling. You're not allowed to do it without the *carte G* real-estate agent classification. That means all the net funds go straight to the host. As an *auto-entrepreneur* (or other independent statute), you'll have to bill them for your time, or your percentage or whatever you've agreed to. This leaves you subject to the whims of when they pay you, how much, or the doubt if you will ever get compensation. Put signature to paper with the host, and hope for the best. Slow/no payers are rampant, and recourse is long, expensive, and damaging to your reputation.

Many established *conciergeries* like Welkeys are looking for city managers. Maybe one is needed where you live. Instead of setting up your own business, you could learn from them as you work independently from inside a successful company you wish to emulate.

Resources: Cohostmarket

Conciergerie

You could start out by creating your own STR property management business or *conciergerie* as they're commonly called in France. Owners provide the property you don't have, and you help them make money on it.

The difficulty is you can get into a bit of a catch-22. Only licensed real estate agents with the *carte G* for *gestion* or property management, have the legal right to handle money on behalf of owners. Do so without this and you'll be in for heavy fines and jail time.

However, if you bill owners after the fact for money they've been paid directly, you're taking a chance you may be working for nothing. Will they pay you all that you're owed? How long will you have to wait for your compensation? Even when things work well with an honest owner who pays on time, they'll certainly get tired of a system which has you bill them regularly an amount they'll have to verify and pay. It's much easier for them to work with a property manager which has the *carte G* and simply deducts their fees without the owner having to do anything.

One way around this situation is if you contract with a PMS which offers split payments. Using their own Stripe account, the PMS automatically takes the payout from the OTA, and splits it- the owner's share gets deposited into their bank account, and the property manager's share is transferred into your bank account. You've respected the letter of the law, and you didn't need to beg to get paid.

RentalReady can do split payments and handle guest funds on behalf of the owner because they have the *carte G*. Smily and Guesty claim to do this (unverified) and likely don't have the *carte G*. The latter is headquartered outside France, so check on compliance in general. Inquire with them to see if split payments could be a solution for you.

Resources: CLF, SPLM, RentalReady, Smily, Guesty

Property Management helper

You could offer your services to landlords doing LTR. This could consist of finding tenants, ongoing tenant relations and upkeep of property. As usual, the fees you charge are up to you.

Investing in 2nd before buying main residence

It would surprise a lot of people to discover that 37% of French property investors don't own their primary residence. "How can that be?" you may ask "So, they don't really believe in the value of real estate?" Hardly.

This could be for several reasons, some beyond their control. They could be renting when they inherit a property. In the UK, 17% of landlords are 'accidental.' The landlord might have moved into an assisted-living facility which the rental income is financing. They could be forced into renting while waiting for their new build primary residence to overcome many delays and finally be delivered.

We know a couple who tumbled into this situation under bizarre circumstances. While renting, they bought a home which was occupied by a tenant, who was given notice in due and lawful form. Their intention was simply to change primary residences. But they were denied access to the property by the tenants, who refused to leave. So, they became accidental investors.

This stalemate went on for five years, when the courts, bailiff (*huissier*) and police finally got the tenants to vacate peacefully. Thankfully, the recourse has improved for owners experiencing this type of situation in the future.

Or, the investor could be making a purposeful choice.

They could live and work in Lyon, an expensive city where they rent, and own an investment property in nearby Saint-Etienne, a growing economy where the price per square meter is four times less. Renting in Lyon gives them much more space than buying, and with their higher salary they can afford to be in the city-center, where they don't need a car and can commute by public transport. Meanwhile, the net yield from their Saint-Etienne property could be close to 10%, a phenomenal return one could only dream of in rent-controlled Lyon.

That return, coupled with a rent that's much less than a Lyon mortgage, may help our investor build a nest-egg faster. If they count on savings from their salary alone, their money may never run fast enough to catch up to a rising market.

From 2000 to 2020, apartment prices rose by 138% in France, which were way above rents, which increased by only 42% during the same period. Rents grew by an annual average of just 1.13% from 2006 to 2020. French wages from 2000 to 2020 grew just 25%, a slower rate than either.

In many cases it's easier to get a loan for investment, based on the potential rental income produced, than a loan for habitation, based on the owner-occupier's salary. If a buy-to-let shows positive cashflow, lenders may think that's a slightly better bet.

One expectation for owner-occupiers is that their primary residence will increase in value, giving them a capital gain. But this isn't always the case. In France, there was a big downturn which started in 2008 and lasted a long time. Our investor may be timing the property market the way some do the stock market, getting out at the peak, and buying back in at the bottom of the dip.

Bargain basement

Auctions: This topic was covered in the beginning of the Big Budget chapter. Check out organizations like Agora Store, Kadran and WinUp, which specialize in auctions (*enchères*).

Take over a wreck: Every once in a while you hear about a dying village in the boonies in Italy, or the backwoods of Greece or some other area offering property for $1 if you agree to move there. You even hear about these things sometimes with one of the 40 000 *châteaux* in France, albeit the ones in the worst of shape. Taking on one of these requires accepting renovations using the tools of the time, by specialized artisans, and bringing it back to 'stock' without any custom improvements.

It's true, England has 1 million abandoned homes. Maybe France has similar numbers. It would probably take knocking on a lot of doors and the *mairie* of the town you're interested in, to see if there's a hovel you can take off their hands for a pittance.

There are agencies which focus on selling patrimonial properties, like Histoire Patrimoine, but we doubt they have any stock for someone without deep pockets.

Each one of the ideas or "plays" mentioned previously in this Expand section warrants further exploration. Entire books have been written about many of the topics, such as 'Buy-to-let' and 'de-fiscalisation.' Still other books have tackled the related areas of financing, renovations, hospitality and such. If you're in need of greater depth in one subject area, you may wish to read some of the books mentioned in the bibliography.

You've reached the end of the first My Property Payday book. We hope the information shared in these pages have helped open your mind to possibilities you didn't know about before.

Wherever you've started on your rental income journey, whether with several or no assets, we hope this book has encouraged you to keep pushing forward, to realize your personal goals through property rental.

CHAPTER THIRTY-ONE
Acknowledgments

We at My Property Payday would like to thank you for your concerted attention throughout this tome, and your courage for taking on the challenge of transforming your space into a money-making enterprise.

There are a number of people who were instrumental in making this book possible, looking sleek and professional.

Fellow artists and authors Tony De Souza, Charles Timoney, Alain Cournoyer, Aleah Niemczyk and Adrian Leeds. Friends who have shared their experiences like Dave and Lynn Demeda and Dave Krumland.

Colleagues and friends at GuestReady and RentalReady who I've learned from, including Alexander Limpert, Andreea Petrisor, François Lavie, Alexandra Jourdan-Astruc, Aura Pana, Carolina Dias, Márcio Jesus, Marie Rupin, Ronan Boiteau, Raphaël Oren, Charles LeGuennec, Ilo Steffenoni, Lorenzo Ritella, Kasia Aubier, Sinan Sattar, Rui Silva, Antonio Fragateiro, John Severino, Burhan Hayat, Hadi Hijazi, Romain Giacalone, Camille Texier, Benjamin Niel, Victor Bosselaar, Aline Mostachetti, Noémie Gourdon, Théophile Wagner and Jihad Sebgui.

Clients and partners too numerous to mention.

Former colleagues William Tonnard, Charles Wanecq, João Cristóvão, Elena Velte, Sara Ceia, Duarte Ramalho, Luis Rosa, Miguel Soares, Roman Renke, Edouard de Feraudy, Matthias Kégl, Stéphane Bâlon, Brad Jensen, Grégoire Werth, Marc London, Urban Lingmerth, Charuta Fadnis, David Lewis, Alexandre Fitussi, Emma Malha, Axel Dufour, Romain Valverde, Pierre Gaslorowski, Antoine Elias, François Ehret and Matthieu Havette.

The authors have been inspired by the founders of RealEstech, Robin Rivaton, Vincent Pavanello and Florian Freyssenet. We also greatly appreciate industry leaders and spokespeople Thierry Vignal, Geoffrey Reiser, Mickael Zonta, Manuel Ravier, Thibault Masson, Martin Menez, Vincent Pineau, Jamie Lane, Thomas Lefebvre, Gail Boisclair, Marie

Pristinier, Jeremy Nabais, Jasper Ribbers, Mark Simpson, Liam Corcoran, James Varley, Damian Sheridan, Paul Stevens, Antonio Borlotti, Vanessa Guérin, Dominique Petit, Xavier Demeuzoy, esq. and Dmitri Bougeard, esq.

All those we've been educated by at industry events, and all the associations carrying the flame to professionalize the property rental industry owned by individuals, who are regular people like you and me.

Finally, to the two foundational people who were flipping houses before Robert Kiyosaki published his first sentence. Who camped out overnight in line to be the first to buy into new developments. Who renovated, decorated, repaired and improved with their own hands. Who lost their shirts several times because there was nobody to guide them, and no books like this available. To Jack and Kathy Siart, who parlayed a modest single-income into a comfortable existence for their family, and a retirement far better than the average American, all through dozens of seat-of-their-pants real estate plays over 50 years.

Thank you, all.

Resources

GLOSSARY

Glossary

Lexicon and definition of property vocabulary and translation of terms used commonly in the field in France. *French* to English:

Abonnement / Charges = standing charge, typically for utilities
   Acompte = deposit nonrefundable
   Acte authentique = The final contract for the purchase of a property established by a notary.
   Acte en main = The total cost of a property including agent and notary fees
   Acte de vente = Deed of sale or conveyance document; Conveyancing is the legal term for where you transfer the ownership of property
   Agent immobilier = real estate agent or sollicitor or buyer's agent or property finder (aka '*chasseur d'appart*'); Estate agent only represents the seller. Fédération Nationale des Chasseurs Immobiliers (FNCI) and *La Fédération Française des Chasseurs Immobiliers* (FFCI)
   Amortissement = amortization or reducing debt in equal payments on a mortgage
   Arrhes = Deposit (refundable)
   Attestation d'acquisition = Proof of purchase
   Avec tout le confort = with all mod. cons.

Bail = lease
   Bail mobilité = Mobility lease
   Bailleur = landlord or lessor

CCI *chambre de Commerce et de l'Industrie* = regulating body for estate

agent licensing; the closest UK equivalent is NAEA Propertymark, however estate agents don't require certification like in France
   Cadastre = land registry
   Caution = security deposit (usually not refundable)
   Cave/cellier = Cellar
   Certificat d'urbanisme = Town planning permit
   Cession = transfer of ownership
   Chaudière = heater (US) or boiler (UK)
   Chauffage collectif / chauffage individuel = communal heating / individual heating
   Clause particulière = special condition
   Clause pénale = penalty clause in a sales contract
   Clause suspensive = A conditional clause in a contract which must be met to ensure its validity
   Clé-en-main = bespoke or end-to-end or tailor-made (*sur-mesure*)
   Co-host = Co-host or someone who helps you self-manage your property
   Colocation = Houses in Multiple Occupation (HMO) or flatshare; Coliving also sometimes expressed in this way, even though each lease is individual
   Conciergerie Airbnb or *Concierge meublé de tourisme* = STR property manager
   Comble = loft
   Comptable = accountant
   Comptant = All cash purchase
   Compte séquestre = deposit held in a special escrow account
   Compteur = meter measuring usage of utilities like water or electricity
   Conditions suspensives = Opt-out conditions
   Courtier de prêt = mortgage broker
   Coûts courants = Running costs including loan interest, prop mgt fees, insurance, maintenance, tenant deposit protection, advertising
   Conservateur des hypothèques = District land register
   Constat d'huissier = irrefutable statement by a bailiff
   Copropriété = "co-ownership or copropriété" like condominium where owners share charges and responsibilities
   Cuisinière = cooker (UK) or stove (US)

Dépôt de garantie = deposit paid when renting
   Devis = quotation or estimate
   Diagnostiques = diagnostic studies by a professional prior to sale. Diagnostics
   Disjoncteur = Circuit breaker
   Domicile fiscal = main residence for tax purposes

Droit d'enregistrement (fais partie des frais de notaire) = part of stamp duty or tax on property purchase paid by the buyer

Émolument de négociation = finders fee for introducing the buyer to the seller's agent
Emprunt = loan
Encadrement des loyers = rent control
Expert géomètre = land surveyor

FAI *frais d'agence inclus / commission compris* = Price including estate agent commissions
FNAIM or *Fédération Nationale de l'Immobilier* = regulator for estate agencies; also *Professionnels Immobiliers* (SNPI)
Forfait = fixed price for all items
Fosse septique = Septic tank
Frais de Dossier = Arrangement Fee (sometimes called a Completion Fee or Booking Fee) is an administration charge made by lenders for arranging credit
Frais de Gestion = Property management fees / Letting agency fees
Frais d'acte / frais de notaire = notarial fees for producing a deed plus stamp duty and land registry

Gérer les locations sur une plateforme = listings management
Gestion immobilier = Property Management
Gestionnaire patrimoine = Wealth manager or financial advisor or director of family office

Honoraires = commissions paid to an agency
Hypothèque = non-possessory lien, typically 1% of the purchase price, paid by the property buyer, it provides further loan insurance to the mortgage bank in case of default. Returned after full loan repayment or house sale. Doesn't exist in UK or US.

Impayés = unpaid rents
Impôt sur les plus values = CGT or capital gains tax
Indivision = joint ownership
Inventaire / État des lieux = Inventory of contents and condition of property either prior to rental or upon vacating

Jouissance = exclusive usage

LCD - for *location courte durée* or *court-terme* or *location saisonnière* or *meublé de tourisme* = STR or Short-Term-Rental

Location = rental

Locataire = tenant

Loi ALUR of 2014 for *"accès au logement et un urbanisme rénové"* = also known as the '*Loi Duflot*' this legislation was all but fully replaced by the *loi ELAN*

Loi Carrez - living area as defined by legal measurement system. A sanctioned technician (called a '*géomètre*') must be hired to establish the official surface area by taking the interior floor plan, then subtracting partitions/walls, stairs, balconies, terraces and any interior area without at least 1.8m clearance

Loi ELAN of 2019 = completes and updates the Loi Hoguet, forming the two main pillars regulating real estate in France

Loi Hamon = consumer protection law

Loi Hoguet = regulating real estate representation and practices in France; the UK equivalent is the Estate Agents Act 1979

Loi Nogal = rental deposits held by a 3rd party instead of the landlord

Loi Solidarité et Renouvellement Urbain (SRU) = law about sustainable building

Loi Scrivener = Rules regarding mortgage finance and the preliminary contract

LLD or *Location Long Durée* = LTR or Long-Term-Rental

LMNP ou *Loueur Meublé Non-Professionnel* - Owner renting furnished property who's not acting as a professional landlord as it relates to the French tax code

LMP ou *Loueur Meublé Professionnel* - Owner renting furnished property who is acting as a professional landlord as it relates to the French tax code

Loyer = rent payment

Mainlevée = release or withdrawal of charge

Maison secondaire = holiday home or rental property

Mandat de vente = Mandate to sell required before agent may perform duties

Mandat exclusif / simple = exclusive or non-exclusive giving of rights to an agency to represent owner for the purposes of sale

Mandat de recherche = agreement with agent to find a property

Marchand de biens = property developers and speculators

Mètres carrés = square meters, although square feet is more common to measure surface area in the UK; a square foot is approximately 10% of a square meter

Meublé / non-meublé = furnished unfurnished

Mobilier = Furniture

Mur mitoyen = shared wall (US) or party wall (UK) with neighbor

***

Nantissement = collateral for a loan
 NV or *Net Vendeur* = Price seller receives once agency and other fees are deducted
 Notaire = notary public handling conveyancing for property sales similar to a solicitor or lawyer

Offre d'achat = formal proposal to purchase
 Offre préalable d'un crédit immobilier = preliminary offer of a bank loan

Permis de construire = Building permit
 Plein pied = Single storey
 Plan d'amortissement = Mortgage repayment schedule itemizing interest and capital
 Plan cadastral = cadastral plan showing the dimensions of a property's land area
 Pleine propriété = freehold
 Prélèvement automatique = Direct debit
 Prêt classique or *prêt amortisable* = capital and interest mortgage
 Prêt immobilier = mortgage
 Prêt in fine = interest only mortgage almost non-existent in France
 Prêt relais = bridge loan
 Procuration = Power of attorney
 Projet d'acte = draft or preliminary deed of purchase
 Promesse de vente = preliminary or promissory contract to buy a property (binding after 14 days); There's also a version called a '*Compromis de vente*' which offers fewer protections to the buyer
 Promoteur = property developer
 Propriété et terrain = property and land are almost always intrinsically bundled in France
 Publicité foncière = obligatory registration of a property

Règlement de copropriété = rules and regulations of an apartment building
 Rendement brut = gross yield
 Résidence principale / secondaire = primary residence / secondary residence
 Responsabilité civile = third-party liability insurance
 Révision de loyer = rent increase
 Renouvellement = renewal of a rental lease
 Rez-de-chaussée = Ground floor

SCI ou *Société Civile Immobilier* = SPV Special Purpose Vehicle; A company or Building society with real estate holdings. Could be held by

members of the same family in the case of an *SCI Familiale*.
Séparation des biens = marriage regime were each spouse retains own assets
Servitude = Rights of way or easements
Sous-seing = preliminary contract
Syndicat de copropriété = condominium association

TEG or *taux effectif global du prêt*, also TAEG = Annual Equivalent Rate (AER) in the UK or APR in the US
Taxe foncière = annual local property tax equivalent of council tax in the UK
Titre de propriété = title deed
Tout-à-l'égout = mains drainage system
TVA = VAT or value-added tax or sales tax

Usufruit = Life interest in a property; in France you can separate the ownership of a property with the usage rights of that property and each has a separate monetary value.

Valeur cadastrale / vénale = assessment price for land tax purposes versus market value
Vacance, taux de = Vacancy rate (US) or Void Weeks (UK) where property is unoccupied; the opposite is the Occupancy rate
VEFA (*vente en état futur d'achèvement*) = buying a new build on plan which will

Further resources: Lodgify; Vesta property

PROVIDERS

Service Providers

Here are hundreds of companies who can help you manage your property business, or run it for you. They are either based in France, or actively operating in the country. A complete and updated list can be accessed by members on mypropertypayday.com

Platforms
Where you can post your listings

Accommodation, STR:

Atypical
Abracadaroom	www.abracadaroom.com/en/
Bedsonboard	www.bedsonboard.com/
Cool stays	www.coolstays.com/owners/
Host Unusual	hostunusual.com/
Mon Hebergement Insolite	monhebergementinsolite.com

E-commerce marketplace (which also has vacation rental listings)
Craigslist	paris.craigslist.org/
Eversy	www.eversy.com
Facebook	facebook.com
Gens de Confiance	gensdeconfiance.com/fr/s/locations-vacances
Le Bon Coin	www.leboncoin.fr/carte/_vacances_?
ParuVendu Vacances	www.paruvendu.fr/location-vacances/

Gîtes
A Gîtes	Agites.com
Gers Gîtes France	www.gers-gites-france.com
Gîtes de France	www.gites-de-france.com/en
Gîtes Normandie	www.gites-normandie-76.com
Gîtes dot com	Gites.com
La Clef Verte	Www.laclefverte.org

Luxury (or curated)
Boutique Homes	boutique-homes.com
Dream Exotic Rentals	dreamexoticrentals.com
Le Collectionist	www.lecollectionist.com/en
Luxury Retreats	www.airbnb.com/luxury

Oliver's Travels	www.oliverstravels.com/
OneFineStay	www.onefinestay.com/
Plum Guide	plumguide.com
Smiling House	smilinghouse.ch/
Solmar Villas	www.solmarvillas.com/
Stay One Degree	www.stayone.com/
Time and Place	timeandplace.com
Top Villas	www.thetopvillas.com/en_us
Villa Finder	www.villa-finder.com/
Villas of Distinction	villasofdistinction.com

Real Estate generalists (which also have vacation rental listings)

Barnes Luxury Rentals	barnes-luxuryrentals.com
PAP Vacances	papvacances.fr
SeLoger vacances	vacances.seloger.com

Regional

Charminghouses	charminghouses.net
Location Pays Basque	location-paysbasque.fr/
Perfect Experiences	www.perfectexperiences.com/
Perfectly Paris	www.perfectlyparis.com
Vacances Cote d'Azur	vacances-cotedazur.com

Rural

Accueil Paysan	www.accueil-paysan.com/en/
Bienvenue à la ferme dormir	https://www.bienvenue-a-la-ferme.com/
Fleurs de soleil	www.fleursdesoleil.fr/maison-adherer-label.html
Inspiration Montagne	inspiration-montagne.com

STR specific

Abritel	abritel.fr
Agoda	www.agoda.com/vacation-rentals/
Airbnb	airbnb.com
Belvilla	www.belvilla.fr/
BungalowNet	bungalow.net
Cityscan	cityscan.fr
CoinPrivé	coinprive.net
Coinsecret	coinsecret.com
Cybevasion	www.cybevasion.fr/index_en.html
HomeAway	homeaway.com

Locations Vacances Part.	locations-vacances-particuliers.com
Media Vacances	mediavacances.com
Vacances Location	vacances-location.net

Vacation generalists (which also have short-term rental and hotel listings)

Booking dot com	booking.com
Cléavacances	www.clevacances.com/fr/
Expedia	expedia.com
Flipkey	www.flipkey.com/
France-Voyage	france-voyage.com
Holidu	www.holidu.com/about-us
Maravista	maravista.fr
Opodo	www.opodo.com/
Orbitz	www.orbitz.com/
Poplidays	poplidays.com
Sejourning	www.sejourning.com/fr/location/new
Travelocity	www.travelocity.com/
TripAdvisor Vacation Rent.	www.tripadvisor.fr/Rentals
Voyages Pirates	www.voyagespirates.fr/

Camping overnight (unequipped tourists)

Camping dot fr	camping.fr
Campings dot com	campings.com
Campspace	campspace.com/en/host
HomeCamper	www.homecamper.com/land/new

Caravanning (equipped with RVs)

Yescapa	www.yescapa.fr
Camping car on line	campingcar-online.com/fr/
Outdoorsy	outdoorsy.fr
Campanda	www.campanda.fr
Hapee	www.hapee.fr
Indie Campers	www.indiecampers.fr
Wikicampers	www.wikicampers.fr

Accommodation, LTR:

Standard Lease

Bien'ici	www.bienici.com/recherche/location/france?mode=galerie
Figaro Immobilier	immobilier.lefigaro.fr/annonces/immobilier-location-bien-france.html
Le Bon Coin	www.leboncoin.fr/locations/offres

LocService	www.locservice.fr/
Logic Immo	www.logic-immo.com/location-immobilier.php
Meilleurs Agents	www.meilleursagents.com/location/
Mitula	www.mitula.fr/
Particulier à Part.	pap.fr
SeLoger	seloger.fr
Trovit	https://immo.trovit.fr/
Wizi	Wizi.io

Mobility Lease

Badi	https://badi.com
Click&Bed	https://www.clickandbed.com/
Morningcroissant	Morningcroissant.fr
WeekAway	https://www.weekaway.fr/

Coliving and Roommates

Chez Nestor	www.chez-nestor.com/
Co-living et Co-working	www.co-living-et-co-working.com/professionnels-2132/
Cooloc	cooloc.com/
Koliving	www.koliving.fr
Lacartedescolocs	www.lacartedescolocs.com/
Roomlala	https://fr-fr.roomlala.com/

Students

Adele	adele.org
Appartager	appartager.com
Immo Jeune	immojeune.com
Leavy	www.leavy.co
Location Etudiant	location-etudiant.fr
Lokaviz.fr	lokaviz.fr
Recherche colocation	www.recherche-colocation.com/
StudyLease	www.studylease.com

Activity (recurring):

Business function (recurring):

Coworking

Bee My Desk	beemydesk.com
CoWop	cowop.co/

Activity/Amenity (one-off):

Outdoor day use

Jardins privés	jardins-prives.com
My Garden Party	my-gardenparty.com

Preter Son Jardin	http://pretersonjardin.com
We Peps	we-peps.fr

Swimming Pool

Louer une piscine	louerunepiscine.com
Swimmy	www.swimmy.com

Corporate/Teambuilding (one-off):

Corporate/MICE

Bird Office	bird-office.com/en/
Comet Meetings	https://en.comet-meetings.com/solution
Kactus	kactus.com
Lieux Atypiques	lieuxatypiques.com/
Office Riders	Officeriders.com
Snapevent	Snapevent.fr
Spacebase	www.spacebase.com/en/

Creative endeavors (one-off):

Creative industries (film/TV/photo/ads)

20000 Lieux	20000lieux.com/
Agence Repertoire	Agence-repertoire.com
L'Association des répereurs	asso-repereurs.fr
Cinedecors	cinedecors.fr/en/choose-a-region
InSitu	insitu.space/
Mires	miresparis.com/proposer/
Peerspace	www.peerspace.com/fr

Celebration/Party (one-off):

Private Events

Mynöx	mynox.co/en/home/
Privateaser	privateaser.com
Une Salle A Paris	unesalleaparis.com
We Peps	We-peps.fr

Dining/Drinking (occasional):

Experiences

Cookoon	Cookoon.fr
Eatwith	eatwith.com/

Parking (daily access):

Agencies

Finapark	www.fipark.fr
ParkAgence	www.parkagence.fr
Parking Nomad	www.nomad.immo

Cars (mainly)

MonsieurParking	Monsieurparking.com
Parkadom	parkadom.com
Prends Ma Place	prendsmaplace.fr
StockOn	www.stockon.fr/
Valopark	www.valopark.fr/
WePark	wepark.fr

Motorcycles and Scooters (mainly)

12p5	www.12p5.com/
Gare ta Becane	Garetabecane.fr

Storage (long-term):

Boxes/Furniture

Costockage	costockage.fr
HomeBox	homebox.fr/en
Jestocke	jestocke.com
Kiwiiz	kiwiiz.fr/location-particuliers/costockage/stockage-en-cave/

RV/Campers

StockOn	https://www.stockon.fr/

Boat winterizing

Allovoisins	www.allovoisins.com/r/4359/93/0/0/location-Hivernage-bateau
BoatOn	www.boaton.fr/en/rent-my-space

Tools
   Technology to help you manage property yourself

Accommodation, STR only:

Communications

Duve	duve.com/vacation-rentals/
Host Tools	hosttools.com
Smartbnb	www.smartbnb.io/
Your Porter App	www.yourporter.com

Pricing management

AirDNA	airdna.co
Beyond	https://www.beyondpricing.com/
PriceLabs	pricelabs.co
RateGenie	www.rategenie.io/
Wheelhouse	www.usewheelhouse.com/

Staff/Cleaner scheduling

Care dot com	www.care.com/fr-fr/join-now

Operto Teams	www.operto.com

PMS built in France

Concierge Me	www.conciergeme.fr/
RentalReady	www.rentalready.com
Smily	www.bookingsync.com/
Superhote	www.superhote.com/

PMS for owners of one property

Beds24	https://www.beds24.com/
Bookerator	www.bookerator.com
Bookerville	www.bookerville.com
Booking Automation	bookingautomation.com
Bookster	www.booksterhq.com
Freetobook	https://en.freetobook.com/
Hostfully	www.hostfully.com
Mr. Alfred	https://mralfred.com/
My VR	www.myvr.com
Rentability	www.rentability.gr/en-us
Travelnest	https://travelnest.com/

PMS for owners of several properties

365 Villas	www.365villas.com
Bookalet	www.bookalet.co.uk/
Booker Tools	booker-tools.com
Estarbooking	www.estarbooking.com
Futurestay	www.futurestay.com/
Guestline	www.guestline.com
Hospitable	hospitable.com
Hostaway	https://www.hostaway.com
Hosthub	https://www.hosthub.com/
Hostify	www.hostify.com
Lodgify	https://www.lodgify.com/pricing/
Rentalspms	www.rentalspms.com
SabeeApp	https://www.sabeeapp.com
Smoobu	smoobu.com
Stays	stays.net
Streamline VRS	www.streamlinevrs.com
Suitech	www.suitech.es
Turisoft	www.turisoft.com
Uplisting	http://www.uplisting.io
Vacayz	https://www.vacayz.com/propertymanagers
Yesbookit	www.agents.yesbookit.com

Accommodation, STR and LTR:
PMS

Avantio   www.avantio.com/
Guesty   www.guesty.com/
Lavanda   getlavanda.com/
myRent   www.my-rents.com

Accommodation, LTR only:

Coliving and Roommates

Glynk & Cosine Labs   glynk.com/#solutions
Obeyo   www.obeyo.com
res:harmonics   www.resharmonics.com
Sowebuild   www.sowebuild.com
Spaceflow   www.spaceflow.io/en
TheHouseMonk   https://monktechlabs.com/housemonk
Wicomico   www.wicomico.dk/home-en

PMS for LTR

Appliceo   www.appliceo.com/fr
GererSeul   gererseul.com
Insitio   https://www.insitio.com/
Pandaloc   www.pandaloc.com/gestion/locataire
Pinql   www.pinql.com/
Rentila   rentila.fr
Ublo   https://www.ublo.immo/

Activity (recurring):

Other

Bookinglayer   https://www.bookinglayer.com/
Checkfront   https://www.checkfront.com/

Providers

Outsource all or part of your property business

STR Property Managers
    Appart'Tourism   www.votreappartaparis.fr/en
    At The Corner   atthecorner.fr/
    BNB Conciergerie   www.bnbconciergerie.fr/a-propos
    BnBkeys   bnbkeys.com
    BnBsitter   en.bnbsitter.com/
    Charminghouses   charminghouses.net
    CLICK YOUR FLAT   https://www.clickyourflat.com/
    Cobblestone Paris Rentals   cobblestoneparis.com

Coinsecret	coinsecret.com
Concierge BNB	www.concierge-bnb.com/ville/
Flateo	www.flateo.fr
Freehost	www.freehost-conciergerie.com/
Good Job Charlie	www.facebook.com/page.GoodJobCharlie/
Groomlidays	www.groomlidays.com/
GuestReady	www.guestready.com
Homepilot	www.homepilot.fr
Hostnfly	www.hostnfly.com/
Houst	www.houst.com
Keypers	www.keypers.paris
La Conciergerie Royale	www.la-conciergerie-royale.com/contact
La Tour Immo Gestion	www.latourimmo.com/
Le Logis Versaillais	https://www.le-logis-versaillais.com/services.html
Le Relais D'Anjou	https://www.hotesanjou.fr/
Leavy	www.leavy.co/en/happy-leaver
Les Clefs Occitaine	https://www.conciergerie-occitane.fr/
Les Demoiselles a Versailles	https://lesdemoisellesaversailles.com/contact/
Les Petits Apts de Versailles	lepetitappartversailles.com/reservation/
Location Prestige	https://www.prestigeconciergerie.fr/intendance-locative
Logistiloc	www.logistiloc.fr
Merci Alice	www.mercialice.com
Mon Concierge Parisien	https://www.mon-conciergeparisien.com/
Premiere Conciergerie	www.premiere-conciergerie.com/
Sam'Loc	samloc.fr/
Smartflux	www.smartflux.fr/
Smartrenting	smart-renting.com
Sun Key Locations	thesunkey.com
Team Tattoo Gestion	www.ttgestion.eu/
The Heart of Paris	theheartofparis.com
TranquilleEmile	tranquillecmile.com
Tybnb	www.tybnb.bzh/offre-de-conciergerie/
Weekhome	weekome.fr/#estimezvosrevenus
WeHost	www.wehost.fr
Welkeys	www.welkeys.com/

***

LTR Property Managers
- Blue — www.lagenceblue.fr/gestion
- Click&Rent — www.clickandrent.fr
- Cozy Home — www.cosyhome.net/
- Excelsior Lodging / Rentalls — rentalls.fr
- Flatlooker — www.flatlooker.com/gestion-locative-innovante
- Gest'in — gest-in.fr/
- Homepilot — homepilot.com
- Kaliz — www.kaliz.fr
- Les Meublés de Madeleine — http://va.appartementmeubleversailles.fr/
- Mon Agil — monagil.fr/
- Monsieur HUGO — https://www.monsieurhugo.com/blog/a-propos/
- Owwner — www.owwner.com
- Pure Gestion — www.pure-gestion.com/fiches-conseil/location/frais-location
- Valority — www.valority.com/gestion-locative/agence/
- VPat Immo — www.vpatimmo.fr/activites/locations-meublees

BTL or Buy-to-let turnkey operators
<u>for Investors only</u>
- Beanstock — beanstock.fr
- Bernie — www.bernie.re
- Bevouac — www.bevouac.com
- Brickmeup — brickmeup.com
- ColocR — colocr.fr/
- Greenliving — www.greenliving.fr/
- ImAvenir — imavenir.com/investissement-locatif-cle-en-main/
- Immocitiz — immocitiz.fr/
- Investissement Locatif — en.investissement-locatif.com/
- Lokizi — www.lokizi.fr
- Masteos — www.masteos.fr/
- MyExpat — www.myexpat.fr/

Coliving Property Managers
<u>Your home, their operations</u>
- Co-Liv — www.co-liv.org/
- Colivys — colivys.com/en/contact/

Colonies	www.livecolonies.com/en/private-investors
Finestate	finestate.eu/en/coliving/
Friendlyhome	friendlyhome.fr
Hife Coliving	https://hife-coliving.fr/en/the-gains/business-offer/
Koliving	www.koliving.fr
La Casa Coliving	lacasa.io/
Lamaiz	www.coloc.fr
Mutinerie Le Village	sites.google.com/view/la-residence-verte/accueil?pli=1
Roof	weareroof.com/
Sharies	https://sharies.co/en/about
Tendoors	www.tendoors.fr
The Babel Community	www.thebabelcommunity.com/en/partner/
The Collective (UK)	https://www.thecollective.com/about-us
Vitanovae	www.vitanovae.com/#contact
DoveVivo	dovevivo.com/en/
Habyt	www.habyt.com/

Fractional Ownership turnkey operators
<u>for Investors only</u>

Altacasa	www.altacasa.com
Barak	webarak.fr
Mansio	www.mansio.com/
Pacaso	www.pacaso.com/
Prello	prello.co

In-home helpers
<u>Check-in, Cleaning, Maintenance companies</u>

Paris Suite Services	www.parissuiteservices.com/en/
DoInn	doinn.co/en-GB
Brigad	https://www.brigad.co/en-gb/find-a-workforce
o2	versailles.agence.o2.fr/
Saint Honoré Cleaning	sainthonore-cleaning.com/
Shiva	https://www.shiva.fr/tarifs-femme-de-menage
Aladom	https://www.aladom.fr/devis/menage/femme-de-menage/
Spic'n'span	spicandspan.fr/en/
Untempspourvous	www.untempspourvous.fr
Opago	www.opago.co/
askAndy	https://www.askandy.co/
Gofer	www.gofer.fr

Prestadomicile   www.prestadomicile.com/menage-location-saisonniere

Miscellaneous
Other resources and folks to help you

Freelancers

Independents in France: JeMePropose, Gofer, Yoopies, AlloVoisins, HelloCasa, Pwiic, Yoojo, BeFreelancer
   Maintenance/renovations: NeedHelp, Frizbiz
   Independents general: Malt, Side, Fiverr, Upwork, Speedlancer, Freelancer.com

Financial

Banks, specialising in non-residents
   Banque Palatine (very high net worth individuals only)
   Banque Transatlantique (very high net worth individuals only)
   BNP Paribas International Buyers +33 3 20 18 18 44
   Britline affiliated with Crédit Agricole +33 2 31 55 67 89 contact@britline.com
   Crédit Agricole, Normandy FRANCOIS QUONIAM jeanfrancois.quoniam@ca-normandie.fr

Brokers for Mortgages, specialising in non-residents
   Paris Loan Broker   https://www.parisloanbroker.com/
   ICE   https://www.icefinance.fr/services/courtage-en-credit-immobilier/
   Blue Sky   https://bluesky-france-finance.com
   Carte Financement   https://www.cartefinancement.com/
   PretGuru   www.pretguru.com/courtier-immobilier/expatries-non-residents/
   So2fi   www.so2fi.com/pret-immobilier/
   French Mortgage Xpress   www.frenchmortgageexpress.com
   France Home Finance   https://www.francehomefinance.com
   French Private Finance https://www.frenchprivatefinance.com

Associations
   Professional Host Alliance, ASTRHO, LPGI, Trampoleen (FF2i), UNPI, FNAIM, ESREA

BIBLIOGRAPHY

Bibliography

Books

<u>English</u>

The Complete Guide to Property Investment in France, a buy-to-let manual - Gerry Fitzgerald

Buying a Home in France - David Hampshire

Earn Money From Your Home - Stewart Whyte

Rich Dad, Poor Dad - Robert Kyosaki

The ABCs of Property Management - Ken McElroy

Idiot's guide to Making Money with Rental Properties - Kimberly Smith

How To Invest in Airbnb Properties Create Wealth and Passive Income Through Smart Vacation Rentals Investing - David Leroux

Investing in International Real Estate For Dummies - Nicholas Wallwork

Optimize Your Airbnb - Daniel Vroman Rusteen

Hospitable Hosts - a book of chapters from a dozen different authors who run STRs

HOW TO RUN YOUR AIRBNB IN ITALY The Ultimate guide to manage your holiday lets in full compliance with the Italian laws - NICOLÒ BOLLA

<u>French</u>

Doublez vos Revenus en Louant votre logement sur Airbnb - Julien Chorbet

Consommation Tout se Partage, Tout s'échange Le guide pratique - Le Particulier Éditions

Gérez votre location meublée ou saisonnière - Le Particulier Éditions

Louer à des touristes 2021-2022 - Assistant Juridique

Vive l'immobilier et vive la rente - Mickael Zonta

Comment investir en immobilier locatif ? - Leo Nardecchia, Daniel Vu

Airbnb Master : les 200 secrets des nouveaux millionnaires de la location courte durée - Pierre Tellep

L'investissement immobilier locatif intelligent: Itinéraire vers votre future semaine des 7 dimanches – Julien Delagrandanne

Investir dans les parkings pour créer sa liberté financière: Un investissement accessible, rentable et simple à gérer - Alexandre Lacharme

* * *

Joe Siart

Magazines

25 millions de Propriétaires - La Presse immobilière (90% of readers belong to trade association UNPI)
The Good Life France - Janine Marsh, Editor
Le Particulier Immobilier - Figaro Média
French Property News
International Living magazine

Online

French Property magazine and website
Rentalpreneur France-based blog in English
Podcasts: in English- Holiday Cottage Handbook, Boostly, Get Paid 4 Your Pad, Good Life Property Mgt., STR Success Stories, TechNest, Propcast, Short-Term Rental Profits, Vacation Rental Machine; in French- Mon Podcast Immo, Frenchweb Future of Proptech, Investissement Immo, Le Podcast de l'Investissement Locatif - Manuel Ravier and Mickael Zonta, Ça Fait Un Bail podcast - Jeremy Nabais; in Spanish- Kasaz, Spanish Proptech

Blogs: Int'l Hospitality, VRMB, BiggerPockets, J'affiche Complet, Louer Efficace, Eldorado Immobilier

Pundits/Influencers: on Youtube in English: Rentals U., GuestXperience, Mark Simpson, Rental Scale-up, Optimize my Airbnb

Forums: Quora, AirBnB hosts (official), Property Hub

Groups: LinkedIn in English- Vacation Rental Pros, VRMA; Facebook in English- Airbnb Profit Club, WeHost, Concierge Club, Airbnb Mastery, Bnbook, Pro Hosts, Holiday Rental Owners, STR University, Best Hosting Tips; in French- Location Saisonnière, Les pros de l'immo, Gite Owners; in Portuguese- Alojamento Local; in Spanish- Barcelona Hosts

Reports and White papers

English
Global Proptech confidence index end 2022 from Metaprop
Sifted Proptech report 2022 with contributions from venture capital firm Pi Labs and law firm Shoosmiths
Blevins Franks Guide To Taxes In France
Buying in France property guide by: The Overseas Guides Company
The growth in short-term lettings (England) 2023 House of Commons report
WHO'S WHO GUIDE of the Vacation Rental world 2020 - VR TECH sponsored by RENTALS UNITED
Study_europe-s-travel-and-accommodation-sector-in-44-charts Statista Booking.com
The Ultimate Airbnb Host Checklist - Guesty

2022 Hospitality trends in the vacation rental industry from Hostully French

Immobilier ancien : les étrangers non résidents 2020 report by the *Conseil supérieur du notariat* (CSN)

Wuest Partner 2022 Observatoire de l'immobilier en France

Tourism Observatory of the Côte d'Azur 2020

Tourisme Observatoire Provence-Alpes-Côte d'Azur 2021

LE GUIDE DE L'INVESTISSEUR LIBRE - Investissement Locatif

LE MARCHÉ DU COLIVING EN FRANCE 2019 - BNP Paribas Real Estate

Réglementation des locations meublées touristiques 2019 - Xavier DEMEUZOY Avocat au Barreau de Paris

Renovation Energetique Hors-Série N°214 - juillet/août 2022 - 60 Millions de consommateurs.

Les chiffres du logement neuf au 4ème trimestre 2021 et bilan annuel - FPI

Baromètre du Coliving 2023 - FriendlyHome

Event keynotes and speeches

From presenters at:
the France Property Show in London 2022
RENT, Paris 2022
Short Stay Summit, London 2023
Scale Rentals, London 2023
Vacation Rental World Summit, Barcelona 2023
Scale Rentals, Paris 2023

AUTHOR BIOGRAPHY
Author biography

Joe Siart is the principal author and creator of online magazine My Property Payday, where he developed an algorithm, enabling selection of the ideal rate for maximum revenue of different uses of renting space. He has worked in travel, hospitality and real estate for more than a decade.

Since 2019, he's been an executive director in the Proptech sector: a CEO for a 60-person short-term rental property management company overseeing 250 apartments and villas in Portugal and the Alps, a commercial director for a 20-person residential real estate agency in Paris, and head of expansion for a 40-person investment firm and mortgage broker in France.

Today, he runs his own property management company, Sun Key Locations in Versailles, where he's personally earned Superhost status since 2018. He's also managing director of a property management system (PMS) used by conciergeries to oversee large portfolios of thousands of vacation rentals in EMEA.

This is the third book he has authored, the other two being a memoir about his adventures as an American expat abroad, and a photobook companion to his audioguides, both written under a pseudonym. He has also written and narrated audio content heard on four walking tours in Paris and Versailles.

Please let folks know what you thought by reviewing on Goodreads, Amazon, Colibris, Book Riot, or your own blog.

Subscribe to My Property Payday magazine here: http://eepurl.com/dMDj9s

***

Consultation: discussion - plan - estimation - then choose which management level is right for you.

DIY: renter search, contracts, then once lease signed you, the owner, self-manage

Outsourced: provider search, vetting and contracting, ongoing liaison or oversight

Active property management: (depending on location and usage)

For STR: Sun Key Locations operates physically around Versailles. Remote management considered if automation possible (smart locks, etc.)

For LTR: We refer to agencies or consult with owners who self-manage.

For Storage, Parking, Amenities, Events and Activities, we offer remote management (listings, pricing, search, communications, paperwork) if the owner handles logistics in-person.

www.ingramcontent.com/pod-product-compliance
Lightning Source LLC
Chambersburg PA
CBHW051544010526
44118CB00022B/2568